I Am Yolanda

I Am Yolanda

A journey of hope

YJS Toussaint

DEDICATION

I dedicate this book firstly to my sons. I cannot imagine life not as your Mother. Having you has given me a new lease of life, granted me with strength I never imagined I could possess. You are the reason I strive to be better with each day I am blessed with. You have challenged me to see tomorrow when today was hard to survive. I love all three of you, and my fourth, with everything I have. Thank you for giving me your full support in writing this book, for believing in me and what I stand for.

To my sons, Our Future, Our sons.

CONTENTS

FOREWORD

For me, the noun 'Yolanda', over recent years, has become synonymous with words such as 'strength', 'inspiration,' 'bravery,' and 'compassion'. For me, Yolanda epitomises pure kindness and wisdom. As you will learn once you dive into the depths of this memoir: she is full of contradictions, sure, but she is made up of juxtapositions that make perfect sense when embodied by her; contradictions that you never knew would fit perfectly until you see her laugh and cry in the same moment; fight and protect in the same instance; break your heart and heal it at the same time. You will know this for yourself as you venture through this journey with her, she moves seamlessly through emotions and you will too. I have heard snippets and anecdotes over the past few years but it has been an emotional rollercoaster to read about this phase of her life from beginning to end; needless to say it is one that pays off in catharsis and lessons. I am happy for you as a reader, I am glad that you too get to experience the gift that is her words. I've personally experienced the healing power of her words and this book is evidence of her Divine gift. She was born to write; she was born to be heard. And how fortunate are we to bear witness. The writer of this book is a phenomenal, remarkable woman. But above all she is Yolanda - and that in itself is more than enough.

Mina Abdi

PREFACE

I have tried to recreate events, locales and conversations from my memories of them. In order to maintain anonymity, in some instances I have changed the names of individuals and places, I may have changed some identifying characteristics and details such as physical properties, occupations and places of residence.

ACKNOWLEDGMENTS

Firstly, I'd like to Give Thanks to The Almighty for seeing me through. For blessing me with the faith to understand my journey as just that, my journey, not my destination. For giving me the courage to share my story fearlessly. For this I am eternally grateful. Thank you for giving me Purpose.

I'd like to Give Thanks for my Mum, who gave me all she had, so I could experience a life less challenging than hers. Believe it or not, those challenges were written for me to endure, yet somehow both spoken and unspoken, you taught me to Survive. One of the greatest gifts bestowed upon me. Thank you for teaching that a Mother's work is never done. For unconditional love and commitment. My Superwoman!

To my Granny, I wish you were here to read this book. I feel so much of who I am, intrinsically starts with you. For allowing me to talk you into insanity whenever we visited, for giving me advice on life, love, relationships in the most transparent way it can be given. Grandma you will always be my Sheroe.

To my Baby Brother, M, the thing I love most about you is Loyalty. It goes beyond our bloodline and bears a love of a different kind. Without perhaps realising it, you always encourage me to embark on one project to the next. That there, is faith in me, it is support you can't buy. I love you for this. Thank you for being there, for being you and in being you, being the best Brother Ever.

To my Husband, 'Bubba', I don't know where to start. I have isolated myself, spent hours in silence in the same room as you, just to write this book. And you allowed me, without question or complaint, occasionally asking me 'how's it going'. That in itself spoke volumes to my soul. It demonstrated to me your belief in me, without ever reading a word I had written. I can't Thank You enough for allowing me to be me and standing right behind me while I do so. You must be one of my biggest fans in absolutely everything I do, because it sure feels like it. Thank you for believing in me unselfishly. I am so glad I Chose You.

To each of my Aunties, who are individually **phenomenal** women and **mothers**. Thank you for being a true example of Strong Women throughout my life. I watched you struggle, overcome and through it all be the Best Mother's you could possibly be. Thank you. I love you all and owe so much of who I am to who you are.

To my 'Girlfriend' aka GF. Who knew life would deal us the cards it has, but at least through it all, we've had each other. I dedicate this book to you, to us, because we have truly lived and continue to strive and be victorious. You always tell me how important my story is and why I must share. Now I can confess that I secretly fight the tears because your belief touches a different element of my soul. Thank you Gf for the love, the hugs, the conversations, the memories and for too, surviving above all.

To my soul sisters, Zalika, Lisa, 'Mimi', each of you speak my language. A language that cannot be understood by all and has to bare a core of Spirituality.

To Zalika for challenging me to see life as the complex navigation it is and thus challenging my thought process. You have added so much value to my growth in one-way or another. Nothing can change you as my Sister, it's organic, it is written and so it shall be. Love you 'Moonie'

Lisa, from way back then until now. Wow. I admire you more than I think you possibly know. Not just because you remind me that I am normal or sane. Lol. But because you love from a place so deep within, and so selflessly, it baffles me at times, but still challenges me to be better. I am so grateful for having a friend who I know I can share my thoughts without fear of judgement. One who supports my evolution. You inspire me, and I am so grateful to have you as part of my family. Oh and the world needs to read your work…

To Mina, 'Mimi', Can I start by saying thank you. Thank you for being in my corner, pushing me to 'trust the process' and be fearless. Thank you for understanding the fragments of my thoughts and unpicking them patiently with me. For believing in a story, you did not even know. That takes some Faith. Thank you, Mimi, love you 'deep'. (Wink)

To Lorna my sister-friend, for being a guiding star in my life since the very first day we met. I learn so much from you, from what you say and ultimately from what you do. Thank you for believing in me. For taking time out with me, for being there for my family. Love you Lorn'.

'Sir' Ewan Briscoe, thank you for pushing me to complete this book. Without any idea of its content, you have believed and encouraged me to be consistent and it worked. I cannot Thank You enough for your support.

Lastly to all the women who paved the way for me in one way or another, knowingly and unknowingly, to friends, family and of course to you for choosing to read this book.

CHAPTER 1

It was 5am, and the sun was silently sneaking through my bedroom window. The alarm had just started to buzz (a minute too late might I add), as I opened one eye only minutes before to check if it was still the night before, and I had dozed off for 20 minutes. Of course, only to realise that it was not the night before and indeed it was time to get up.

I hit the phone to silence the alarm and pulled the sheets up as not to expose any part of my upper body to the early morning chill. Opening my other eye slowly, I quickly slammed it shut. The sun was no longer sneaking in; it had now forced its way in! And now I had a clear view of my lonely bedroom. I lay still and gazed up at the ceiling; I hated the paint on the ceiling. It was off white and made the room appear unloved. Somehow if the ceiling were to speak to me right now it would probably say, 'listen I don't know who you're turning your nose up at, you're a sight for sore eyes too'.

I looked at the time it was 5:05. I had at least 25 minutes before I simply had to, no questions asked, get out of bed. The house was silent, the only sound the annoying tick coming from the clock in the sitting room. Funny how the clock was always silent when you were sitting in the front room; but the moment I went to bed and switched off my TV, the clock would start ticking as loud as I imagined Big Ben to sound if ever I had to sleep within the large stature where it was housed.

I could hear Cassius snoring gently from the boys' bedroom. I knew it was him because he had a distinct breathing pattern when he slept. Kwame, on the other hand, was a more silent sleeper. He instead opted for what could be referred to as the 'turn and kick' as he slept. I considered how lucky they were or how unlucky I was. They would stay sleeping for at least another hour before I had to wake them. I, on the other hand, was left with the unfortunate task of getting up. I decided after a few minutes not to focus on the dreary paintwork on the ceiling and instead turned my focus to the TV. I knew there would be nothing of interest on TV that might beat staring up at the ceiling. I knew it was too early for GMTV but I decided anything had to be better than what I was currently watching. I flicked through the channels and decided the only thing I could possibly consider watching at that ungodly hour was the news. Not quite what I was after to start my morning positively. Depressing news on lives lost unnecessarily to heinous crimes, at the hands of those with psychotic imbalances and cruel intentions. To end it all and of course, to offer viewers some solace after the volcano of negative features, was the amazing news of the dog that could play football, or the cat that has died not nine but 10 times.

'Really?' I sighed, staring back at the ceiling. The ceiling seemed like a much better option. I turned the volume down on the TV. I could barely hear it now so turned my focus to the wall. At least my photos would make me feel better. Photos of my brother, photos of the boys hugging each other ever so tightly. Yes, much better than watching the news. I smiled as I recalled them in the earlier years. They were beautiful boys inside and out. Funny how it was so much easier to see that when they were fast asleep. I reminded myself that was the beauty of quiet moments in my room. Without the noise from loud and boisterous playing, the 'he won't give that back' arguments. I could enjoy the beauty of just being. I had to be grateful for those moments and allow myself to bask in gratitude irrespective of where I was at that moment.

It was 5:30. I must have been lost in the moment because now I had to get up and start moving pretty fast. I turned on the shower while I made my way to the sitting room to turn heating on. I liked the house to be warm when the boys got up in the mornings. It didn't seem right for them to sit and eat breakfast in a cold room. As a child, I still had memories of my mum and my aunties Calor Gas heater turned on so that the room was hot when we came out of the bath. Come to think of it, I have visions of them positioning our pyjamas to lay somewhere where the heat from the Calor Gas would catch it. That way, when we finally snuggled into our pyjamas, my cousins and I, we were warm despite how cold the room may have been. So, to me this was standard practice. I'm afraid to say, it was also my idea of good parenting. If my mum and my aunties did it, it was what 'good mums do!' And besides I hated the cold as well.

The shower was what I needed. I stood still as the water rained down on my skin. Now I felt ready to take on the world. I got partially dressed, leaving only my skirt left to drag on later and started to warm some milk for the boy's cereal while boiling the kettle for a hot drink. I entered the boy's bedroom quietly and as I did; I saw a Cassius' eyes open looking up at me.

'Morning Mummy', he grumbled in his sleepiest voice.

It was no surprise he was awake already. Cassius, five, was like an alarm clock, always the first to wake, ready for breakfast. I kissed his face. He was so cute. 'Mummy's little dumplin'.

I looked at Kwame, still fast asleep. I stroked his cheek.

'Time to wake up," I uttered gently. 'It's morning time,"

Morning time was the title given for anything before 11 o'clock in our house. For some reason the boys just couldn't fathom that it was just morning; it had to be morning time.

Kwame, seven, peered through one eye. It made me smile inside, how he somehow managed to replicate daily, waking up in disbelief that it was now the morning. He closed his eyes and tried to turn around. I nudged him again 'come on its time to get up'

'It's morning time Kwame, its time to get up', chorused Cassius as he climbed out of his bed.

"I don't need you to tell me, I heard Mummy,' Kwame replied, still with both eyes closed.

It was almost always the same story Cassius would try to wake up his brother and then would in turn be greeted by the bad-tempered ladybird from the storybook. The joys of motherhood, these sleepy head sons of mine bickering even first thing in the morning, was slightly hilarious. I left the room as Cassius was putting on his dressing gown and went to start preparing breakfast. It was easy. I didn't ask what they were having I knew. Cassius would have the same thing every day: Weetabix. Whereas, Kwame: anything but the cereal that his brother was eating. I selected Cassius' boring regular weeties. Then choose a different box of cereal for Kwame and that was breakfast done!

The TV in the sitting room was on GMTV as per usual. I barely watched the screen, but I listened attentively, glancing up at the screen every so often, when something interesting caught my eye.

I carefully laid the well-pressed school shirts onto the radiator to warm up until the boys were ready for them. Another trick I learned from my mum and aunties.

Once the boys were dressed, and face shined ready for the outdoors, I threw on my skirt, smeared on my lip-gloss and started loading the boys in the car. It was 7:38 we were doing good for time. This rate we would make it to school just after breakfast club had begun. Where I imagined Kwame would have his second breakfast for the morning. Whilst Cassius would be playing with some of the girls from his class.

Cassius was popular in his year and the girls were always fussing over him. He didn't say much, his face said it all. He loved it, his cheeky grin, his shy demeanour. My son had them eating out of the palm of his hand. Silently clever he was.

We pulled up at the school and I took the scooters out of the boot and unfolded them, ready for the two-minute scoot to the gates.

The school had launched a 'walk to school' initiative whereby the children and parents were being encouraged to save the environment by walking instead of driving. All the parents knew this was more an initiative to stop parents blocking the road, while dropping and collecting their children to and from school. I had to explain to the boys that because we didn't live close enough to school, we couldn't 'scoot' to school. I explained to them that if they wanted to, we could leave home two hours earlier, meaning I would have to wake them up two hours earlier. After which we agreed we could scoot to school, but only from the car to the school gates. Seemed like a fair compromise to all. So that is what we did every morning. 'Mummy muggins' here, would put the scooters in the car and unfold them when we got to the school so the boys could scoot happily down the road with their friends for two minutes and then I'd kiss them goodbye, fold up the scooters and carry them both back to the car and throw them in the boot. Looking back, even I'm shaking my head.

I signed the boys in at Breakfast club, kissed them goodbye and made my way back to the car, scooters in each hand.

I started the engine and immediately turned the cd on full blast. I needed a bit of music therapy before I got into work. I exhaled deeply.

There was something about the way in which I seemed to exhale after dropping the boys to school. It was as though my purpose for the morning was successful, I could breathe now. You know like the breaths an athlete must take after he completes the 100 metres. I myself could only merely imagine as the chances of me ever really knowing what that feels like are like one in a trillion. And I say trillion because honestly, past a billion is a blur to me. I'm going on a limb with a trillion. So, as I exhaled, and the music blurted through the speakers, I started my journey to work. The other thing I had to do most mornings.

Recently it had been a whirlwind of seasons. I had changed the boy's school to one slightly closer to home but more importantly to one which was not Independent, yet the standard of education was at least still on par with their previous school.

I had made the difficult decision of withdrawing the boys from their previous school for a few reasons but the icing on the cake, came after I felt the head teacher was trying to almost typecast Kwame into being something, he felt that he should be. Which just so happened to be an athlete, a runner.

On its own, I have absolutely no objections to either of my sons being athletes. However, I do experience slightly raised eyebrows when my children attend an interview at an alternative school as it just so happens on the day the school had hailed Sports Day and somehow, The Head teacher found it necessary to write to me to advise me that I should have requested permission for the boys to be absent etc… and that he was 'thoroughly disappointed' as he feels Kwame in particular, 'would make an excellent runner.'

I'm not sure how that sounds as you read this. I'm not sure if my ears are more sensitive to certain verbatim. But I didn't like it!

What didn't I like? I didn't like that this man somehow felt like he could presume my son's future at seven based on what? It was Sports Day, not the Olympics! Although I had made both my sons' teachers aware of the planned absence, this fat faced chubby bellied Santa Claus looking Head teacher was now apparently scolding me and asking me to place my hands on my head until I understood my shortcomings! No. I am afraid I am not a pupil at your school. Nor will I, the parent of these boys, (my sons), allow you to converse with me as though we are unequal. These are indeed my sons! Not our sons. Mine!

The more I thought about it I wanted to write back to say;

'Dear Mr Chubby face,

Yes, my sons missed sports day, but what you may have missed is the memo that reminds you, that you are the Head teacher of a school, not me, neither my household! Furthermore, was it necessary for you to write me a letter and waste school finances on a stamp and envelope to post it, when it may have proven to be more resolved more swiftly, had you spoken to Miss Bates who would have advised you that she was indeed, aware of my sons' prior appointment, scheduled in advance for that very day!' However, I didn't write that. I opted instead for something like this:

'Dear Principal,

Thank you for your letter regarding my sons missing Sports Day yesterday.

I had informed Miss Sharpe, Head of Juniors, in advance that the boys would be attending another school for an interview and this was authorised.

However, I was slightly taken aback by your strongly worded remarks concerning the value you place on Sports Day in relation to my sons and in particular Kwame.

I accept that both my sons have a multitude of talents, however running is not one I wish for him to be pressured or type-cast into.

Whilst I wish for my sons to take part in as many school-based activities as possible, it was unfortunate that this appointment resulted in them missing Sports Day.

Nevertheless, I feel it is important that children are supported into what may become their future endeavours, and not coerced into them based on possible cultural expectations that lack any solid foundation.

I am sure your letter was not intended to offend me. However, it is vital that I am transparent with you in my response. Kwame and Cassius are my sons.

Decisions pertaining to their lives are mine to make as I see fit.

Please refrain from attempting to mould my sons in the direction of what you feel is best for them without my agreement, as I am available both before and after school, should you wish to discuss my sons progress and development.

Please do not hesitate to arrange a meeting with me if you wish to clarify the contents of this letter.

Kind Regards

Yolanda'

I decided not to post the letter but instead to hand it to his PA first thing in the morning. In all honesty I asked if I could wait to hand it to him in person but apparently, he was out of office for the morning and would return at 11am. The term 'timing' sprung to mind, but it was fine. I would be available at the end of the school day if something in my letter required clarifying. I smiled a stern smile, but kept it buried within my freshly ironed white shirt the following morning. I greeted the parents I liked with the same love I always gave them. I had no reason to share 'Chubby face's' letter with the other parents. I didn't think it was necessary. Perhaps after the situation was firmly in the past, but not right now. Right now, I would smile on the inside despite feeling chubby face' had some nerve writing me that letter in the first place. Let's face it, was the real issue the fact I was hoping to withdraw my children from his prestigious school to obviously one I felt was better. Most likely!

'Yolanda!' I heard a voice calling me from across the road. I looked up; it was one of the parents from the school. Her son was in Kwame's class. She seemed like a nice woman. An Asian lady. She was older than me, married and had two children. A baby around 18 months and a six-year-old. Her husband seemed to work quite late most days, he was a Doctor or something, so she managed the school runs single handily. I must admit having watched her most mornings I somehow felt sorry for her.

Here's me managing on the outside, but struggling on the inside, although I had no husband or significant other. Then there's her, Sushma: married, stay at home Mum, a nice house, fancy car. Yet in her face, she just looked like another woman screaming for 'time out'. I'm sure if offered, this parent would gladly sit on the naughty mat for ten minutes, just so she could enjoy some me time. That's the impression I got from looking her in her eyes and listening to some of the terminology she used to describe her day: 'exhausting, same old, manic'. This woman had what I thought I wanted for my future, but looking at her, made me rethink what that could look like in reality.

I was already managing school runs myself, I was already Mum and Dad to Kwame and Cassius, I was already the only person in charge of housework and cooking. Frankly there didn't seem to be much difference. No wait, there was a difference. I didn't own my own beautiful four-bedroom house, and 4x4 to chauffeur the family around.

On the other hand, if that was the price I had to pay, I'll stick with what I've got!

I shouted back across the road Morning' and gave her a friendly wave. She waved back at me whilst balancing her 18-month-old daughter on her side. I smiled at her and gave an extra wave to the baby balanced carefully on her side. She was small in her frame, and watching her hold her daughter as she did, balanced on her side, reminded me of a balancing act witnessed at a circus where someone small would lift something larger than themselves to show skill. She signalled for me to wait, whilst she hurried her son through the school gates. I waited patiently, by the gates, although patience was not one of my strengths, exchanging pleasantries with the other parents as they entered the playground. By the time she had returned, her baby was now waddling cheerily along beside Mummy, carefree. Brand new first walkers coming to terms with solid ground, mums' hand firmly in grasp, I watched as they approached me in what many would consider, slow motion.

'How was Sports Day?' one of the parents asked. I looked up to see if her question was directed at me. Luckily it was not. I didn't really want to share the details of the letter I received, nor the response I fired back. In hindsight I think this was due to the fact that based on the little I knew of these devoted women, mothers, and wives. I knew their character was different to mine. I knew their lives were different to mine, and most importantly, I knew their personalities would rarely have them speaking against something the precious Principal had said.

These women were perhaps considered more dignified, if dignified meant you suppressed your own feelings as not to upset anyone else. To me, these women simply highlighted that I was different. I mean despite them all being older than me, the differences were greater than that.

In my mind I imagined sharing the details of my war with words with 'Chubby face', and I imagined a look of shock, possibly absolute horror as I described to them what I wrote and more importantly why I wrote it. I imagined explaining to them that with my son being one of two Black boys in his class, of course my son would be an athlete. I imagined, eyes tunnelled as each parent silently whispered to another parent with their eyes, 'Oh my, can you believe she said that out loud!' I imagined how they would repeat the conversation at home to their husbands. 'Well you know Yolanda, the young Black girl, you know her son is in the same class as ours… the unmarried one.' Yes, of course, husbands would likely reply. Perhaps I have a vivid imagination, but in my opinion, this was a practical assertion. I was accustomed to being judged, accustomed more than anything to being misunderstood, so much so that I tried not to let it concern me.

Even as a child I had to learn to silence the voices of others, because voices can steal from you. They can steal confidence, dreams, beliefs, and expectations. I worked hard on this as a teenager particularly when I discovered that having my own mind, and the confidence to speak it, was not favourable. So, whilst you may escape having stolen my voice as I was a child that was now a speck in the distant past. As for the parents I conversed with briefly during school runs, I accepted their unspoken, unknowing apologies for misunderstanding me.

Another lesson learned as a teenager, was that we are all the result of where we come from. And judging by where I was coming from, I could see as clear as day that I would be hard pressed to find one of these parents who were coming from the same place as me, but that was okay. We assume what we do not know and often that becomes a judgement of character and a misunderstanding of an individual's intention.

CHAPTER 2

I peered through the curtains, the weather was welcoming, outside for the first time in ages looked like a summers' day. I loved it. Perhaps it was something to do with the time my mind began functioning, that break of dawn feeling. Maybe it was the expression of beautiful flowers, and blossoms that just made me experience love of a different nature. I could only imagine how the flowers must feel as they bloom and witness the sun for the first time. I guess for the flower, it's a birthday, something to be celebrated. Well I suppose my observation is not dissimilar to that. Spring, summer, sun, all had an impact on my overall perception. It was like a birthday, in fact no, it was more like being reborn. Although I was used to practising a moment of reflection. A moment where I stepped outside of myself in silence, and could then and only then, take a look at my life, my journey, daily occurrences, and conclude if this was what I wanted to see, feel, or experience. Spring seemed to be the onset of a deeper reflection period for me. One where it seemed simpler to see all the blessings I had been bestowed with. And today on this Spring Saturday morning, I lay in bed, whilst stepping out of myself into my tranquil of reflection. At first my mind was all over the place, it was a classic tale of my thoughts masquerading as Tarzan, frantically swinging through the trees in my brain faster than I could say 'is it a bird, is it a plane!' I tried to slow my thoughts down, attempted with sheer determination to centre my thoughts on just one thing at a time, it was no use. Tarzan just kept swinging as he shouted from the treetops 'Oooooh ooooooohooooooh'. I sat up frustrated with my lack of concentration, my lack of dedication to a practice I enjoyed, a practice I knew was helpful to my survival in this game of cards, which I just didn't play well. I knew that this practice was dependent on me being able to recognise my shortcomings, subsequently striving to be better. This daily practice of reflection was who I was, I needed it today, and I needed it right now. This morning whilst our home was basking in absolute serenity. I looked over at the clock on the wall, Cassius was sure to wake up soon, expecting his breakfast, I knew I didn't have long. I lay back down, glanced at my half open door at the same time, listening attentively to the silence of my sons sleeping.

Oh, how I loved those boys. They were my world, my true loves, my little handbags that accompanied me almost everywhere I went. They were so different in personalities. Chalk and cheese would not even begin to describe. They were as different as is oil and water. The only stark difference was that they came together in absolute harmony when they needed to. Perhaps not when one had the others toy, but definitely when one was tired in the back of the car and needed the others lap to act as a pillow. Inevitably the one needing to sleep was Cassius, and the lap substituted for a pillow was Kwame. He was a honourable big brother from the moment he had met his brother when we returned from the hospital. He fell in love with his baby brother. Even at two years he somehow found it in himself not to feel jealous of the new arrival. The bundle of joy, family and friends flocked to meet soon afterwards. No, he embraced it, in a way that can only be described as natural, perhaps a spiritual connection. The way many mothers view their new-borns, during that moment of initial existence outside of their womb. Kwame was drawn to his brother, fetching bottles, trying to feed him and being sure to alert the adults if Cassius should whimper, even if in a minuscule second whilst sleeping. Kwame was dedicated. A dedicated big brother, and in honesty this impacted my view of him as my first-born. Upon reflection I understood that he was special, that the circumstances prevailing my decision to welcome my pregnancy were ordained by a Higher Being: The Almighty.

That going into labour four weeks before my expected due date, and then being told whilst still in the delivery room, that his lungs were fine, and he needed not to be placed in the Intensive Care Unit. Those were all part of the blessing. That was intended for my journey. Even though the financial impact was often a strain, I soldiered on knowing that this boy, this tiny little son of mine who could not even fit into a premature baby grow, would be like a new-born King born in a fairy tale palace. All would one day be in awe of him and most importantly. I would not allow society in its array of racism, prejudice and violence to steal his greatness. He would go on to exceed expectations and prove to the world that your circumstances do not determine your future. Single mothers. No Single Black mothers are not the cause of a destructive society. On the contrary, they can produce some of the most revered humans. Kwame, my son, would go on to do just that. I was sure of it. Furthermore, each time I reflected on my life and how I had reached this point of Blessing. Although through immense difficulty, heartache, and more. Almost miraculously, my assertion remained the same. It was difficult at times, but we would soldier on and be happy.

Why? Because, it was ordained.

CHAPTER 3

There was traffic everywhere. Cars were driving at maximum speeds of approximately 4mph at best, horns were tooting aggressively, drivers impatient with the actions of another. I had travelled into hell without paying attention. At this rate I would just make it to the school before the end of after-school club. 'Great,' I thought. I didn't like leaving the boys at after-school club until the end. I didn't want them to be the last children collected at the end of what must be a long and arduous day for the keen staff. I liked to arrive at least an hour before 6pm. For some unknown reason collecting my sons at 6pm made me feel like a terrible mother. Already I dropped them to school at 8am most mornings, now picking them up at six made me question my ability to be called a mother. Perhaps it was because I didn't really have an experience of breakfast and after-school clubs. Although my mum worked two jobs when I was a child, a day job and a night job. I on the other hand neglected that whole experience of attending such clubs. It wasn't a bad thing. But I realise it influenced my view of how I should be able to function as a mother.

I thought about how my mum's day looked when I was younger. As it so happens when I was the boys' age, my mum had only me. I was still an only child. However, in hindsight her struggle was apparent. I mean a Mother who attends work approximately all day after dropping her daughter to school and then collects her, drops her to her sister's house, my auntie before then dashing off to a night job until what I recall must have been about 6am or so, can eventually give you the impression of a Superwoman. In fact, Supermum, because quite frankly if superwoman had to raise a child and save the world, I'm sure she'd quit one of her jobs.

Nevertheless, my Mum did not quit! She soldiered on. She worked, she studied, and, in my opinion, she succeeded. Upon reflection it was becoming as clear as day why I thought collecting the boys at the end of after-school club made me terrible. Because my own Mother despite her struggle, her fight to raise me... had not asked an outsider to look after me. She had relied on her sisters and at times, my Step Dad, as my real dad was unfortunately not as committed to raising me as my Mum.

Yet I didn't have a sister, (or sisters) I could lean on in desperation. I had close friends, in particular my Best Friend, Girlfriend (AKA GF), but she lived at least 30 minutes from me and too had to do her school run, single handily.

My brother on the other hand was studying, and he didn't drive either so attempting to get the boys school would not have been practical. Everyone had their own struggles to deal with, their own school runs and their own lives, it wasn't fair to expect everyone to drop their priorities in place of mine. Or to fill in, because perhaps I had chosen this life for myself. I had made my own decisions that resulted in my current situation. I had been the one who expected too much from others and ultimately had been left with two children under the age of five, by myself. I was the one that chose to go to work and study knowing I had these responsibilities. In fact, I was the one who chose for them to attend a school in an area where I had 'diddly squat' support system and now I was here sat in traffic feeling like crap. The traffic had moved on slightly and I recognised the faint red light I knew to mean there were temporary traffic lights in the distance.

Now I understood why a thirty-minute journey was taking me close to an hour. At least now after spending what felt like an entire afternoon in traffic, I could see the light at the end of the tunnel. In this case, the much appreciated traffic light. Sitting in front of the traffic light, I tried to avoid looking at the time on the dashboard. I really didn't need the reminder of the current time or the voice inside that kept asking 'what kind of mother are you?' I had begun to feel hopeful that my sons would not be the last children to be collected so 'Ha, I am a good Mum after all!' I felt smug having this conversation with my mind, but deep down I knew that my response to the question was not correct. It was not appropriate for the situation. That response was merely a defence, an opposition to a point of view. The response to such an argument needed to be absolute; it needed to be a clarification, accurate, a matter of fact, (and in no uncertain terms), the last word on the subject.

Yet I knew within myself that, this would not be the case. I would go on to have another row with my mind. Perhaps next time, a blazing row, a battle. Who knows? For now, I would settle for the half-hearted win and still claim my 1-0 defeat.

CHAPTER 4

I arrived at the school half an hour before after school club had ended, pleased with myself at the accomplishment.

'Sorry I'm late Sandra', I said smiling though wearing a look of embarrassment.

Sandra was one of the staff at the after-school club and my favourite member of staff. I'm not sure of the moment at which I realised that this woman was someone I didn't mind leaving my children with. Yet I can recall it was almost instantaneous. Sandra from what I gathered from previous conversations with her had worked at the after-school pub for many years. Her children had attended the school when they were younger and since then she had worked there. I remember her talking about how the job allowed her to balance work and the kids as it meant that the kids would stay with her during the hours she worked at the after-school club. Sandra had explained to me that after she took her children to school, she would go home and cook dinner. That way when they arrived home in the evening, dinner was already prepared. I admired Sandra and that admiration earned her my respect as a woman and as a Mother. Talking to her resonated with me, although Sandra was single with five children. I often wondered how willing her heart must be to have more children than me and still believe a man could guarantee her their love and commitment. Though experience had taught me that it wasn't always as simple as that. Things change, people change, and life will deal you cards whether you're sat at the table or not, you will still be expected to play them. Sandra reaffirmed that for me.

Although I personally could not consider more children, I admired her for braving the unknown and taking chances despite not knowing the outcome. She was a strong Black woman and I respected her struggle and her ability to soldier on.

'Oh please', Sandra said rolling her eyes at me. 'Half of the parents haven't arrived yet, nuff of them said they're going to be late because of traffic, you obviously didn't have any issues with it'

'I wish!' I replied widening my eyes. 'I thought I was gonna be the last parent here' I exclaimed.

'Well you're not, as usual'.

I smiled at Sandra, oh how that comment made me feel better. I wasn't the worst after all. There was me dreading the walk down the plank into the after-school club when admittedly I was allowing my mind to stir a reaction in my metaphysical. A reaction that led me down a path of doubt and for want of a better word baptism in a sea of depression, where all our deepest fears and doubts go to congregate. If such a sea existed, I would probably have been a frequent visitor throughout my life. Better still not a visitor because visitor implies consent of some kind. No, I'm referring to non-consensual visits, much like a kidnapping. The mind is overcome and dragged to the edge of the cliff before being hurled into that sea with colossal strength, and told to figure its way out, despite not having a body with both necessary and vital elements it would need to swim to safety. That was what I was referring to.

'Mummy!' A voice shrieked excitedly by my feet. It was Cassius, he had spotted me first and run over to greet me.

'Hey Mummy's dumpling', I said as I bent down to hug him. He was so cute with his cheeky face and sly grin. He made my heart smile to look at him.

'Mummy', it was Kwame this time, charging from the other end of the room where it looked like he had been sat drawing a picture.

'Look I drew a picture of me, you, Cass' and daddy at home', he waved the picture excitedly under my nose, 'here you go Mummy.'

I looked the picture grinning, it wasn't hard for me to make out amongst the multitude of colours, that there were two extremely large people and then two distinctively smaller ones. I imagined myself and daddy were the large ones and that Kwame and Cassius were the smaller ones. We looked as dysfunctional as the Simpsons, but with the beauty of things through a child's eyes.

'This is beautiful 'Kwame-bug' (a nickname gained at nursery for having two of his plaits sticking up out of place on a daily basis)

'Brilliant colouring', I commented, as I glanced at the picture boasting an array of colours some even mixed together to create new colours. 'Mummy really likes this picture baby'.

I gave him a hug and kissed his cheek. Watching him beaming with pride as he placed the picture neatly in his bag.

When we arrived home the boys changed out of their uniform into house clothes and I did the same. The boys had mentioned that they weren't hungry yet so I could afford to sit on the sofa and relax for a moment before either one started explaining that they were starving. Not hungry of course, no starving, for some reason my children were never hungry always starving.

I joined both the boys on the sofa where they had already begun the argument over what to watch. This too was a daily occurrence, neither boys ever wanted to watch the same thing at the same time. They would both much rather bicker over the remote about why the other should choose. Eventually the argument would end in one of two ways:

Either I would snatch the remote alternatively selecting something that I would rather watch, which inevitably was not something either of them wanted to watch. Or I would demand they take it in turns watching one programme until the end, in turn, letting the other person watch what they wanted until the end of that programme. This was everybody's preferred option, including mine as TV wasn't my dearest friend, I didn't watch soaps and it seemed most of the selection seemed to be an on-going soap opera. I stuck to mainly American comedy or CSI Miami. A friend of mine once told me that I watch 'middle class comedy' as opposed to comedy. He referred to me enjoying countless episodes of Frasier as that being 'middle class comedy' whilst I wouldn't watch an episode of Red Dwarf or 'Father Ted'. We disagreed for several hours each criticising the others taste in TV programmes before agreeing to disagree as we both had invariably different taste in programmes. Or as I put it in my mind, he chose to watch a load of ridiculously daft behaviour and I did not! I took the remote out of the clasp of Kwame's huge hands (by anyone's standards) and asked them both to state what they wanted to watch. As last time Kwame had watched his programme first, I turned the TV to Cassius selection and settled down to watch Power

Rangers with my sons. We were watching kid's shows for about an hour before I went into the kitchen to start sharing out dinner. Luckily, I had cooked enough the previous day, all I needed to do was heat it up. I started sharing dinner onto plates when Kwame entered the kitchen, 'Mummy do you think Dad can pick me up from school one day?'

I stopped what I was doing and put the serving spoon down turning to face him. 'I don't think so Kwame, daddy's got a lot to do at work, he can't get to the school baby'

'But why can't he leave earlier Mummy…?'

His question was valid, yes. However not quite under the circumstances. The Daddy he referred to was not here. It had been that way for a while but the boys, particularly Kwame, had experienced a hard time in understanding that. One day he was here. The next he simply wasn't, as far as the boys were concerned. They couldn't understand why he never came to visit, or to school plays, trips and other events. They could not fathom why he would choose to do that. The bewildered questions that followed, were the consequence of that lack of understanding.

The questions were always my unwanted invitation to a party I'd rather not attend but had to anyway. These questions were at the very core of my metaphysical battles and not having the right answer, the truth, or an answer that resolved their curiosities in any way, shape or form, just added to the weight I was so weary of sustaining.

'Maybe one day baby' I said as reassuring as I could. Just not yet. If you want, we could post Daddy your picture, I'm sure he'd be happy with that'.

'Yes Mummy, can we post it!'

Phew he was back. The sadness in his eyes had been replaced with a gleam in his eye and the excitement we were all accustomed to experiencing when he was around, had returned. Goal! Many a time the conversations had lasted much longer, leaving me stumbling over words clumsily, as I tried to make sense of adult material for the ears and understanding of children, until eventually I would shut the conversation down in defeat and retreat to my room only to explode into tears, at the realisation that I had let them down. I had let down my sons whom I loved beyond words, by failing to ensure that they had a Father to carry out school runs with, one to make breakfasts, dinners and lunches. One to run to, when Mum was in a foul mood, and one to just sit on their laps and have sensible, childish conversations about the woes of being a child. Yet I had not delivered that. I had failed to provide that. Of course, this did not help me out of my sea of depression. It only made my immersion more violent, tumultuous, waves attacking me more uncontrollably each time my head peered above water.

This sucks, I thought opening my eyes as wide as possible to avoid the droplet of tears I could feel patiently waiting for its cue. Cassius entered the kitchen.

'Mummy can I do a picture for daddy too?' He looked up me eagerly awaiting a response.

'Yes baby, of course, daddy will love that'

'Yes!' He shrieked with excitement. 'Kwame, Mummy said I can do a picture for daddy to and post it'.

Cassius was so smug about it. It was as though each had been awarded exclusivity to a Private event. I smiled at him as he turned to run back to the living room. Shit! The tear had fallen. I had succeeded up until that point in keeping the dam intact and held back the force of water. But as I watched and listened to the excitement of my sons at the prospect of sending daddy a picture… I melted. The tears fell as silently as I could allow as I wiped them away sure not to leave any evidence that I was in any way less than happy.

It was time for dinner. That was my priority for the moment.

CHAPTER 5

The house was silent, not eerie mind you, just dead silent. Even the usual unwanted ticking of the clock could only be heard in a sort of faint like whisper. A siren screamed loudly as I heard the wheels screech past outside. There you go, I knew it was too good to be true. One thing you were guaranteed, living where we did, was sirens. It wasn't as though crime actually ever took place within the walls of neither ours nor our neighbours. It just so happens that we seemed to reside along the most common pathway for Police attending to an incident or rushing back to the station to clock out and go home early. Either way we lived on route, so this was the familiar tune where we lived.

It had been a month since the boys had started at the new school. They were settling in okay, I guess. Well actually Cassius had settled in okay. He was apparently very quiet at school, yet his teacher, Miss Franklin, referred to him as being the most popular boy in his class. One afternoon in the playground, as I was collecting the boys, she went on to describe a typical scenario in the classroom whereby the children (in particular the girls), would argue about who was his girlfriend. Yes girlfriend! My cutesiest little son had clearly made an impression on the excitable little hearts of some of these unsuspecting daughters, of equally unsuspecting parents. But it didn't end there, no. We haven't touched on the boys yet. So, what was the story with the boys, I'll tell you. All the boys had decided my Cass' was their best friend and apparently, he could only choose one. So, every day his teacher explained to me, the boys would attempt to corner Cassius to demand clarification on who was his best friend today? This was a recurring event on the daily schedule, and Miss Franklin, explained with what seemed like genuine honesty, that she had never seen anything like it.

So how do you think little Cass' coped with the turmoil of selecting a girlfriend and best friend daily...? Simple. He smiled adorably, much like a child trying to convince his parent to buy a nonsensical toy in the toy store, or the box of cereal that the child categorically does not eat but tries to convince you to buy so that they can get the free toy.

I knew that smile only too well. No words, just a smile. When you have a child, who chooses not to talk to people outside of his literal immediate family. Or better still did not talk fluently until approximately three or so years old! You learn to understand and translate an alternative language, one that is unspoken. You learn to read eyes, yes eyes. Not as straightforward as blink once for 'yes' and twice for 'no'. We had to understand the difference between sadness or joy in his eyes. We had to understand the meaning of various sounds accompanied by gestures.

The language Cassius taught us to understand was different, you had to read silence or actions. Like hiding behind mummy's leg at various points, that could mean 'I don't like that person, don't leave me with them'. Or it could mean, 'I don't want them to touch me, they can talk to me from over there', or perhaps he simply didn't like the sound of their voice. There was a multitude of translations we had to learn to decipher, in order to understand Cass', but it was interesting at best, maybe a tad frustrating at worst. Come to think of it, I remembered when the boys were still at nursery. At first Cassius would only speak at home or when I collected him. This son of mine seriously spent an entire day at nursery and uttered only 'yes please' or 'no thank you' if asked something that required an actual answer, until home time. Imagine that!

I collected him from nursery once and he started talking to me about something and the Nursery Manager, Amina, told me that she didn't know he could speak that much. Laugh out loud is the best term I can find for that moment. That was a perfect example of how my son could have you fooled. I mean I know adults who cannot demonstrate that kind of behaviour or discipline even as adults. Me included!

Think about it. How many of us women give ou
partners the silent treatment to apparently teach them a les
to respond to something they say then realising perhaps muc.
your dismay, that you're talking to them when really, you're suppose
to be mad at them?

Am I alone here? Hopefully not. In fact, if I am, please can
somebody, anybody try intentionally not speaking to anyone outside
of your home.

In other words, speak only to the people you reside with and
when anyone else speaks to you: simply ignore them. Only resume
speech once you are home, in familiar surroundings, with your
familiar people. At the end of the day, email me, tag me, somehow
contact me, and let me know how straightforward or challenging it
was.

I challenge you. My hope I confess to you, is that you are able to
understand how difficult that behaviour is on a daily basis. Then
hopefully you too in turn, will understand that this little boy of mine
was truly something. But there was someone else, he would always
speak to, his big brother. Even when no one else knew what was
wrong, it was guaranteed that Cassius would tell Kwame. He
wouldn't necessarily say 'hello' to someone when we were out and
they spoke to him, but if Kwame happened to say hello, or show
some affection, maybe a hug or spudding of fists, only then did
Cassius apprehensively acknowledge your existence. But don't push
it! No hugs, or holding of hands, no conversations lasting more than
three words, i.e. none longer than 'how are you?' And all remained
well.

Otherwise, we may have a fit of hysterical tears and frantic
climbing of imaginary wire fences and walls whilst trolls, giants and
two headed monsters chased him away. Well that was how turbulent
my son's reaction was to strangers in general, or just anyone else. If
you didn't know better, you would almost certainly be worried, and
as for what you may have been thinking...well who knows. Again, the
beauty of my (then), youngest son.

So as Miss Franklin went on to share Cassius' progress, I rubbed
the tight curls on the top of his head lovingly, kissing his cheeks. He
smiled at me. There goes the smile again, adorable. I thanked Miss
Franklin for the progress update and walked over to Kwame's
classroom to collect him. His teacher Miss Reynolds had not begun

dismissing the class. There were at least nine parents stood anxiously waiting outside the door eagerly, to collect their children. Some of the parents were complaining amongst each other, about the fact the children were never dismissed on time, some went on to compare the teachers of their additional children in older years, who were always dismissed on time. I stood silently, unwillingly eavesdropping, as Cass' and I waited patiently on the outside but impatiently on the inside. I had to admit that I did agree with the other parents about the children not being dismissed on time. I mean I had just had an at least five-minute conversation with Miss Reynolds and then made my way casually over to Kwame's class only to find the children still sat at their desks. It was a bit annoying. I mean unlike a number of the parents I still had to make my way home, further than a ten-minute walk, and prepare dinner, and get the boys ready for bed. This woman was screwing with my schedule to be honest. But we were new here, so whilst the boys were still settling in, as was I. So, for the minute Miss Reynolds was going to escape my quiet word with her on why I need my son dismissed on time after school, but only for the minute.

I felt a tap on my shoulder and looked round to see Priti, another parent whose son was in the same class as Kwame. I liked Priti, she was the most interesting parent I had met so far and to be fair, she was less conceited than some of the other parents who lived in the area.

Furthermore, when the boys started, she just happened to be one of the three parents who struck up a conversation with me, the 'new mum', that didn't appear too inquisitive or outright faas. Priti was deaf, I hope I am using the right term for her. But in short, she had a hearing impairment and could not speak. Priti however demonstrated an unbelievably phenomenal skill in communication, which she had mastered without words, or sound hearing. She was able to speak to anybody and I mean anybody, and they would be able to understand her (well at least I could). I remembered our first conversation. Embarrassing as it was to admit, it had taken me all of about three minutes to identify that the parent stood before me was in actual fact deaf. I assumed she spoke with an accent, yet I listened attentively and could comprehend her every sound. As I explained, it took me all of three minutes to decipher between what I thought was an accent, to embracing her skilfulness at attempting to talk to me using broken sounds and hand gestures, despite knowing that due to her disability, I may struggle to understand any of it. Yet that thought, clearly had not crossed her mind. Or better still Priti was not willing to let that stand in her way, of perhaps trying to make me feel comfortable, in the unfamiliar surroundings. In fact, I commended Priti, she had gained my respect. Why, because her actions showed courage. Here was a woman who was clearly not going to be isolated within society. She was not going to allow her own differences to hold her hostage and cower in the corners of the world where others would be least likely to suspect her existence. She was Bold, adventurous, fearless! Priti, to me, was as the super-humans are, to the rest of the World when they compete in the Paralympics. She refused to be held back, disadvantaged, typecast into some sad old 'poor me' feature length movie. Priti was as good as badass, just missing the leather jacket, shades and loud sneakers to embody the full character.

Women who defy all odds appeal to me, they are frequently on my radar, from the famous heroes to the local ones such as my granny, my Mum, my aunties. I notice these women as I journey through life and commend them unreservedly. Priti was probably the most recent addition to my list. Turning to face her, Priti used a mixture of hand gestures and word sounds to complain about the children having not been dismissed as yet. I agreed with her, making sure to allow my lips to intentionally pronounce each word as to help her comprehend that I too, was unimpressed with the delay. I explained to Priti that thanks to Miss Reynolds, now I'd be caught in traffic, the boys were going to eat later than I wanted them to, and now bedtime would be later than usual and so on. As futile as my complaints may have sounded, for me it was a real issue. I wasn't interested in bitching behind Miss Reynolds' back, I felt like perhaps just a quiet little word privately to explain that the children have various activities in the evening, and after being at work all day I need to get them home in time to sort out the dinner, homework and bedtimes. Standard as this was to me, I had come to understand in life that what comes naturally to us is not necessarily natural to everyone.

Take Priti for example, she too was unimpressed with Miss Reynolds and her antics, but I can tell from previous conversations with her that the delay didn't faze her. It didn't affect her routine. She was as relaxed as anything. A little delay might tug away at her skirt the way a toddler pesters his mother in the supermarket for lollipops, but it wasn't detrimental to her evening. Not as it was to mine. I caught a glimpse from the corner of my eye as the children finally began filing out of the classroom, one by one. I turned my attention to the door eagerly looking for a glimpse of Kwame's head. I noticed Priti was now almost on tip toes trying to see over mine as she stared past Miss Reynolds, who seemed to be guarding the door ever so attentively, for her son Ash.

'Afternoon mums and dads, the children are coming out now, so please, allow them enough space to get by'. All the parents, myself included, immediately moved back against the wall to create a clear path for the escapees.

Kwame was still sat at his desk in the class, waiting for his name to be called. I noticed there were only four more children, including Kwame, left sat at their desks. In actual fact to me it seemed a bit strange that with only four more children left to dismiss, she didn't feel it necessary to just dismiss them in one go. And why on Earth did my Kwame have to be among the four?

'Do you mind waiting behind just a moment so I can have a word with you about Kwame? Miss Reynolds requested quietly, almost uncomfortably.

'Yes, no problem I replied smiling with the uncertainty of what the conversation could be about.

Miss Reynolds rather swiftly ushered out the last few remaining children to their awaiting parents and then politely signalled with open arms for me to enter the classroom where Kwame was still sat at the table. Miss Reynolds sat at her desk. 'Great now I'll be here forever' I thought rapidly looking over the children's displays on the wall and anxiously looking for the artwork that would be signed by my son.

'Yolanda, thank you for waiting behind...' began Miss Reynolds 'Kwame has had a pretty mixed day today. He found it hard to sit on the carpet during news time and struggled a bit with his handwriting task'.

I looked up at Miss Reynolds and then at Kwame. Somehow, I was sure she was talking about another child, she obviously thought I was someone else's mum and had confused me. Of course!

'I have tried sitting with Kwame, but he just refuses to do the work I set him, and often begins running around the class while the other children are working quietly'

I glanced at Miss Reynolds this time, and then turned to face Kwame. He was holding his face down, while shuffling his feet. He was guilty. Why on earth did my son have to make his guilt so obvious? I sat there wanting to shake my head.

Miss Reynolds was not sat at home fabricating a tale worth telling the masses. She had not mistaken me for another child's parent. She was definitely talking about my son, Kwame. That boy she described was my boy … but that behaviour? Not familiar to me.

'When you say 'he struggles to sit on the carpet … can you explain for me what you mean by 'struggles'?

I was confused. Bemused. Why on earth was I sat here, at what was starting to feel like the graveyard shift as the only visible faces were teachers with rucksacks on, ready to exit the building, or cleaners with trolleys of cleaning products, ready to tackle a days' worth of childhood spillages and mishaps. I was possibly the only remaining parent on site. The last one. I felt captured for a moment, but quickly snapped out of it as Miss Reynolds responded to my question.

'He tends to sit still for about a minute and then he begins crawling around the carpet making jokes with other children. The problem is the other children know that he is not demonstrating the correct behaviour, so they do their best not to engage with him. However, he becomes louder, more disruptive, causing me to request assistance from another member of staff, to allow me to continue teaching the other children.

I shot a look in Kwame's direction. I was not happy. I didn't need to ask him if it was true. I could see it on his face. On one hand, I felt that I didn't need to give Miss Reynolds the added pleasure of asking Kwame in front of her so his admittance would be almost public. Yet nevertheless, I did it. I asked the question, because no matter what. I knew that what this woman was describing was not behaviour that we condoned as a family.

'Kwame did you do that? I asked in what emerged as a surprisingly understanding tone of voice, considering I felt let down and annoyed at being asked to wait behind for this ridiculous behaviour.

'Yes Mummy', came a mumble from behind his school bag, conveniently perched high enough on the table, preventing me from seeing his face clearly.

'Why weren't you sitting still with the other children?'
I was becoming more confused, irritated, yet trying not to sound it.

'I don't know Mummy'.

I heaved an internal sigh and told Miss Reynolds that I would talk to Kwame about this at home that evening.

'Also,' she added 'Kwame seems to find it challenging when he has to do most writing tasks. He seems to be struggling with writing his letters.

'You f***** what? My son is struggling with letters. I don't think so! Let me tell you, this boy has been reading fluently since he was about three, and his spelling is outstanding, so don't tell me about struggling with letters. My son ain't struggling with no damn letter writing!' I almost very nearly replied. But I caught myself, and just in time to alternatively respond 'can you elaborate please Miss Reynolds?' I was sure to emphasise her name, because I needed her to know this conversation was now becoming serious. Therefore, however she wanted to proceed, this conversation was going to be at her risk.

As I write this, I know it sounds drastic, perhaps I sound defensive, but I was not as naive as my age may have led this teacher to believe.

I had spent my childhood listening and observing teachers putting down any non-Caucasian children. Or trying to convince children of any colour that they would not amount to much, so to stay within the safety realms of small dreams. Perhaps not in those exact words but definitely with that exact intention. You see, intention (I know) is a very powerful tool. However, you use it is up to you. Intention can be the start of segregation as we have seen historically when you consider rulers such as Adolf Hitler, who used his intention of a 'pure race' to cause turmoil and commit and instruct countless heinous crimes.

Alternatively we only need to look at the history and the starting point of Windrush or immigration, to understand that a dream was sold with ulterior intentions, only for my parents to get to England and be subjected to poverty racism and signs that said: 'no dogs, no Blacks, no Irish'. I mean the order of that notice in itself is degrading, but you just for a second allow me to stray so I can regain my position of the story.

They did not tell my parents (or their parents) that they would be scorned, mistreated as second-rate citizens and physically abused because of their appearance and accents. Why not?

Because they had work for them to do. And with that our Grandparents and parents have had to fight, struggle, and adapt in order to survive the injustice in order to then teach the next generation and so on, so they too can survive. So, whilst I may have thought my Mum had exaggerated when she impressed certain principles on us about our foundation. I have very quickly realised that she did not. And even now in this day and age, I too experience racism both directly and indirectly. I quickly recognise when my confidence in who I am causes others to want to 'cut me down to size'. When the colour of my skin does not match my language or verbatim, or even intellect based on another pre conception. You'd be surprised what I notice. Therefore, in terms of my son's, and what that meant to be the mother of my sons, I noticed more than others would care for me to. So as for 'cutting me down to size'?

It's too late! Do you know who my Mother is? Then you know it's impossible! Mum taught us about achieving from the moment we could understand and with me, once I understand something, it cannot be taken away, forgotten or retaught. So, at school most teachers didn't like me much. They assumed, I learned later in life, that I was a know it all.

Not that my Mother is a well-educated strong black woman. Not that my mum had to fight to see to it that I too, would be educated, articulate, and driven.

And certainly not that I was determined to be the best I could be, and that meant not adopting the labels people would try to attach to me.

I was certain that never occurred to other people. Let's face it, most people see only what they want to see, and use those ideals to reaffirm illogical facts that in turn result in misconceptions misjudgements and discrimination. All hail the Mum who taught me to read from a young age, and then fed my love of books with even more. So much so, that when I arrived at Primary school, I was bored stiff. The work was too easy, the teachers kept trying to suppress my ability, and on several occasions my mum had to visit the school and be firm in her assertion of her daughter's capabilities before teachers realised I did not need handwriting assistance, or books with one sentence a page. No. I needed chapter books and access to the library please and thanks.

So, I sat before Miss Reynolds with my first-born son, whom she was advising me, was 'struggling with writing tasks'. I looked her dead in the eyes whilst I waited for her to elaborate. Another skill my mum had successfully taught me as a child: 'look at me when you're talking to me.'

'Kwame tends not to be able to get on with the writing tasks once I have given the class instructions, he doesn't ask for help either he just wanders around singing or disrupting the others'.

I shot another look over at Kwame, who was now looking back at me almost anticipating the words that would follow. Bearing in mind I didn't really have any words; little did he know. I was sat with this woman who was telling me all this crap and then insinuating my son was stupid or senile or something.

'Can I see the work that Kwame has not done today please Miss Reynolds?'

She reached over behind her desk to where the stacks of books were kept and handed me my son's book. I flicked through the pages from the start of the book, slowly until I came to today's date. There it was. Two lines of work in the untidiest scrawl I had ever seen from any of my sons, (let alone one who has been writing long before he started at this school). I noticed immediately that all of the work in the exercise book was unfinished. I could see where the teacher had begun writing sentences for him, in a bid to get him started but still the work remained incomplete. As I turned to the present day, I could see a repeat of the same thing, only I also noticed, where Kwame had done some work, albeit poor work, based on his usual standard, and his teacher had written excellent!

'Sorry Miss Reynolds, can you explain why you have written the feedback 'excellent' here?' I tried not to knit my brows as I awaited an answer.

'Oh yes, I wanted to encourage Kwame to do his best work, so I like to give positive feedback'

'I'm afraid that does not sound positive if it is as far from the truth as this is, Miss Reynolds. Your comment of excellence gives the impression that there is very little left to do to exceed this. Yet, judging by the standard of work and the feedback you have just sat here and given me, this is not excellence. Kwame is indeed more than capable of delivering excellent work, and I believe he has demonstrated that previously.

However, this is definitely not it. In fact, I think that kind of feedback limits an individual if it is not accurate, and I don't want that to happen to my son'.

Miss Reynolds appeared taken aback by my comments. On one hand I wanted to say, 'good now it's your turn'. But on the other hand, I couldn't, because I could see that this was bigger than that. This was not about me getting 'one up' on her or her getting 'one up' on me. This was about the fact that this teacher may well want to make a statistic out of my son, my first-born, my articulate, intelligent child. This was the case, I needed to stay on top of this. In any case something wasn't right here.

'I assure you that I do this with all the students, and it helps them improve upon their work, and Kwame requires a lot of encouragement'

'I'm not for a second disputing the power of encouragement, however what I will say, is the way in which you are using it, could turn out to have an adverse effect, and I would prefer you to use an alternative method with my son. Also, if it's okay with you I'd like to take the exercise book home so that Kwame can have the opportunity to finish what he did not do today, that way tomorrow he is not falling behind'

'Yes of course' Miss Reynolds didn't sound sure, but she did it anyway.

'And if at all you have any issues with Kwame, please do not hesitate to contact me or to speak to me when I'm at school in the morning or the afternoon. Thanks'.

I got up as I finished my sentence and signalled to Kwame using my finger to do the same. He stood up immediately.

'Thank you Miss Reynolds for your time', I said leaving the classroom.

'No, thank you for your support,' she replied (relieved, I'm sure) that I was finally leaving. Kwame scurried behind me and took my hand.

Cassius had been patiently waiting in the corridor and playing with what looked like a soft ball.

'Let's go baby,' I said walking towards the exit. He took my other hand.

'That was a long time Mummy you were talking to my brother's teacher.'

'Yes, I know, sorry about that, let's get home so you two can have dinner.'

Besides Cassius talking to his brother about a story he heard from his teacher that day, the walk to the car was silent. I was deep in thought and knowing Kwame as well as I did. So was he, because he knew his behaviour at school had let himself down and in turn left me feeling let down. The silence continued in the car. Cassius, for some reason, was talking non-stop, giving a minute-by-minute account of his day. Both Kwame and I remained silent. I didn't bother to turn the radio on, I just wasn't in the mood for music. Perhaps usually that would be my chosen blankie, but today that blankie just wouldn't do. Instead I chose to listen to the sound of traffic passing as the car took us on an arduous ride home. Each time I was forced to halt the car due to a beaming red light, it was as though the car was saying 'think long and hard about what you've done...' resulting in me responding only loud enough for the universe to hear me, 'I am!' Even if it didn't take heed. Although I wasn't sure what part I had played in today's spectacle, I was sure I did indeed need some time to think.

CHAPTER 6

I ran myself a piping hot, deep bath that evening. Considering the events of the day, the boys had still gotten to bed on time. I was grateful, knowing that I had been thinking about this bath since we had left the school earlier. In fact, whilst Miss Reynolds had been droning on about my son's conduct. I had stood there planning dinner and dreaming of the steam rising from the waterfall of hot water as it entered the bath at full speed. For the first time I realised it was much like adding hot water from a kettle to an already prepared tea bag. Like the tea bag all that I needed at that moment, was to add water. Mind you, I was under no illusion that the water would in some miraculous way wash away the events of the day, cleanse my heavy heart, or at the very least, drain every ounce of negativity down the plughole. Yet somehow, I still looked forward to my bath. Because above all else, experience had taught me previously that when all else fails take a moment. The bath, I knew allowed me to have that well-deserved, much needed, moment of freeness. Freedom to think, freedom to feel, freedom to just let it all out, and the freedom just to be. That was all I needed. Just the freedom to be and feel. I watched in a subconscious daze as the water reached its limit. Before I knew it, like the person in the movie who falls asleep on the boat only to wake up and realise the boat has drifted out to sea. I too was startled back to reality, just in the nick of time. I reached over and turned off the hot water tap. I had neglected to add cold water purposely, reserving it for the end, as I knew I needed to sit in the bath long enough to watch my troubles rise up and away with the flow of the existing steam. Tepid or lukewarm were not the temperatures I sought. I needed heat! I guess somehow, I associated hot water with thorough cleansing. I mean come to think of it, I had grown up with the notion that in order to clean something thoroughly you used hot water. You mop the floor with hot water. You wash dishes with hot water, not cold. Yes, hot water clearly had an association to deep cleansing for me. Perhaps it wasn't that deep, but whatever it was I needed hot water in my bath at that moment. I dipped one of my feet into the bath slowly. For some reason I was cautious about the temperature, although I knew the likelihood that the bath was too hot was almost inevitable. Yet just in case it was as I anticipated, scorching, I decided to trial just one foot to begin with. Yikes! I yanked my foot out of the scalding water. So much so, I almost threw myself backwards into the doorframe, with my head literally missing the sharp corner of the latch.

'Woah!!... could have been worse' I said thinking out loud. 'Well actually could it?' I replied to my own question as I recalled the day's events. Could it get worse than my son having a complete out-of-body experience at school and behaving like a child that even I was unfamiliar with?

Could it be worse than the teacher talking to me as though my son was a statistic, the very thing I had prayed for him not to be? Come to think of it, a scalded toe, foot, and leg at the very worst, still did not feel like the catastrophe of a day that I was currently going through.

I realised then, and I realise now that what was bothering me may well not be a bother for other mothers. In fact, I may well sound like a hypochondriac. However, my intuition told me that this had the potential to be bigger than it seemed at present. And I trusted my intuition.

When we were children Mum always highlighted the differences in the experiences that we would inevitably go through at school, in life, and ways in which we could always protect ourselves. I admit, back then I thought she was balmy, stuck in a time warp even. But as I grew older and paid attention, I saw through my mother's eyes. And this situation highlighted everything my mother had taught us, because I felt like Miss Reynolds was trying to bring us down.

Extreme, it sounds (I'm sure) but based on behaviour that I had seen with other children, of different races to my son, even if my son was doing all that Miss Reynolds described, it actually still wasn't worse, than some of what I had seen children doing in that school playground after school with their parents and teachers present. Things that where I come from would result in stern words, sanctions, discipline. Nonetheless they instead just seemed to be left alone. Each to their own, I guess. It was already clear to me that where you come from determines how you raise your children. So, while I could stand back and watch in shock and horror at times at the behaviour of some of the other children at the school, I make no apologies for the fact that, that was not where we came from. Where we come from, children do not behave like that. It is frowned upon, not accepted. You will get a good slap for it too. Oh, did I say 'good'? I meant 'well earned!

I twisted the cold-water tap on, ever so gently because I couldn't afford for the water to get tepid. After only a few minutes, I decided to brave it, and step into the bath feet first. Funny I didn't hesitate this time. This time I felt ready for whatever. Too hot, too cold, whatever it was, I was ready for it! I eased myself back into the bath and rested my head right back onto my pale Pink bath pillow. I sighed and expressed gratitude at the comfort of the hot water as it encompassed my body, 'Give Thanks'. I mumbled out loud, as I sighed a huge sigh of relief. Hot baths always released something in me that led me to a chant of extreme gratitude. I say chant because what I did was something unlearned, something so far from the religious beliefs shared and taught with absolute enthusiasm by my dear Auntie Barbara. If I'm honest, my precious Auntie could pray the ears off anyone. She had a way of praying that always seem to sound like a full-blown discussion or an unrehearsed song. As a child, her method of prayer intrigued, excited and confused me, all in one. I used to think that God responded to her in a voice only she could hear. I had convinced myself that my Auntie was probably one of God's favourite people, and for that reason, her conversations with him were unheard by my ears. I wonder if she would think me crazy if she could hear me now. Perhaps she could explain to me, why the bath seemed to have that effect on me, who knows? All I was certain of, is that it had been this way for as far back as I can remember, and I loved it. Somehow when I entered the bath, I felt at one with a bigger spirit than myself. Not necessarily religious, but definitely a spiritual experience that embodied God himself. Somehow when I sat in the bath and laid back, the water went to work on me. As I lay still, chanting verses of gratitude all beginning with 'thank you for....' I slowly began to feel at one with myself. I could see myself in conversation with Miss Reynolds, I could see my son regrettably watching Miss Reynolds describe his abysmal behaviour. The disappointment was so apparent, I could visualise the disappointment in his eyes, he was embarrassed. Much like a child who just couldn't make it to the toilet in time before the dreaded 'accident'. He was ashamed at the information regarding his behaviour, being translated to me. My heart sank; my chanting seemed to cease like a cassette tape used to before you turned to side B for the rest of the album. Sinking lower into the water, I closed my eyes foolishly thinking that tears fall only when you open your eyes. Yet still I kept them closed, and in closing my eyes I caught myself again chanting out loud.

'Keep my sons out of this!'

I had no idea who I was talking to. No longer speaking to God whom I trusted with all my heart. I had subconsciously spoken the term out loud, but knew that I had meant it, for whomever the message was intended. I knew I meant every last word.

Keep my sons out of this!

CHAPTER 7

I sat in the canteen at University, the noise was unbearable. If it wasn't students playfully flirting, it was the clanging of dirty plates. Even if unlike me you were allergic to too much noise, I think this was the noisiest eating area I had ever come across. Desperation and laziness had partnered together to force me to buy a dry, crinkled Jacket potato which much rather resembled a baked new potato. However, I chose not to mention it to the lady serving me in the canteen as she abruptly told me it would cost £3 without butter, beans or cheese. Eyes rolling, I accepted the subpar lunch substitute.

Something I know well about myself is that if I am not in a good mood, it's probably best not to mention to someone else the thing that they are doing that I think is unacceptable. In this case it was the nerve of the lady in the canteen selling me a new potato with cheese and beans for £3.75. It was taking everything out of me not to say, 'how dare you, I could've bought two bags of potatoes for that price!', but I didn't. Simply because I hadn't. I knew I was still feeling a lot of things that I hadn't yet been able to shake. Kwame's behaviour at school had not become worse, so to speak. Nevertheless, the complaints were still coming. Each day still felt like something. I eagerly anticipated seeing my sons after a long day at work or university, only to get to the school and see Miss Reynolds' face in the playground eagerly awaiting my arrival. Then came the 'we had a so-so day today didn't we Kwame?' In her stupid pathetic, whiny tone. It was only a few more hours until I had to collect the boys, yet as much as I looked forward to seeing them. I was dreading having to listen to the woman's patronising nasal complaints.

I had resorted to setting aside specific sharing time at home with the boys just to try and ascertain if I was missing something. I mean if the school was right and there was something wrong with my sons then I wanted to identify that. I didn't want for external professionals, outsiders, to identify it and strategize without me. No. I needed to stay ahead of this, I needed to remain on top of this because something wasn't right, I knew that much. I had begun being even more attentive. Making sure we were having conversations about the school day. I was hoping I could somehow gauge some picture of their day, perhaps figure out where I was going wrong. I mean if, my children are playing up, then it must be something I'm doing wrong ... right?

For some reason the assumption seemed fair.

I imagined how the teachers would talk about my son in the staff room. They probably thought my family was a disaster waiting to happen. A dysfunction in every way.

Yet deep down I disagreed.

We were imperfect yes.

'Single parent home' yes.

'Young black mum' check.

I felt it all. Somehow, despite viewing my family as more of an 'against all odds' type of family. I viewed our structure as challenging, yes. Not having someone, namely a father there to share the joys and woes, not having the option to share school runs and extra-curricular activities. I felt it. I felt the overarching stigma. The energy when some of the teachers had spoken to me about my son. It was as if they saw my family as a lost cause. Almost defected at the point of conception. My thought process infuriated me. Somehow the conversations the teachers chose to have with me at the school gates, amongst the other seemingly 'traditional, have-it-all together' families, was gnawing away at my outer layers and seeping into my spirit. I no longer felt together. Rather I was beginning to feel like I was missing pieces of my own puzzle. My heart told me they didn't have my son's best interest at heart, so why was I allowing these no gooders, these destructive educators, to gnaw away at me, burrowing their way into our lives, our home. I didn't have the answers. I was blank. I looked up at the Herculean clock on the canteen wall. I didn't have long before I had to attend my next lecture. I contemplated calling my

Mum, I needed to clear my chest, dissect my thought process, and get answers. My Mum always had something to say, at times just the thing, other times not. Yet I had come to realise that it didn't necessarily have to be the perfect thing to say. I came to understand this about my mum as the years passed. It could be the most obvious assertion, ordinarily one that may have eluded me. Yet one thing was always guaranteed with my mum. Whatever she did say would provide me with ample food for thought. Whether I agreed or disagreed, at the end of the conversation I would be left with something to think about. And that is how I best operate. Giving thought to everything, on a number of occasions in retrospect.

However, I appreciate having the capacity to get lost in my thoughts. Boarding a train, destination undetermined, with a standard ticket, requiring all passengers on-board to explore the surroundings of each stop in detail. That was the only drawback. Well actually, getting off the train was never an easy task either. You could not simply abandon the journey due to sights seen at any given stop. No, it was compulsory that you faced what was presented to you and fathomed how to make it better before the next stop. There was so much I (almost) detested about that train. Needless to say, deep down, I knew I boarded the accelerated steel tube, often of my own accord. Not kicking and screaming like you would imagine. No, I willingly boarded the train and sat comfortably awaiting its departure.

The phone rang a few times before my Mum picked up.

'Hello'

'Hi Mum, you okay?'

'Yes, I'm good. How you doing? The boys okay?'

'Yes Mum, they're good. I'm just at university on lunch.'

'Okay, how's it going, did you get your assignment done?'

'I've started it,' I said' conscious not to stretch my truth. What I didn't add was that I had literally written a mere introduction. Much of which was I'm sure, a repetition of the same sentence for the duration of the short paragraph. I was not finding the assignment difficult. On the contrary. I was simply finding it hard to get my head in gear. To focus on absorbing the relevant information to evidence the basis of my understanding.

'How are the boys getting on at school?' Mum asked.

'They're okay Mum. Cass' is alright, he likes his class and his teacher. She keeps going on about how he doesn't speak much in class.

'Did you explain to her that that is his character?'

'I did Mum, however for some reason she still going on about it every now and again'

Mum kissed her teeth.

'What about Kwame?'

'Mum I don't know. Every day his teacher has something to say. She tells me he's walking around the class when he should be sat doing his work. He's playing with objects in the classroom when he should be sat on the carpet, refuses to do his work.'

'That doesn't make any sense!' Mum said sternly. 'All of a sudden he's doing all of that in class. He never behaved like this before!'

I could hear the frustration in my mums' voice, despite the fact I knew she was trying not show it.

'But Mum when I ask him about the things the teacher says, he admits it Mum, so I can't say she's telling lies. This is actually what he's doing.'

'Why does he say he's doing it?

'He says 'I don't know Mummy.' Though the other day he was telling me that the teacher said he doesn't have to do the work if he doesn't want to'.

'I beg your pardon!'

'Yes Mum' I replied in agreement with her thoughts.

'Listen I may have to have a word with that, whatever her name is, because I don't know what the hell they're trying to do with my grandson. She must think he doesn't come from nowhere.'

'Exactly Mum!'

I was grateful for my Mum. Grateful for the fact that her love for me immediately extended to my sons from the moment they were born, even conceived. It helped that I didn't have to face anything alone, that my mum was far from con formative, and in being that way, encouraged me to stand up for what I believed in, to fight, to have my voice heard.

My mum taught me that the law, when I was a child, started and ended with her. I feared no teacher, no one else's parent, the police, the army. No, instead I feared my Mum, the real Law. As a child, I often imagined what I would do if I was ever arrested and the police had to contact my mum. As a now adult, I'm telling you that if I had ever found myself in that position, my concern would not be the police. For me, it would be what happens once they let me out. Some children I suppose, feared the police, but I have never felt that way. In fact, as I sit here imagining it. My greatest fear would be when they open my cell door and tell me my mum is here to collect me. Would I beg them to protect me from this woman, ask them to send me to anybody else, just not her? No, I wouldn't.

Do you know why?

The way I viewed my mum. The police couldn't save me from her. That was my mum. They had no authority over my mum! She was not a criminal. She did not break the law. She was the woman who had given me life. She was my mum. So, what on earth were they going to do, try and tell her how to raise me? I don't think so. My mum was the law!

So, as I listened to the aggravation in her voice pertaining to the boys. It reminded me that despite Miss Reynolds' constant griping, I was the law! And always would be, where my sons were concerned.

'I need to sit down with the boys and understand what's happening at school', mum started to say. 'It doesn't make any sense that all of a sudden the behaviour has changed so dramatically'

'I have tried Mum, but I dunno'.

'Yolanda...' I felt a tap on my shoulder.

'One second Mum' I said as I turned to acknowledge Tracey, a woman from my class.

'There's been a room change Yolanda, we're on the 3rd floor today room 311'.

'Oh, thanks Tracey, I'll be up in a minute'

'No probs' Tracey replied 'I'll save you a seat'

Tracey was a woman in my class. She was older than me, her family were from Sierra Leone. She was a nice lady, quite kind, and thoughtful. Sometimes a bit slow in class, but she had a good heart. Always trying to help others. I appreciated that although I was clearly sat at this table as not to have to socialise, Tracey still felt the need to come over and give me an update on the lecture room change. Other people (I realised after looking around the canteen) had already left to make their way to class. None of them had tapped my shoulder to update me.

'Awww well' I thought. I was glad I always took the time out, to help Tracey understand the work, because bless her, she clearly wasn't leaving me out.

I got back to my phone call.

'Mum I'm going to have to go now my lecture starts in 5 minutes. I'll call you this evening after I get the boys.'

'Okay then, you have a good day and keep your chin up'

'Yes mum, you too' I said, before ending the call and quickly silencing the phone before putting it back into my bag. I put away my tray with most of what I ordered, still on it, and hurried to the third floor, the last thing I needed was to be late for class.

CHAPTER 8

By the time I was ready to collect the boys from school, my day had already begun to improve dramatically. Despite the upheaval of the room change, the lecture was surprisingly interesting. Not interesting as to provide the impression that ordinarily these lectures were boring. No, I was surprisingly impressed by some of the information we received. We discussed the impact of social class and stigma on families. I'm sure this was not for my benefit. However, as I sat there at the back of the class, I felt this lecture was easily relatable to my family. I had taken at least four pages worth of notes in the space of half an hour. Not notes containing letters the size of two lines. No. I mean notes in small writing, extensive notes, highlighting things to read up on. Cases to look up. The lecture had intrigued me. Learning things, I didn't know, things I thought I knew, and further causing me to evaluate how a person in that situation, manoeuvres their way to a better outcome.

I guess for me one of the most interesting things about the lecture that day. Was learning from someone else how stigma impacts the lives of others. How it somehow has the right to diminish opportunities, as it saw fit. That stigma was not as many would have you believe, an excuse for self-pity. Rather it was a fact! A social manifestation of judgements prejudices and ingrained discrimination. And as the lecturer discussed thought leaders, their opinions, experiments and scientific anomalies. It reiterated to me, the mantra my mum had taught us when we were small, about not just doing well but doing 100 times better than that, in order to be recognised for it.

My mum fortunately had arrived in this country when stigma, discrimination and prejudice were an acceptable factor of society. I'm pretty certain that some of the stories my mum could potentially share, may perturb some. You had to pay homage to the fact that my mum never saw herself as a victim, she simply knew she had experiences, and those experiences she chose to learn from. As she learned, she taught us. So, as I sat taking notes vigorously as though my life depended on the information, I also knew that my mum had given me this very information in her own way, throughout my childhood. It's just that at the time, I thought my mum was just being too hard. I take that back now, mind you. And whoever the thought leaders were, hats off to them for acknowledging that there is a distinct difference between the way society treats poor people and those considered wealthy. You did not have to go too far to decipher the academic differences between the schools available in the most prestige residential areas, as opposed to the schools in the surrounding areas where I currently lived. Neither did you have to go far to witness the differences between the way Black people were criminalised for illegal behaviour as opposed to those who were not of Black descent.

And how about the rate of permanent exclusions in school. Take a look at the statistics on the race of the children who tend to be most likely to be permanently excluded from school. Then for the sake of having fun, compare that with the rate of permanent exclusions from independent schools for instance. This was the gist of the information that had improved my day. My mum, in fact we, were clearly not alone in our assumption of the disparity of equality within society. So, as I pulled up outside the school gates, waiting patiently for the school bell to ring. I felt reassured that society doesn't always have your best interest at heart, so you do need to learn how to fight. I took a deep breath before walking through the gates to collect the boys. In all honesty I had a plan to collect Kwame from Miss Reynolds without making eye contact, thus minimising the opportunity for her to drone on about my son. I was on a high, a legal high obtained from intellectual enlightenment received at University. I did not want this simple little woman to mess with my high. I had an objective which involved going home and researching this intriguing topic in much more depth. I didn't have time to hear her today. Today was not the day.

I collected Cassius first. I wanted to charge straight right back through the gates after collecting Kwame. If I could I would have given my son's the ready steady go, as though we were about to take off in a race against Usain Bolt, an amazing great race, they even they had the possibility of winning. Quite frankly I would have, because that's how I felt.

Cassius was already holding my hand. As we approached his brother, he instantly let go running over and throwing his arms around his brother's neck. The excitement he showed towards Kwame was funny at best. You would think they were in two separate schools, only seeing each other for the first time at that moment. I saw Kwame rub the top of his brother's head appreciatively before hugging him back.

'Did you have a fun day at school?' I heard him ask his brother as though there were at least a 10-year age gap between them.

'Yes Kwame 'Cassius replied excitedly almost bouncing up and down before going on to give his older brother a lengthy synopsis of his day.

'Let's go boys' I announced loud enough for Miss Reynolds to acknowledge that I was taking Kwame, yet swift enough that she was unable to share all of her pessimism of the day with me. Perfect. I noticed her mouth open as though she wanted to call me back, I smiled, waved and kept it moving. Not today b**** I said in my mind, holding the boys on either side, swinging their hands as though we were going to see the Wizard of Oz. Awwww that's one day down, I thought to myself, as I bundled the kids into the car.

CHAPTER 9

The weather had taken a turn, becoming a bit chilly, considering it was supposed to be summer time. To top it all, winter was my least favourite time of year. Icy winds, the sting of the breeze, as it touched my face and ears. No thanks. I had brought the boys winter coats already, whilst I could afford to buy them both, so the boys were well prepared.

Me on the other hand, I knew I would end up probably still wearing my leather jacket, unable to fork out the extra money for a much-needed winter coat for myself. After all I was driving, I could cope with my leather jacket for the limited time I was outside of the car. Besides, I could think of much more important things I needed to do with that money. Pay for swimming, after school club and football, which the boys, particularly Cassius, enjoyed doing. Not to mention my rent and council tax, that for some reason, the local authority had assessed that I was able to pay on my low, single parent income. Yeh right. As if! At the end of the month I could barely cover the essentials. Nevertheless, I did tell myself the other debts could wait. Like my much-needed winter coat, I was putting off buying, until maybe the January sales when it would cost me only half the price. Beats me, how the local authority even assessed people's incomes. To me it was as though no consideration for individual circumstances was taken into account. How on Earth could I be expected to manage my income, with my outgoings, if they expected me to contribute so much to council tax and rent? However, I was beyond arguing. I had already contacted them and spoken to an extremely unhelpful call centre operative, who told me under no uncertain terms, was it the local authority's problem, and swimming, in addition to any other extra-curricular activities, were not considered priority debts. As were car payments.

Now firstly I hated contacting the local authority no matter what the reason. However, pride aside, I had told myself that the reason for the disproportionate assessment was because I must have in some way, been unclear about my family's income. Only to make the dreaded phone call and learn that actually, they didn't, no couldn't, care less about how we survived. It was a vivid reminder and reality check, that reiterated to me that my family's survival, my son's survival, was my problem! And you know what, despite feeling hard done by, or insignificant. I accepted it as fact and continued my struggle knowing that one-day. I would not need to communicate with them again. One day I would be able to do this myself, with no assistance. Everything for a time my Mum had always taught us, and I believed this. Much like the trauma I had experienced previously in my life, which somehow, I had managed to overcome. I too would overcome this, looking back on it with a feeling of great satisfaction. Knowing that once there was no light, then suddenly the sun would shine on all that was blessed in my life.

Although I was yet to see the light, I reminded myself why I was working, studying for a degree, and trying to raise my children. I could do this, I thought reassuring myself.

Many had achieved it before me, my Mum, my Auntie's. They too had studied and worked, often two jobs just to make sure we had what we had needed. Unlike me, they did not have the added luxury of housing or council tax benefits. They merely had the mind-set of soldiers fighting for survival, coupled with dedication to the children they had conceived, carried and subsequently brought into this world.

That momentum had extended to me. The tenacity, the dedication, the 'I can do it alone' attitude. I have to say it was hard to maintain this momentum consistently. Some days it was easier than others.

However, I had mastered bad days as momentary, cry though I may when feeling low, or lacking the necessary resources. I knew once the tears had fallen. I would be okay again. In essence, the feeling of inequality drove me that little bit more. Gave me the extra push I needed to soldier on.

I would gain my social work degree, my children would survive with want for nothing, and I, me alone, would make sure of that.

I pulled up at the school, feeling empowered. Today felt like a good day. I was up to date with my assignments, bar the last one which in part, was focused on a 90-day placement within a social care setting. My reputation with a local authority I had previously worked for, had made it easy for me to secure a placement within Social services. So, my placement would begin quite soon, sooner than I thought. Placement would act as a full-time job without pay, meaning I still kept my permanent role within a semi-independent home for young people in the meantime. Perfect. Tiring yes. But perfect, because I could not afford to work for free, and still survive.

I glided into the school oblivious to everything around me. We had one more week of school before the half term began, and I couldn't wait. The excitement must have shown on my face because I could see Cassius' teacher smiling at me before I had even reached the classroom door.

'Afternoon Miss', I said extending the joy I was feeling, as Cassius ran towards me grinning. I hugged him and asked Miss Franklin about his day.

'He was fine' she replied reassuringly. She updated me on the homework that had been set, before wishing Cassius a wonderful evening.

Hand in hand, Cassius and I made our way to Kwame's classroom. Almost all the children had already been dismissed. Shocking. I looked at the parents stood in the corridor; I definitely was not late. I gave Miss Reynolds a smile,

'Afternoon Miss'. Although she was far from my favourite teacher, I thought perhaps I could extend some joy her way too. She seemed like she needed an injection of positivity. She looked at me sheepishly and then walked over to me 'err Mrs O'Connor would like a quick chat with you'

'Is something wrong?' I asked, smile slowly disappearing.

'I think she just wants a quick chat with you about the boy's transition.'

Somehow her sentence seemed to be missing some detail or the other. I looked her square in the eyes, she avoided my gaze. I could feel the anxiety in my stomach. What now I thought. What do they want now?

The boys were doing okay. Kwame was still refusing to complete his work on some days, but I had already arranged with his teacher that for each piece of work he refused to complete at school. We would take it home and complete for homework. This would mean less TV and time to play with toys for Kwame and I knew he hated that. However, I needed him to obtain his education. He was more than capable and showed this at home when he was doing work, so I continued to be confused as to why he simply wouldn't complete the work in class.

Kwame ran over to me hugging and kissing me excitedly.

'Afternoon son' my smile returning briefly.

'You can leave the boys here whilst you see Miss O'Connor', Miss Reynolds offered still sounding uncomfortable.

'No that's fine Miss' I replied faking a smile and taking the boys by the hand.

I did not like this woman's body language and no I did not need you to watch my sons I heard myself saying as I made my way to reception where the Head teacher's office was. The joy seemed to have left me. Not gradually either. No this was more like when you yank the plug from the bath and the water starts disappearing rapidly down the plughole. I felt anxious; my stomach still uneasy. Anxiety always got me in the stomach, ever since I was a child. Awaiting something major, good or bad, had the ability to give me what I refer to as nervous belly. Knowing I did not wish to speak to this woman and not knowing why she had indeed requested to see me made me feel unprepared. I gave the receptionist my name and advised her that Miss O'Connor had requested to see me although I did not have an appointment. Her response gave me the impression that she had been expecting me. Hmmm.

Miss O'Connor stepped out from her office behind the reception desk, glasses perched on her nose like the head-teacher from one of the classic storybooks at home.

'Thank you for coming in Yolanda, please come this way' she said smiling and using her hands to gesture.

I put the boys to sit down on the green chairs in the reception area and told them to wait there quietly while I spoke with Miss O'Connor.

'Okay Mummy' they chorused.

I entered the office and sat down at the oak table in the centre. I looked around the office at the certificates on the wall. Some of them looked quite old and were dated over seven years ago. The shelves were full of books to do with education and child development. I sat there wondering if Miss O'Connor even read the books or if she kept them there to assert her position as head-teacher when parents were present. Quite frankly I didn't care because whether or not I knew for sure if she read them. It probably wouldn't impact my opinion either way. On the desk was the picture of a little girl. She looked older than my boys but not quite of high school age. I assumed it was her daughter. Sitting down on her expensive looking lumbar support chair, Miss O'Connor began to talk.

'I really appreciate you taking the time to meet with me' she began.

You already said that, I wanted to reply but instead opted for 'you're welcome'

'How are Kwame and Cassius settling in to our school?' she asked as though she had no idea. I found her approach a bit testing. I mean if you have something to say just say let's not play games, we're all adults here.

'Well as with most things, it takes time, but okay thanks' I replied hoping she would get to the point quickly.

'Yes, I agree these things do take time and each child has different needs when it comes to transition.

Cassius' teacher has commented that he is relatively quiet in school, he gets on with his class work and peers but does not actively participate in lessons much'

'When you say 'does not actively participate in lessons' can you explain that? For example, his teacher will spend a few minutes discussing the learning objectives and subsequent task to be completed. After which she would ask the children a question to check their understanding of the task. Cassius does not put his hand up to answer questions. However, if his teacher selects him to answer he does know the answer. Therefore, she questions why he did not put his hand up to answer'

I listened to what she had to say. Repeated it again in my mind and tried to ascertain if I had missed the purpose of what she was telling me. Had she seriously called me to her office to tell me my son doesn't put his hand up in class. I think Miss O'Connor could see the bemused look on my face because she went on to say...

'Kwame as you know has been finding it difficult to settle in. Miss Reynolds has said that he regularly refuses to do his work and has very little interaction with his peers except for one child, with whom they seem to have a negative impact on each other, often resulting in a temporary fallout or verbal altercation. We are concerned that he may have social and emotional needs resulting in some of the challenging behaviour we have seen so far. Having looked at his class work, we are also looking into whether Kwame may have additional learning needs. He has been struggling to complete his class work unaided and is often unable to follow whole class instructions, appearing disengaged'

'Sorry to interrupt you' realising how defensive I now sounded. 'Firstly, I have already told Miss Franklin that Cassius has always been that quiet. That is his character. He will play with his peers, engage in his class work but only speak to his teacher if he has to. That is how he has always been. Have there been any occasions whereby Cassius has not understood the work, and subsequently not asked for help?'

'I would have to double check that with Miss Franklin she replied clearly taken by surprise with my question.

'I would find it hard to believe that Cassius would sit in class without any understanding of what to do, and not ask for help. He may well not answer questions voluntarily. However, he doesn't seem to be unable to comprehend and complete the work based on what you have explained to me a moment ago'.

'That is correct, however we would love to see him taking a more active role in class'.

'Miss O'Connor, I do, understand what you're saying I personally don't think you're paying enough attention to the character of the child you are speaking about. Cassius has always been that way. It is not a defect, nor a need of any kind. It is his innate personality and I feel that what you are saying, is requesting him to alter who he is, so he appears more like a traditional pupil or learner. It seems that what you want is for him to conform, assimilate'.

'Yolanda, I assure you that is not what...'

I interrupted her again.

'And with regards to Kwame, I am aware of his refusal to do his work and I have asked Miss Reynolds to send him home with any incomplete work for him to complete as homework!' My tone of voice had changed from calm and composed to irritated and defensive.

'What my son is demonstrating is in no way acceptable. However, since when is defiance a social, emotional or even learning need. Kwame completes the work at home unaided, in less time than is even allocated in class so I don't see how you assess his behaviour as a 'learning need'

My legs were crossed now, and my back assertively straight. I meant business with this woman sat in front of me!

'Yolanda, please don't be defensive' miss O'Connor pleaded 'I understand it must be difficult. I have a daughter and I remember when my husband and I split up, I found it difficult on my own...'

My eyes opened wide; brows joined together in unison.

'Sorry Miss O'Connor, are we having the same conversation?'

Foolishly she continued to speak.

'I was simply saying Yolanda that we are here to support you Kwame and Cassius, and whatever we can do to help with the boys transition we are happy to do'

There was so much running through my mind it felt like I was sat in silence for over 10 minutes. I was in shock; this woman was sat here telling me to my face that she knows my struggle. No f***king way you don't! Here she was talking to me like we were a pity case. Like we were the same. What the hell did she think she knew about me?? What because I was young Black and single with two children?? That made me a case for pity. No, I don't think so.

And I'm sorry but without any racism intended, she was white, and I am Black. There is, and will always be a stark difference between you and I. My struggles are nothing like yours and come to think of it. How dare she even assume to know my life?

'Firstly, Miss O'Connor I think the most helpful thing both you and your staff can do is stop assuming there is something wrong with my sons.' I replied regaining composure. 'That way you can look at ways to stretch them further, as opposed to diagnose them. I have told Miss Reynolds that I do not tolerate Kwame's defiance, and I find it hard to understand why he doesn't behave like this with everyone. Nevertheless, Kwame is a bright child. You give him an inch he will take a yard. If he thinks he can get away with something, he will push the boundaries. I can accept that about my son.

I was not in any way recognising my son's behaviour as ok, but I felt it prudent to highlight his character because what they were getting was basically what they were allowing.

'Perhaps Miss Reynolds should try sanctioning him instead of keep giving him Gold stars for sitting at his desk! He's not a dog training for the Crufts, he is a child, my son!'

'I think you're taking this the wrong way Yol…'

'I don't think I am Miss O'Connor', I said standing up. I could feel the tears in my throat, I was angry, frustrated. I almost wanted to sweep all of her paperwork to the floor with one swipe. I refused to let even one tear fall from my eyes whilst I was stuck in her dingy cave listening to the sad sack of a woman. Miss O'Connor stood up from behind her desk and tried to plead further.

'Yolanda if you could just sit back down for a moment. I don't want to end our conversation like this'.

I looked at Miss O'Connor's face, she was old. Well, at least she looked it. Probably in her 50's judging by her crows' feet and stringy silvery grey and brown oily hair. 'Bitch' I said in my mind. I don't want nothing from you or your school. I left my thoughts for a moment.

'Can I sit in one of Kwame's lessons to see what exactly he is doing to cause such concern? I'll sit in the back and simply observe'.

It sounded like a request, but I think both Miss O'Connor and I knew that it was neither a request nor a question.

'I can speak to Miss Reynolds and arrange that for next week. Do you have a preferred day?'

'No any day is fine'. I replied wondering what I would tell work to get the time off.

'Okay so we can tell Kwame you will be sitting in the class an…'

'No Miss O'Connor, Kwame does not need to know I am coming in. I will wait for Miss Reynolds to settle the class and then enter. That way I can hopefully see some of the behaviour he is displaying which is clearly causing you some concern'.

'That is entirely up to you' she replied almost throwing her hands up, had she not gained control over them just in time.

'Yes, that's fine'. I had the tears under control for the moment, but it wasn't going to last. The tide was bursting.

'I'll wait for your confirmation of a day' I said before walking towards the door.

'Thank you.'

I left the dreary head teachers office and called to the boys extending my two hands for them to hold. They immediately jumped up from the chairs putting down the old leaflets lying on the table that they had evidently been looking at. Briskly walking through the entrance doors that now served as a perfect exit. I was unsure why I said thank you. I had no reason to thank her and her pathetic team. A teacher that could not even manage a small child refusing to do his work. A head teacher who thought I would start pouring my heart out to her because all of a sudden, she knew what it was like to be me. Was she crazy or something? I could not believe the cheek of what she had said to me. Why did she think that was okay? Did I look like a victim to her?

Furthermore, I should have called her out on her racism, her prejudice. Why didn't I?? I asked myself the question a few times before I could answer myself. Because anything I would have said, irrespective of my sound evidence, I knew would have sounded like I was playing the 'Black card'. You know the one where you attribute every loss, challenge, and statement to 'it's because I am Black. That would have made me sound more the victim they wanted to assume me to be, so no. I will not give you the satisfaction. In fact, not even for a moment to tell you that I choose to be single because I haven't met anyone, I feel I can be with. Or that actually you have no clue about my struggles. Both statements gave the impression in my opinion, that their assumptions, their prejudices were accurate. They were not accurate, and I was not sharing my life with them!

Having successfully concluded the argument with myself left me feeling less victorious than I expected. Instead the tears started to roll, from the deepest corners of my eyes, down my cheeks and onto my stupid leather summer jacket. I inhaled in an attempt to act as a plug for the falling tears, but it was too late.

'Are you crying Mummy? Cassius' asked with his inquisitive innocence. He was the first to notice.

'What's wrong Mummy?' It was Kwame this time.

I could see the sadness in their eyes. The last thing I wanted for them to witness me crying. For what seemed like already the hundredth time since they were born.

'Nothing, mummy's okay', I said trying to reassure myself. Yet with every word I could feel the tears flowing with absolutely no communication from my brain. Kwame gave me a used tissue from his pocket. I looked at it questionably, saying thank you all the same and dabbed my face. Bless these little soldiers of mine. As we climbed into the car Cassius put his seatbelt on then stared at me and said, 'Mummy I really don't like it when you cry' and without warning tears started to fall. Like a domino effect Kwame too started to cry. I got out the car and climbed into the back in between both boys pulling them into me with each arm.

'Why are you crying, mummy's okay, don't cry' I held my head up in hope that my sons could not see the tears still rolling down my cheeks, and I held them tighter until they knew that everything was okay. I felt bad for them. Bad for the fact that they had no idea what was going on, no idea that sometimes Mummy just needed a release and tears gave me that. My tears personally reflected my emotions at that moment, frustration. These boys my precious sons, were too young to understand what was being said to me and why those words attacked my spirit in the way that they did. I didn't need them to know. What I did need them to know was that everything was ok. I was ok. They were ok. And we would be ok, because I wouldn't have it any other way.

As we sat there for a moment, I swore to myself that these two boys of mine, my sons would not become a statistic. I didn't care what they thought. I didn't care how much they thought they knew about us. I did care if their intention was to destroy mine.

Note to self

You cannot control the opinions or judgements of others. Rather you can prevent them from defining you.

CHAPTER 10

Despite the unexpected turbulence of the day, the boys and I made the most of our evening. We watched 'You got served' for the millionth time. The boys jumping and prancing up and down our front room, doing all types of suspect dance moves. I held my breath to stop myself from visibly laughing, overtly filming them for future humiliation. I mean memories. They were too funny these sons of mine. Cassius was jumping over imaginary hurdles, before landing in a finishing position that resembled a gymnast. Only the main part of his move wasn't quite as gymnastic as the gymnasts we might see on the TV.

Kwame on the other hand had opted for more complex moves of course. These included what I assumed from experience, was a combination of the snake. Picturing my son lying on his stomach and trying desperately to propel his body up and down, not very successfully might I add. Teamed with some floor spinning Turbo and Ozone type breakdance moves that resulted in him crashing into the dining table nestled in the corner of the room. Ordinarily the bang, crash or broken pieces would prompt me to declare 'pyjama time'. Yet today was different, nothing was broken, well at least not noticeably and there was so much joy in just observing. I'm not sure what my favourite part of being a mum is. What I do know is that it's somewhere between watching my sons laughing, playing, excited or simply being the individuals that they innately were. It warmed my heart, filled me with joy and gave me hope. These simple things inspired me to go on, to keep trying, to stay strong, to remain undefeated. These boys prancing around the house, near mashing up my front room, gave me life. I realised in that moment that if not for my sons, I wouldn't even try. Their sheer existence was the reason I wanted to breathe again tomorrow, even if my life was a never-ending booby trap. Welcome to my version of the 1980's classic Goonies. It was the reason, I wanted to create a better future for myself. I knew that if my future was better, there's would be phenomenal. And that was my sequence of thoughts, my motivation, I guess.

On a bad day I thought about giving up. Packing in university so I could spend more time with my sons. Packing in my job and claiming income support so I wouldn't accumulate even more debt, not to mention my rent and crippling council tax could be paid, but then I had to play devil's advocate with myself.

If I did quit university, and my job, how would I then feed and clothe my sons. Then let's say I could clothe and feed them. How would I pay for my car, their extra-curricular activities? No actually let's say I could pay for all of the above. How long would I need to be unemployed for? Until the boys started high school, or until they left high school. Either way neither option seemed more appealing than the other. The way I saw it, I made a choice to bring them into this world without a concrete career, although with a decent job. Therefore, I now had a duty to create my career, and raise my sons. Of course, things may have been easier if I had been pregnant at 29 instead of 19. That would have given me enough time to build my career, have ample savings, a house of my own and then the flexibility of being able to decide on working or staying at home. But no. That was not my life. I knew I could not provide them with the all the things I wished for them, not just to have, but to experience. I wanted them to have a life of experiences. Memories. I wanted as much as physically possible to give them, what perhaps my mum was unable to give me. I didn't know how to be unemployed and survive. Of all the skills I had acquired from my mum that was not one of them. So, I did what I knew best, I worked and lived in hope, directed by faith. Nothing is forever, right.

CHAPTER 11

The morning was dull, I could hear the uninviting sloshing of puddles each time a car drove past my bedroom window. The sound alone, was enough to make me consider skipping the day, strict bed rest, evacuating only when necessary to relieve myself, or for food and water of course. It was like being surrounded by a moat, I imagined. We sat comfortably within the castle gates, the water surrounding us, swerving repeatedly into the stone infrastructure insisting on being recognised as the force of protection. The only thing was the water did not make me feel protected. It made me feel attacked, disheartened. Rain happened to signify real storms in my eyes, storms of life. Rain for me was indeed a force. For me this was the term that seemed most appropriate to the devastation that was often left behind after its visit.

I felt I was often up against the storms, me vs. them. A force of nature perhaps, but more discerning. Rain happened to be a force of provocation for me, like the sibling who snatches your favourite toy then says, 'whatcha gonna do about it'. That was my relationship with the rain. Its force edged me on with its potent damp misery, demanding to know what my next move was, until I rose to the challenge. Did I mention that I hate rain! So, here I was knowing that the day ahead of me was going to require every bit of the last thread from my worn but still intact, imperfectly, might I add, structured fabric that constituted me. How I would get through the day. Only God knows. Yet I was willing to give it a go. Willing to courageously take the sling shots, dodging those which I could, but braving those which would inevitably bruise my inner being, even if only for a moment.

'You got this Yolanda' I whispered as reassuring as possible, 'you got this!'

I climbed out of bed, diverted from my usual routine directly to the bathroom and headed straight for the kitchen. I needed a hot drink this morning. Something to ease my tension, take the edge off the anxiety I was beginning to feel. Usually I would opt for a Green tea, yet today didn't feel like the kind of day where the bitterness of the green blend would suffice. I was going to need something stronger.

Coffee it is.

The aroma of the coffee wafted into my nostrils, teasing its way down the back of my throat, as if to say 'you wanna piece of me' gave me a slight sense of aaaaaahhhhh. You know similar to the feeling you experience when you've been standing in high heels all day, then you sit down and take a load off your feet, and it feels like Heaven. Well I won't go as far as to say this was like Heaven, instead I'll say it was relieving. Yes, definitely worth deviating from my usual. Total duration of satisfaction = 1.5 seconds. And despite how miniscule, 1.5 seconds may sound to you, don't knock it until you try it.

I half expected to see Cassius totting out of the boy's bedroom and kept glancing towards my son's bedroom door through the small gap in the kitchen doorway. I had to appreciate living in a home, whereby all the rooms were so close to each other, we could have a fairly sensible conversation through the walls.

From the kitchen I could exit straight through to our front room, or I had the choice of leaving via the kitchen door, which could lead to either my bedroom, the bathroom, or the boy's room, depending on which way you were facing. This was our home, our little four walls. Our home and its dynamics somehow contributed in providing us with the necessary space that we needed, yet still managed to keep us closely knitted together. I mean for Cassius who strategically made his way to my room and then slyly snuggled into my bed most nights, after he was sure I had been overcome by sleep, the layout must have seemed ideal to him. I stood, coffee in hand staring blankly out of the window, still procrastinating at what awaited me, once I ventured out of the warmth, closeness and comfort, of our cosy little four walls. I knew the longer I stood there, would eventually impact my daily routine, but I was willing to take the chance. Even Knowing full well that I would then systematically run behind schedule, causing me to frantically rush around like a blue ass fly, to get us all ready in order to avoid being late, having wasted so much time. Or snapping at the boys while they moved at the daring speed of a snail racing a tortoise. Whatever the semantics, I knew it was time to get my head in gear

and prepare for the next battle, the day ahead. Today, the day I would observe my son in class, only to prove once and for all, that actually, he was not as they assumed, an emotional wreckage resulting from the collision of his Father and I.

Today they would eat their negative words and judgements and wash it down with a tall glass of humility. Yes, all that for diagnosing my son with mediocrity, and thinking somehow that I would accept their prognosis. No chance.

CHAPTER 12

The journey to university seemed further than usual. Every traffic light I encountered opened its eyes wide until all that could be seen was its piercing red angry pupils staring me in the face. Perhaps the traffic light was saying 'now who's gonna be late'. If I was late for class, it was my own fault. I was dreading going into university I had dreaded dropping the children to school even after my 1.5 second high, which inevitably did prove to be futile. Procrastination had the upper hand and clearly he had signalled to his team mate, 'the aggravated traffic lights' not to mention the drivers on the road who were going as fast as Fred Flintstone in his motor-less vehicle bare feet propelling him forward. I kissed my teeth as I slowed down preparing to stop at yet another traffic light. I had about 10 minutes to go and that didn't include searching for a parking space. The University had in total over three car parks but get this. Parking was exclusive to staff. Students on the other hand studying for specific courses were selected to apply for a permit. Key words, selected groups. So basically, if your course was deemed relevant enough, you may qualify for a priority space, which of course you would still have to pay for, and this was not cheap might I add. I had chosen to pay for a space, conscious that unlike a number of my peers, I would routinely be racing from the school most mornings and the journey was already an excruciating 30-45 minutes long, and that was on a good day, providing the A40 was free from queues of lorries, trucks, and whatever else happened to spill onto the already heavily congested motorway when I simply needed to get to university. Not to mention that since starting in September, I had also been one of the unfortunate, defiant students, who had parked without said permit, only to come back and find my car clamped! CLAMPED.

At university, where mature students such as myself, came to study.

Although I'm not sure how mature the decision to park where I did, was. But as with most things in my life, I continue to live and learn. So bottom line, I didn't have time to be faffing around searching for parking 20 minutes away and then getting a bus or enduring a mini hike, just to get to class, panting sweaty and reeking of a boys locker room at high school. No thank you. Eventually, I closed my eyes, dug into my pockets and paid my hard earned, struggled for, money, and purchased a permit. Don't get me wrong, I still had to contend with the battle to find an empty space in one of the tightly packed car parks. But I suppose, my mum used to say, 'if you want good, your nose haffi run'. So, I reassured myself daily, that this was just for a time and was in no way reflective of my entire life story.

However, the number of times, I had managed to charge through seminar doors just in the nick of time...well let's just say there were several times. Particularly since Kwame had been struggling to settle in at school.

As I entered the class slightly late, I made sure I apologised loud enough for the lecturer to know that I was sorry, but not loud enough to disrupt the class and took a seat on the end of the isle, very much unlike me, as I tend to generally associate the edge of the isle with a swift getaway. But this was an exception. Whilst I was not in need of a quick escape, I did need to be considerate to my peers, as I knew, I would be the first to moan and complain about other students disrupting my lecture once I had made the effort to attend on time. Therefore, the edge of the isle seemed both appropriate and sensible, based on my arrival time. So, as I continued my efforts not to disturb anyone else and slipped my notebook out of my bag, slowly separating the Velcro to minimise the jarring sound. I turned my focus to the lecture ahead. The upheaval of the morning had finally started to fade and somehow my anxiety about the afternoon ahead seemed a tad more under control than earlier. Admittedly I failed to take discernible notes during my morning lecture despite the topic being of great interest to me. My mind had been elsewhere, which was an utter shame as it would mean more reading to catch up on, at home. Nonetheless, the truth was I just couldn't think about much else. The moment I had been waiting for was now fast approaching. However, my confidence levels had taken a slight nosedive. The moment where I would get to say 'I told you so! Where finally I could put this whole thing to bed. In fact, the moment where I would bury Miss Reynolds under a gargantuan pile of manure, harvested just for her, and of course Miss 'Trenchbull' for their pessimism, privilege, and ability to freely use a label maker without seeking the proper authorisation or rights. Yes, that was it. They'd be buried in shit for trying to stifle my son's progress, and my son, in fact, my sons, would outlive their assertions. Much like the Wright brothers who had many dispute their dream to take flight, as they tried and failed better, often more than once a day. The Wright brothers too were judged and doubted by others around them. They were judged not only for their dreams of taking flight during a time when air travel was merely a faint hope. No, the Wright brothers were judged for their lack of finances and resources, required to support their big dreams. In fact, the brothers were ridiculed for almost competing with their opponents who were regarded prematurely as the obvious success, owing to the fact they had received extensive financial support and resources in a bid to ensure they would be the first to take flight.

I suppose the general consensus at the time, towards the Wright Brothers, would have been one of, 'who do they think they are' for their brazenness. I read somewhere that the brothers used pieces of scrap to build and perfect the very first plane and its previous contenders, often having to travel for miles after an unsuccessful attempt, to collect pieces of broken metal and other materials so that they could be reused. Imagine the jeers, criticism and calls for the brothers to simply give up and follow an expected path more suited to their social/financial class, each time that they were unable to sustain the altitude, resulting in the need for them to piece together the wreckage of the most recent attempt to soar.

Much like the Wright brothers, my sons would go on to make sure that their ability to transform shrapnel and other bits and pieces of raw materials, into an entire infrastructure would be their testimony.

I was surprised to see Miss O'Connor stood in the reception, seemingly awaiting my arrival, unsuccessfully manoeuvring around the small-carpeted area, as though she was meeting and greeting parents as they entered the school building. Highly unlikely story, I thought to myself, based on the time of the day. I mean how many parents are you expecting after lunch?? Nevertheless, I gathered she obviously didn't want me to think she was eagerly anticipating me, so I appeased her and acted as though I too thought she had a specific purpose within the Reception area that did not involve me.

'Good afternoon Yolanda'

She spoke in such a tone I was forced to look her straight in the eyes to decipher if the tone was one of discomfort or of anticipation. She didn't appear as confident as she did when she had previously attempted to categorise us, as the same. No, this was not confidence, but I suspected it also wasn't positive. However, I wasn't stood here because I thought she was brimming with positive strategies for my son, so instinctively, I reminded myself of this and continued to appease her.

I have learned in life that when something is quite apparent to you. **Trust your instincts and appease where necessary, rather than feel the need to advise the other person of your cognisance. This can lead to your own frustration as the other party proceeds to minimise or categorically refute your assertion.** Already I was tired of people assuming I was far less attuned than I actually was. Fed up of being seeing as young and totally naive, or just pretty with nothing upstairs. Whilst clearly, I didn't have all the answers. I didn't know it all, and I'd be the first to admit it.

However, life had exposed me to experiences that in turn resulted in my current mind-set. Therefore, I could sense negativity like the heightened smell of fresh cookies when driving past the Mcvities biscuit factory. I knew what pessimism, doubt, disbelief and prejudice looked like, even when adorned in fine clothing and attire accompanied by perfect command of the English Language. I could hear both the spoken, and unspoken words within a conversation, despite occasions where deliberate efforts had been made to somehow disillusion me. Bottom line, I had been taught well by my Mum not to play all my cards at once. So here we were again, with me appeasing Miss O'Connor because clearly, she assumed, I was an idiot. More fool her.

'Good afternoon Miss O Connor' I replied giving her the best fake smile I could muster up.

'Thank you for coming in Yolanda'

What do you mean thank you for coming in, you didn't invite me, I invited myself! I was tempted to reply. Then I remembered, 'appease her'

'No problem that's absolutely fine'.

Somehow, I managed to regurgitate the words from the depths of my throat. I turned to the Receptionist who had been silently staring at me since I entered, eagerly waiting for me to sign the visitors log.

'We can go through to my office for a quick chat before we make our way to Miss Reynolds classroom Yolanda'

This was my idea of a statement, yet the tone of Miss O'Connor's voice gave me the impression she was actually asking a question. Either way I proceeded to respond as though it was a question.

'Was there something you wanted to discuss with me?'

'Oh uh.no ... I just thought you may have a few questions before you observe...?

'No thank you, I'm fine'

Perhaps there were unanswered questions, perhaps I had even a slight need, for support this morning. Needless to say, the truth was, I was liable to freeze over before I conveyed that to this woman before me. At this point I had no reason to think she had my best interests at heart. Therefore, as long as there was uncertainty regarding that belief, she would get nothing out of me.

I followed close behind her as she led me to Kwame's classroom. I looked around at all the colourful displays on the walls, safeguarding promises and obligations, photographs of the children at work. It was amazing looking at the displays. One could make assumptions about the type of children who eventually leave this school. If you were particularly judgemental you may even assume that schools like this turn out the best children. You know those with major opportunities and high IQs. Whatever that means. I suppose just by observing the displays, the certificates, accolades, and the inept policies. I could see that school education, at least primary school, was not as it was, when I was a child. Somehow looking around glancing through the glass square of the classroom doors, there was something very different about this scene as opposed to when I attended primary school; something about this seemed more competitive, more dependent on what others see. Perception even.

Possibly a bit like when the doorbell rings unexpectedly and you've been lying in bed all-day binge-watching movies. However, the person at the door as far as you're concerned, cannot afford to see you in that state. Then comes the 60 second makeover where you miraculously brush your teeth, fix your hair, take of the leggings full of holes, replacing them with a more decent pair, void of material mishaps and holes, before going downstairs to the door, smiling and greeting your unexpected guest as though it was nothing. Yes, I admit I know all about that!

But to stay on point, just for the moment as I walked through the school I started to question if I had made the right choice. It wasn't that this was not a good school, because clearly my children were having different experiences. And of course, there were an array of teachers here, each with their own motive for teaching. In theory, it made perfect sense that each child had a different experience of the school as a whole. I continued pondering, until Miss O'Connor finally stopped in front of Kwame's classroom door. His classroom had never felt this far away from the main entrance as it did that afternoon, and as I stopped in front of the door, I began to sense the familiar feeling of discomfort in my stomach. Here we go again I muttered inside. I wanted to excuse myself and take a second just to go to the bathroom whilst my stomach settled.

However, I felt that disappearing at this point would leave the situation open to factors that could potentially contribute to what I was about to observe. Already I had very little faith in the two people involved, so I felt my presence was vital from start to finish. I could disappear to the toilet for five minutes and come back perhaps to learn of something terrible my son did in my absence without any due cause. Call it vivid imagination, where I come from, my mum taught me 'prevention is better than cure '. To me there was no telling what could happen, so I would rather simply stay present. Miss O'Connor explained to me that I could either observe from outside the classroom or enter the classroom and sit at the back. Peering through the door I could see that the class had already begun to settle into their afternoon tasks. Some appeared to be doing what I can only describe as a group-based art activity. The table was full of colourful bits of paper, glue, paints lollipop sticks and acorns. It reminded me of what it is to be a primary school pupil as opposed to the adult learner I currently was. It was always encouraging to see children learning through play and exploration.

Kwame's table of small children were still getting organised, but I could see him sat at the table twiddling with a blue colour pencil, while taking it in turns, to roll a rubber across the table to another boy in his class. Clearly not on task but judging by the actions of some of the other children, this was by no means a huge deviance. I was glad the class was in full swing, as ideally, I needed to be a fly on the wall in what would appear to be an ordinary day in Miss Reynolds classroom.

'Would you like me to wait here with you Yolanda?' asked Miss O'Connor.

I realised that for a second, I had forgotten that she had been stood there with me. I must have drifted off for a moment, observing the actions of the lower Junior School class. I took a second to consider Miss O' Connors apparently kind offer.

On one hand I would prefer her to be present that way my findings would not be a matter of my word against theirs. I envisioned me trying to prove that the information I had been given over the last two weeks or months was not accurate based on what I'd observed, should Miss O'Connor not be present. And then that would turn into a huge battle of words, presumptions, assumptions and all-sorts. Honestly. If it came down to that I would fight tooth and nail. But the truth is I didn't want to have to endure another battle. Not right now. I was still in my first year at university and I needed to keep my concentration levels intact. Of course, the alternative meant that Miss O'Connor would be stood next to me for the duration, irritating me, just by being present. What a f****** conundrum!

'No thank you, I'll be fine Miss O'Connor'

The response came swifter then I imagined. I was certain I was still in the process of pondering the alternatives, however that was definitely my voice, and I was definitely addressing Miss O Connor.

Sometimes you need to trust your inner voice, even when it speaks without your instructions.

That saying was certainly true for me at that moment. I had no idea that I was about to respond to miss O'Connor's request yet there I was, voice speaking ahead of me yet my intuition affirming that, that voice, was right.

'I'll be in my office if you need me for anything Yolanda'

Miss O'Connor was being really helpful. Offering to stay and observe with me. Then offering to be available should I need her for anything ... maybe I needed to reconsider the conclusion I had come to about her intentions. Perhaps in actual fact she was a head teacher determined to make a positive difference in the lives of all of her students. I mean isn't that why you become a head teacher after all...?

Perhaps it was time for me to lower the gauntlet, soften my approach with the school. Ultimately in my heart of hearts I believed and still do, that schools should support parents and carers in ensuring that every child has access to opportunities that amalgamate into them being able to be the best version of themselves possible. I'd like to think that most schools offer programs today for their apparently gifted children, and alternative programs for the children who may have gaps in their learning. This needs to be standard in all schools and parents sending their children to these schools need to be made aware that these programs exist. It need not be a secret program available through initiation. Rather it should be one where parents are introduced to the program if it is felt that their children would benefit. How many parents would be happy to have their children access this?

I am quite conscious, my thinking stems from my own humble beginnings and experiences of primary school. If I think back to my own childhood. My first primary school was a stone's throw from where we lived at the time. An old school surrounded by a flimsy wire fence you could bend if you leaned on it. Yet I remembered clearly that I spent only a short time attending there. I remembered my mum having to come into school to speak to teachers about things that my 5 or 6-year-old self didn't understand. I remembered sticking chewing gum in my friend's hair. Not realising through lack of understanding, that it would only be able to be removed if it were cut from her hair. Not so proud of that memory, however I now know better, and I most certainly wouldn't do that again.

Soon after that I recall my mum moving me to an alternative school, still not very far from where we lived, but this time a short walk or drive from home. Again, I don't know the specifics about why my mum decided to remove me from the first primary School, particularly as it was about three minutes from our doorstep. However, what I do remember is that whatever caused my mum to make that decision caused her to not be best pleased. And by 'not best pleased' I mean don't upset my mum! She's a soldier, a warrior if you mess with her kids! Be warned!

So, my Mum had moved me to this new school facing a well-known council estate. At this point I like to explain that my reference to the council estate is simply to explain to you perhaps the dynamics of the cohort of my school at the time. It was not the school where MPs sent their children or the school where parents are quite wealthy or 'well to do', sent their children to school either. It was a straightforward combination of people who lived in and around the local area. My early memories are that the school was better than my last. I formed great relationships, some of which I still hold dear today. I worked hard too, (not really optional if you had my mum), but I did, and I want to reiterate that. Nevertheless, something about my experience of primary school troubled me when I was a child, yet only as I entered my teenage years; I was able to identify what it was. It was disproportion. The standards, expectations, opportunities, calibre of students, family composition (mainly single parents) ... I'm hoping you can recognise my point. There were a lot of differences and as most differences do, it made me inquisitive. Being as observant as I am, I couldn't help but pick up on these things.

I recall students in my class who the teachers referred to as 'bad news', and on occasion actually told them so. Surprisingly I actually remember the teacher telling a student he would never amount to anything because he was answering her back. Shocking as it may sound, this was my current primary school, with what I'm assuming were qualified teachers whose care we had been entrusted into.

Other occasions I recall students including myself, being sent out and standing outside classrooms for approximately 40 minutes or more. Or what's more, sat on naughty carpets facing walls with hands on heads until your arms hurt. That was my school. In fact, would you allow me to tell you of an occasion at that primary school, where I was perhaps in year 2 or 3 and the teacher had decided to teach us joined up, or cursive handwriting? Seriously. Did I not tell you who my mum was?

My mum had already taught me how to write in joined up writing, buying me numerous literacy and numeracy activity books for me to complete as opposed to being glued to the TV for hours on end. So, guess what there wasn't anything for the teacher to really teach me about cursive writing. However, when I politely raised my hand, to explain to the teacher I already knew how to do that. She bellowed in my face about interrupting her, screamed at me in front of the entire class about me thinking I knew it all, called me a 'right madam', and THEN wait for it…. Told me to do a demonstration so that the rest of the class could see on the blackboard.

I realise now in hindsight, that was a ploy to humiliate me in front of the class for being a 'know it all'. In any case that attempt failed, as I demonstrated I could perfectly write a full sentence in joined up writing, without lifting my pen off the page.

'Ha'

Needless to say, my teachers' affections did not grow towards me throughout my time at that school. But I loved school and that was that.

When I was at school it was apparent that teachers didn't have to care about children and this was demonstrated in language, attitudes, lowered standards and more. In fact, did I tell you that a teacher once washed my mouth out with soap for saying piss? Yep that really happened! And no, I should not have said piss.

Just to conclude my point. I was now the parent recalling my own childhood experiences and determined to ensure that my children were granted equal opportunities at school irrespective of socio-economic background, race, family composition and anything else. All I ask is that my children were judged on their own merit, and under no circumstances, negatively impact their self-esteem and self-belief.

Lost in my thoughts for a moment I didn't notice Miss O'Connor quietly excuse herself, slipping away back to her office. I took a deep breath for some reason, exhaled and then walked over to a small square section of the glass where I could see the classroom activities.

The door was slightly ajar, giving me the added advantage of being able to hear the dialect within the class as well.

'Okay class, I'd like you all to get started with your group exercises. Remember not to visit any of the other tables to borrow colours and materials please, put your hands up and ask me if you need anything else'

I stood there thinking, 'well that was clear enough I guess'. I continued to watch the children in the classroom; some were talking to their peers discussing what they needed to do. Others were touching materials, feeling textures and playing quietly with them. I even witnessed some of the children bickering over who would do what. The sight made me smile, the joys of being a child. I looked over at Kwame's table. He wasn't there.

The rest of the group were still there, all four of them. But Kwame was not. I quickly scanned the room, being sure not to be seen by any of the children. Then my eye caught a familiar figure standing by the window looking out into an empty playground. Miss Reynolds calling to him interrupted my daze.

'Kwame, please will you come and join your group at the Red table'

'I don't want to' he replied turning to face her only to finish his sentence, and then continuing to do what he saw clearly as more important.

'Please can you join the rest of your group I'm sure you'll enjoy this'

I stood there speechless, literally stood still looking on in amazement. All of a sudden everyone else had vacated the school building except Kwame's class and me. I was centre stage, the spotlight on me. I couldn't see the audience, they were hidden in the shadows of darkness, however it felt like the audience were fixated on me, under the bright white lights. I imagined, if anyone could have seen me from a distance, I went from the onlooker, peering through the circular glass in the door, smiling, to gaping through the glass with my mouth wide open, eyes bulging out of its sockets. I wanted to whisper through the door so Kwame knew I could see him. I needed to get his attention, so he knew that his display of behaviour was also being witnessed by me. Mum. I needed him to snap out of whatever it was, wherever he was, right then, at that moment. Now!

Nevertheless, despite standing there hoping somehow, I would develop telepathic powers that would manifest in him being able to feel and hear what I was saying in my mind. My son did not. He continued to aimlessly wander around the classroom, refusing to comply when requested wearily, by his teacher. I was tempted to accidentally knock the door to get his attention, as ridiculous as it may sound. I was feeling desperate. I needed to get his attention so he could stop playing up.

Don't get me wrong; I understood that would not be appropriate. I had requested this opportunity, in a bid to try and get to the bottom of my son's alleged inability to transition into this new school. At the same time prove to these people, that there was nothing wrong with my son. I was not about to behave in a way that would jeopardise my intentions, least of all behave in a way that satisfies the judgements of others. No way! I stepped away from the glass. I needed distance between myself and what was going on in the classroom. I couldn't leave yet. I was not ready to depart, yet. I just needed to regroup my thoughts. Get my head around this. I wasn't sure what I was witnessing. Maybe I wasn't seeing this at all. Maybe this was a figment of my imagination. A mirage, bad dream, anything! But surely this was not me observing my son. My baby.

I gave it a minute before returning to peer through the glass.

Kwame was still not sat with his group. From what I could see, he had not had, a change of heart and decided to comply. No. He was now in the book corner taking out books! No one else was reading. Miss Reynolds had clearly given up and was now assisting other pupils on another table. Yet still Kwame had not engaged at all with the group activity. I continued to listen as Miss Reynolds feebly pleaded with my son to do what was expected of him and watched as my son walked around the classroom willy-nilly, doing exactly as he pleased. Shock does not begin to describe what I was feeling. What I was feeling was beyond shock. It was embarrassment. No, it was humiliation. No, it was a punch in the gut that winded me causing me to fold at the knees. It was something of utter disbelief for me. I half expected miss Reynolds to look over at me as my son continued to be defiant, yet she did not look over at me once. Even as my son continued to dismiss her every request, she kept the focus of her eyes within the classroom. Even when she could probably feel the colour draining from my Brown skin, she did not peek over at me.

In hindsight perhaps she was embarrassed for me and avoided my gaze for that reason. I guess I'll never know, but if for any reason that is what happened that day, then actually thank you Miss Reynolds. Wherever you are. Thank you.

CHAPTER 13

By the time I had finished the observation it didn't make sense for me to go home, only then to come back to collect the boys. So, I decided to sit in the car and have a moment of reflection. Plus, I needed to make a few phone calls, as I needed to secure a place for the boys at a local play centre for the upcoming school holidays. Luckily it was not for the summer holidays as we would be away by then.

Although I had to admit that I hadn't quite achieved the result I had hoped for. I knew that I wasn't done yet. My experience only a short time ago had left me feeling somewhat disheartened, even defeated. After standing at the window watching my son for almost the entire lesson, I could feel the tension in my shoulders. My stance had altered. No longer was I standing with my back straight and my head held high. Rather I walked out of the school building with my shoulders rounded, head hanging low in despair. I was at a loss. I recalled the receptionist trying to call to me as I walked lifelessly past the desk. Not stopping to sign out, or to see Miss O'Connor as arranged. I wasn't in the mood to see Miss O'Connor. I needed time to myself. I needed to digest what I'd just seen. And most of all, I needed to know where I was going from here. I could not pretend I had not witnessed what I had seen that afternoon, nor could I shamelessly defend my son's conduct in place of acceptance or accountability. His behaviour was wrong. I did not raise him to behave in such fashion. I never allowed defiance, particularly when being spoken to, by an adult. It was irrelevant what I may have thought of Miss O'Connor, Miss Reynolds, or either one's intentions. My children were under no circumstance allowed to behave like that. One of the things I pride myself on is my children being respectful to adults.

As children we were raised to 'respect our elders'. I mean we were literally raised on this powerful phrase. So much so, that we even used to use it on each other, depending on who was the oldest in the bunch. I might say to my cousin who was just about one year younger than me, 'respect your elders' when I wanted her to comply with whatever I wanted her to do and so on so forth.

But on a serious note the phrase, is an extension of who I am. You see where I come from, that phrase applied to absolute strangers. It applied to any teachers, who overtly picked on me at school, the old woman at the bus stop shouting at the school children because she needed to get on the bus first, the grown-up who used to be friends with my mum, but now for whatever reason unbeknown to me, they were no longer friends, yet I still had to greet her each time I saw her when I was coming home from school, regardless. Not to mention the old lady who lived across the road, who demanded you post her letters in the post box at the end of the road, without saying please! The phrase literally applied to everyone. You need to know that as far as I was concerned, being disrespectful to an adult, and my mum subsequently hearing about it, was ultimate shame on my family. Maybe it's me, perhaps it could be a cultural thing, or it could just be my family.

However, I can tell you from an insider's perspective, that if you were rude to an adult, it sent the message that your family had not raised you correctly. That you were perhaps lawless, unruly, 'bruk bad' I'd like to add; the entire World would be talking about your Mums inability to parent (not your Dads). For some reason to have a child deviate from anything considered normal, or if their behaviour was not in line with societal expectations, blame tends to fall on the Mothers.

I can't comment on why, I have yet to fathom why the shortfalls fall on the mother's shoulders. Though you are welcome to look into this. Use Google and take a look at the number of young people who negatively make the headlines, count how many of the articles mention the mother with regards to parenting or incapability. Whether the reason given is single parenthood, mother has a new partner, mum works long hours. They never seem to be short of justification as to why that child was bound to end up like that.

I once supported a Mother whose partner murdered her 18-month-old son. I can't begin to imagine what she was feeling, but I can tell you that she faced a barrage of questioning and blame, from others regarding the fact, she had allowed this to happen. Can you imagine? She was almost held accountable for another adults' heinous actions.

So, if I return to the point I was making, to be disrespectful in any way to our elders was unheard of and our mothers would foot the blame inflicted by the rest of the world. Of course, in terms of accuracy that wouldn't be true. But in terms of perception this was perfectly accurate. Yes, it seems quite harsh, perhaps unfair. But in terms of family commandments 'thou shalt respect their elders!' I had meticulously raised my children on the same ethos. Yet today, I myself had a front seat in witnessing my son doing just the opposite.

I adjusted the driver's seat, something I didn't like to do ordinarily because I didn't like having to make sure I got it to the exact position it was in initially. However today was different. Today I needed to adjust my seating to fit my current mood. I needed to sit back and understand what was happening. Also, I was conscious that if I pushed my seat back far enough, parents arriving at the gates early, would not be able to see me sat in the car, and therefore wouldn't be tempted to come over and converse with me. I was in no mood for small talk about play dates or anything similar. I needed to think, to digest what I had just seen. I exhaled deeply, something that was becoming quite a ritual when I sat in my car. I pulled my bag off the passenger seat beside me and took out my phone to call my mum; I knew I needed to let her know how the observation had gone. She would be concerned by now, maybe anxious. Already she believed her grandson was being targeted at school. I suppose I could understand where her thought process was coming from. It got me thinking about some of the stories my Mum and my Aunties had shared with us when we were younger about their experiences of coming from Jamaica and attending school in England. They had told us of times where places displayed signs that said, 'no dogs no Blacks, no Irish'! Of teachers who spoke blatantly about their skin, hair, accents, derogatively. I couldn't imagine having to bite my tongue, whilst teachers racially abused me. No way! I was guilty of answering back when racism was not even a factor of the conversation much less tolerate someone blatantly disrespecting who I am, the colour of my skin.

I unlocked my phone, dialled my mum at work. I would have preferred not to call her at work so she would have at least a little privacy, when I explained to her about her grandsons out of body experience. Yes maybe that would be best I told myself as I decided against it, putting the phone back down. Perhaps that call to the play centre that GF had told me about. After all, school was breaking up next week and I had no idea what I was going to do with the boys. I contemplated calling GF. This was my best friend after all, I could trust her. Perhaps she could help me to feel better about the situation. She had been there for me throughout; there was nothing I couldn't tell her. I pondered for a while longer, subsequently coming to the same conclusion as I had with regards to the call to my Mum.

Although GF had one child and I had the two, in general our children attended the same play centres. I suppose that was just to give us the added security. You see neither of us liked to leave our children with other people. But being single parents, we also knew we had to do something, to allow us to go to work, earn money and take care of our children. How it worked best, is either one of us would find a play centre we considered to be really good, we would check it out. Providing everything was ok we would send the three boys. My two and Gf's one. That way all three could take care of each other.

When we were children this is how my Mum and my Aunties had been with us. My cousins, and myself all ended up at the same play-centres, on the same coach trips, camping trip, (camping, singular, as I was only ever allowed on one camping trip.) Subsequently if one of us wasn't going, none of us were going. Simple. As children this seemed unfair, yet as we became older we came to understand this was fair our parents taught us safety in numbers.

Looking at modern day theories of young people and gangs, maybe we were part of a gang back then. After all when young people are grouped together, some professionals refer to that as a gang. Inaccurately, in my opinion. Now I too, adopted this same principle with my son's.

I looked through my phone for the play-centre number. There it is. The woman I was contacting was the manager, Delores. GF had already told me that the play centre was based within a church and run by a woman from the church, Dolores. It was a mobile number. I dialled and waited for her to answer. When she did answer, she sounded joyful. I wished I had that same joy in my voice at that moment. Although I made an effort to fake joy whilst she made a note of my contact details and the boys names and dates of birth. GF had already registered her son, my Godson. So, it was just for me to register the boys.

Dolores went through the details of the play-centre, explaining to me that the children would require a packed lunch each day, and spending money, if they wanted to buy a packet of crisps or a snack from the tuck shop. The opening times were perfect, it would allow me to work a full day and then collect the boys around 5:30pm. Between GF, and myself we would manage the pickups that would not be a problem.

Dolores went through the daily rate with me. I cringed slightly. Everything costs something I reminded myself. I would be entitled to a sibling discount for sending two children. However, what I wanted to say, was whilst I appreciate the discount, I still barely have enough money. But I didn't. I finalised the details with Dolores, then sat in the car calculating whether or not it was worth me even going to work. But it was. I already knew that. We were going on holiday, and every penny counted towards that. I came off the phone feeling relieved, that was one less thing to worry about. For some reason it didn't occur to me that Kwame would continue to behave in the same fashion at the play-centre. I'm not sure why, but it just didn't.

I again revisited the idea of calling my mum, despite deciding against it a moment ago.

No. I'd call mum when I knew she was home. Furthermore, I knew I needed to call her, preferably before she called me, because I knew she would want to know how her grandson did. Especially as she too had been rooting for him, the way I had been. How was I going to describe to her what I had seen? If she didn't know me better, she would probably think I was lying.

I stared blankly out of the window. My attention drawn for a moment to the house directly facing me. It was a large town house painted bright Yellow and Blue. The house itself had the potential to be absolutely beautiful I was sure of that, but the explosion of primary colours didn't enhance its beauty. I shook my head. As I sat there feeling slightly sorry for myself, I realised I was struggling to see the beauty I had seen on previous mornings when I'd parked here. This afternoon the house was hideous. The colours looked like someone had regurgitated them following a stomach bug. Wow. I realised in one afternoon I had gone from longing to live in a house similar to this one, just painted in a more subtle way, to the opposite end of the scale of, who would want to live in a house like that? Clearly the afternoon's antics had left me feeling notably pessimistic. Unable to see the beauty in everyday things. Absent of my innate desire to dream, visioning things as they should be, forget how they actually were. I didn't like this feeling.

A tear slid slowly from the corner of my eye, rolling down my cheek. Here we go again more tears, more fears. Why was I crying? I couldn't explain. I was I fearful, but what of? Losing my son to society. The possibility of my sons, either of them becoming anything remotely like a statistic. I was sad. Saddened by what I had seen that afternoon. This was not about being right or being wrong. Maybe it is true that none of us like to be wrong. But this wasn't just about being wrong; this was about my son playing into the hands of people who didn't share my intentions for him. I knew he was too young to know and understand, but I wasn't. I knew that the majority did not necessarily share my intentions for my sons, but that was not going to deter me.

Why oh why, could I feel emerging teardrops getting heavier, despite me trying to hold them back. I really didn't need any of the parents to come by and see me crying in the car. Nor was I willing to enter the school building looking as though I had been crying. It would be like admitting defeat. Miss O'Connor would not see that she was getting to me. I blinked the tears from my eyes, picked up the phone beside me, and started to write my Mum a text. I didn't want to go into much detail I just wanted to give her the gist.

'Hi mum, didn't go too well. I saw him myself wondering around the classroom. I'm just about to pick the boys up call you when I get in.'

'Ok speak soon' came the reply within a minute of me pressing send.

Yep mum had been sitting by the phone awaiting my call. I knew she would have been. At least now she wouldn't be waiting in suspense. The actual details I could tell her later.

I looked at the time on the dashboard; the bell was about to go. I checked myself in the mirror, using my hands to wipe away droplets of water, still visible on my face. Perhaps a little cocoa butter would help, make me look normal. I rubbed the cream into my face, took one more glance in the mirror, grabbed my phone and bag and headed back towards the school gates. Really, I just wanted to grab the kids and go. I didn't want to talk to anybody I didn't want anybody to talk to me. Not even the few parents I actually liked. As I marched back towards the school building, I realised it sounded like my feet were hitting the ground pretty hard in my black, leather heeled boots. The sounds of my own footsteps almost convinced me; someone was following me. Each step seemed to command attention. 'LEFT, RIGHT, LEFT, RIGHT' that was the only element missing. The loud burley voice of the sergeant major bellowing directions of which foot to use, at which time. One may even think that I had not a worry in the world, just judging by my footsteps. You often hear the phrase, a woman wears her pain like stilettos, no matter how much it hurts all u see is the beauty'. I am inclined to believe in that, based on my own footsteps in contrast to the way I was actually feeling.

And because when I went out with my GF, one of us would inevitably be wearing shoes that were part of an agility trial. Long before the end of the night, shoes would end up in each hand, and toes would be sore. Before then, all you saw was a beautiful pair of heels adorning my feet, on a night out. No indication of the fact that shoes might have been causing the blood circulation to cease.

To go a stretch further I will also compare myself to a swan that glides beautifully, elegantly along the water. Yet beneath all that is visible on the surface of the water, beneath the outward beauty, underneath that surface of water, is the frantic flapping of feet, keeping the swan afloat. Perfect analogy for myself I think, but perhaps it's the perfect analogy for so many of us women, Mothers.

I entered the playground trying not to lock eyes with any of the other parents, in a bid to discourage any pleasantries. It was another day when I just wanted to get in and out. I went straight to Miss Reynolds class first. I figured it best to 'eat the frog'.

'Afternoon Miss'

I greeted Miss Reynolds as normal at the classroom door. I could see into the classroom and noticed Kwame sitting quietly at the table waiting to be dismissed.

'Kwame, mummy's here'

He hurried excitedly over, hugged his brother first, and then extended his arms towards me.

'How was your day I asked him as though I didn't know'?

'Ummm okay mummy' he replied avoiding my eyes.

'Have you had a word with Miss O'Connor, I think she was expecting you' Miss Reynolds implied.

'No miss, I haven't as yet.'

'Perhaps you can stop by her office on your way out'

I could sense insistence in her tone of voice, although I realised it was supposed to sound like a suggestion.

'Yes, I'll do that' I responded forcing a courteous smile.

Yes, I'll do that my ass! Is what I was thinking. There was no urgency to meet with Miss O'Connor and state the obvious, that my son really was doing the things they had described him as doing in class.

Whoopsie do!

You were right Miss O'Connor, I was wrong.

I couldn't see why she needed to see me so urgently. What did she want a f****** medal?? I said goodbye to Miss Reynolds and excused myself, heading straight for the exit.

'Yolanda...Yolanda!'

I almost didn't look around. I could hear the joy in the voice and knew it wasn't Miss O'Connor calling to me. So, I turned around again forcing a smile. It was one of the parents at the school, Harrison's Mum. She was okay, I quite liked her. Harrison and Cassius were best friends; well at least on most days. I liked Harrison as one of Cass' friends. He was polite, and less spoilt than some of the others. I had heard him answering his mum back before, refusing to do things, but in comparison to some of the other children at the school, and how they treated their parents. Harrison was a good boy. For that reason, I didn't mind him playing with my son.

I openly admit I am that parent who doesn't want her children playing with children who behave in a certain way. Behaviour can indeed be learned, children can mimic the behaviour they see from other children or adults, sometimes even characters off the TV. I don't believe my children are perfect.

However, I constantly try hard to raise them the right way, according to my own expectations, to teach them the basic principles of life, manners and respect. I tried to be mindful of the influences I exposed my children to, particularly because of where we were coming from.

Already life had dealt us some pretty hard blows, I had to be honest and say that they had contributed even more so, to my need to keep negative influences to a minimum. I always maintain that 'children don't ask to be born', so for that reason, don't deserve to be accountable or pay the price for, an adult's actions. I guess that's why with regards to my own sons, I've always been determined to give them my everything. Because I accept that in life, both before their time, and since their existence, I have made choices. Some of which, have impacted my son's lives.

Example, I made a choice to have both of my son's. Yes, I did indeed think things were going to be different. As it just so happens, things, often people, turn out to, or be, the opposite of what I expected, or dreamed of. This was part of the reason why it was just the three of us.

Like I said, although it hurt, all I had, all I could do, was to make the best of a bad situation. That said, it meant trying to identify the best opportunities and trying to surround them with positive influences.

'Yolanda!' Someone was calling me.

Now Harrison's mum was waving her hands frantically from the other side of the playground. There actually weren't that many parents between us, but never have guessed by the way she was waving at me trying to get my attention. I smiled more genuinely this time and turned around and started walking towards her.

'I need to arrange a play date for Cassius and Harrison. Perhaps next week he can come over after school and have tea with us. Harrison keeps going on and on about it' she explained using her fingertips to move her fringe from her eyes as she spoke to me.

'Yes, that sounds great' I responded noticing Cassius and Harrison hugging and jumping up and down with excitement.

'Fabulous' Harrisons mum rubbed her hands together. 'I'll text you our full address' she said excitedly.

'Great, it's a date then'

Harrison and Cassius gave each other one last hug before the three of us set off again towards the exit. I smiled as we headed to the gates, holding each son by the hand. Now I had a more genuine smile. Amazing the difference positive interaction can make.

'Good afternoon Yolanda, hello boys'

I looked up and saw Miss O'Connor standing just a little before the gates. I wanted to believe she was always stood here and that somehow, I had missed her almost every day since the boys had started this school. I knew that was absolute poppycock. This head teacher was not normally stood here at the gates. She was not normally visible outside of her office after the school day. Yet today broad as day and I do mean broad in its literal sense. Here she was stood before us.

'Good afternoon Miss O'Connor'.

I didn't bother to fake a smile; I kept a straight face this time. It was pushing it slightly if she thought I could fake it some more for her benefit.

'Would you like to pop in and have a quick chat Yolanda?'

Here we go again torn between the want to say no way, and the need to say okay, I told myself.

'I can do Miss O'Connor'. I did not want to speak to this woman, but I also needed her to know I wasn't trying to run away and hide. I wasn't trying to act as though my son's behaviour was ok. I told the boys to wait in the reception area whilst I went into Miss O'Connor's office.

'Thank you for stopping by Yolanda'. Miss o Connor sat down and tweaked the glasses on her nose.

'That's fine' I replied disingenuously. I've already had enough listening to you for one day.

'I thought it would be a good idea to touch base with you to discuss Kwame's needs based on his behaviour now that you have seen it for yourself'.

Call me paranoid, I'll take it. But something in the way in which she articulated that statement came across smug.

'Ok what would you like to discuss?

I didn't mean to come across abrupt or rude, just frank.

'Well Miss Reynolds and I had spoken before about our options regarding some of the behaviour that Kwame demonstrates, and his tendency to get quite upset when he can't do something...'

'Okay' I replied, offering no suggestions, but still waiting to hear the rest.

'Well as I have mentioned to you before, we do believe that

Kwame may well have social and emotional difficulties. He tends to burst into tears quite easily and seems to be struggling to make friends.

BULLSHIT!!!! I almost said out loud.

'I-beg-your-pardon' I was not yet raising my voice however I could see the potential to get there fast approaching. Did Miss O'Connor feel that because now I had seen my son's behaviour, I was going to roll over and play dead...? Did she imagine that perhaps they now had the upper hand and I would do as I was told? I guess she could tell by the tone of my voice that I meant business, that if you were going to say something, be sure to be able to support it, because I was listening. Already I had tried to avoid this conversation today right now whilst I was still 'in my feelings', but this woman was intent on us having the conversation today. She was now prolonging my journey home.

'Today during lunchtime, it was reported that Kwame was trying to play with a group of children who wouldn't let him join their game. Kwame then burst into tears'

It was reported. What does she mean it was reported? Who exactly reported it? Why were we speaking as though we were dealing with adults who required reporting to the authorities? Had I missed something? Was this Crimewatch?

'So just to be clear, because he couldn't play a game with a group of children he burst into tears and for that reason he's having trouble making friends and has social, emotional difficulties. One instance at lunchtime and that was the conclusion you came to...?

'Well you know Yolanda, to be honest, just observing his behaviour on a daily basis and his interaction with his peers, it does appear that he is having some difficulty'

'So, what exactly are you suggesting Miss O'Connor?

'Well nothing concrete Yolanda. However, it may well be that Kwame has some SEN needs resulting in some of the behaviour that we've been seeing. In order to be sure, we wanted to discuss with you whether it would be useful to have an educational psychologist come in and observe Kwame. The educational psychologist would provide a report which if you authorise, would be presented to the local authority to try and get Kwame additional in class support'. It would allow them to look at whether Kwame indeed does have social and emotional difficulties, and also to look into his learning needs as well, as Miss Reynolds has reported that he struggles to do his class work when prompted. I know it may sound quite daunting Yolanda, but we have lots of children here with special needs, and we try to make sure that they are all supported.

If Kwame does have any needs, I assure you the school will do everything to make sure that those needs are met.'

I sat there. I said nothing. I looked Miss O'Conner dead in the eyes, expressionless.

'To begin with, Miss O'Connor, I'm not sure that we share the same views about my son having special needs, so I'm not sure about a stranger, albeit a professional or otherwise, observing him for a day and then writing a report based on that one observation. If I had hypothetically observed an athlete one day during training, am I then able to summarise that athlete's ability based on what I have seen?' I didn't wait for her to answer.

'I think the best thing for me to do right now Miss O'Connor, would be to go away and think about this and I'll get back to you.'

I have learned that sometimes in life, you need to digest conversations before responding to them. I pride myself on that. Don't be surprised if you have a conversation with me today, and I come back to you a week later with my response to that conversation. That is how my mind works. Some things require careful consideration. I refuse to let people force me into rushing decisions. I was someone who needed time. I need to ponder over things; I need to weigh things up.

I can't be badgered. I need to be clear that the decision is mine.

'That's fine Yolanda. Thank you for considering this. I assure you we have Kwame's best interests at heart, and will do all we can, to support him.

'Thank you, Miss O'Connor,' I said standing up.

'No thank you again Yolanda, for coming in'.

I chose not to respond to the last thank you I felt like we had definitely said enough to each other for one day.

'Goodbye Miss O'Connor'.

I closed the door behind me, called to Kwame and Cassius and walked back to the car.

When we got in the car, Kwame was the first to start speaking.

'Mummy please can Romar come to our house tomorrow to play with our toys?'

'No baby not tomorrow, because firstly you've not been behaving at school and secondly, I need to speak to Romar's mum first'

'My teacher said I did have a good day mummy'

'Really???'

I turned around to face him in the back of the car raising my eyebrows slightly. He looked back at me, not as confidently that his teacher had said he had had a good day.

'Can I tell you something 'Kwaams'; I came to school today and watched you in your class. You didn't see me, but I saw you.

I watched as my son's expression changed from assertive to, 'oh oh' I may well be in trouble.

'Yes, I saw you today, walking around the classroom, refusing to do as you were told'

'Who me mummy' he asked as though there were two Kwame's sat in the car with us.

'Yes you.'

I am not quite sure if my son thought I did not know what he looked like, or perhaps I was just plain stupid, or better still, he was just so much cleverer than me. Because actually knowing him as well as I did, I could hear the guilt. I saw his face change at the realisation that I had indeed seen him. I wanted him at that point to offer me an explanation for his behaviour, tell me that somebody was making him act like that or something, I don't know. But he didn't.

'Until you improve your behaviour, I'm afraid you're not going to be allowed to have Romar come and play at our house.' I said sternly. 'Every day the teacher's telling me about you not doing your work, refusing to do your work, running around and acting like you ain't got no sense. 'w'aapen to yuh?'.

I couldn't hide my frustration. Kwame knew by the way in which my tone and accent had changed. I was annoyed.

'Huh??!' I shouted as though my question was not rhetorical and I expected Kwame to respond with a valid answer. 'All you have to do is go school and learn that's it. But you'd rather go school and mek da teachers think you don't come from nowhere!'

I was off 'on one' now; there was no holding my mouth. I was ranting about education, manners, and respect. Some of what I was saying didn't even make sense and I knew it. But I felt like I was at breaking point. If this boy, this son of mine, didn't turn his behaviour around quickly, I felt like the label was going to stick. I couldn't have that.

I ranted some more as I drove home, noticing how much like my Mum I sounded. Both the boys sat silently. On one hand I felt bad, I really wanted to say yes to Kwame's friend coming around. Yet I couldn't reward the behaviour that I had seen earlier. I saw the water filling his eyes and watched as he blinked them tightly together to disguise the tears.

'I'm sorry mummy, I won't do it again'

'That's fine, however until I see an improvement Romar still can't come around'

'Can I still go to Harrison's house mummy?' piped Cassius.

'Yes, but just not today'

'That's not fair' whined Kwame 'how comes my brother can g…'

'It is fair Kwame.' I said firmly. You need to earn rewards and privileges. If you misbehave, you'll lose them.

'But mumm…'

'ENOUGH!' I said in my 'mummy means business' tone of voice, turning the music on and pretending to enjoy the song on the radio. As the song played, I reminded myself how much I hated this kind of music, but let it play for the sake of a distraction.

CHAPTER 14

The following day was a placement day. I almost didn't mind that because it gave me the chance to focus on somebody else's life. I enjoyed my placement; I pretty much liked the team also. Everyone seemed to care about the young people that we were dealing with. Yes, they were challenging, sometimes even threatening, but we were in a good position. We, the social workers or in my case, trainee social workers could add positivity and affect change. That is what I was here for. This is why I was training to be a social worker. It was a shame the placement would have to come to an end soon. Although my manager had already talked to me about offering me a job as and when whilst I was still studying. Perfect. Hopefully once I qualified it would be easier to move to a full-time position. As for my current job, which I also thoroughly enjoyed, eventually I would give that up.

This job on the other hand was a social work role in the division that I wanted to go into. I couldn't pass up this opportunity. My manager was great, knowledgeable, and empathetic. She really cared about the young people we worked with. On several occasions I'd watched her make allowances for a young person's subsistence (like pocket money/living allowance) even though she knew they had squandered it. However, there was something about when she made these discretionary decisions that didn't give the impression, she was a pushover, more so it earned her respect, and a reputation for being human. People liked and respected her, as did the entire team. And as for me I was in absolute awe of her. I was lucky to have her as an example of an excellent social worker and team manager. It was clear she was not in this field for the money as I had seen with many others. She was in it, to make a difference, and I was happy to be part of her crusade!

#BestManagerEver I entered the office, bright, bubbly, and as always excited. I loved placement days.

'Morning' I exclaimed to no one in particular, or better still anyone who was listening. The team were used to my excitement and enthusiasm. I was a tad famous for it actually. Colleagues had asked me on occasion, 'why are u so happy all the time'. And I reassured them that I was definitely not like this all the time, I just loved my job! They assumed it was because I was young, the youngest member of staff on the team. Most of them had been in the field for some time and were perhaps a little less enthusiastic about showing up to work on a daily basis. Not me! I felt like my role, the team, everything here, was perfect for me. And everything that constituted part of my role made me feel fulfilled. Utilised. I couldn't wait to gain my qualification. I already knew the type of social worker I would be. The mere thought excited me. I would not be an overzealous social worker. The kind that runs in, 'all guns blazing' when parents discipline their children, their way. No. I would be the type of social worker that looks at context. One that is able to make a more thorough assessment as to whether a child is being sanctioned or abused, because believe it or not, there is a huge difference. And if by any chance I encountered a family whose parents were sanctioning but perhaps not in the most appropriate way. I would do everything in my power to put support in place to help them learn new strategies and to be empowered in using them. First! That was my idea of a social service. An authority that provides, a social service.

I mean we currently have the Metropolitan Police service, who some would argue is not much of a service, as it is. We do not need further policing we need to empower people. Whether they are parents, carers, young people, the community, disadvantage groups. We need to give them tools, resources and support, because one thing that I think we will all agree on is that parenting does not come with a rulebook. So, in order to provide a social service, we should be coming together to look at what support strategies parents can benefit from. One size does not fit all; therefore all parents cannot follow one manual, because each child is an individual. Therefore, the point I'm making is that I had in mind already, where I would be going with my qualification. The kind of service I wanted to be associated with. Even if I would have to create it myself.

'Morning Yolanda'

The voice came from behind me. I turned to see my Manager, Jean, smiling at me. Jean was Black woman, a mature woman, not necessarily old enough to be my mum but definitely older than me with older children than mine. Her hair was always immaculate, and her clothes perfectly clean, and pressed. She was always calm and made everyone feel like a favourite by the way she interacted with him or her.

'Morning Jean' I responded with the same high-pitched childish enthusiasm I always had. 'How are you?'

'I'm very well sugar'

Just the way Jean spoke to me, somehow made me feel like she cared. If as it has been suggested, we each have a different superpower, then making people feel valued and cared about was definitely Jean's.

'I'm good thanks' I replied

'You haven't really seemed yourself, how are the boys doing?

'They're okay thanks'.

'You sure? How has everything been at school?'

'Okay' I lied.

'Did I tell you that I sent my kids there'?

'I don't remember' I replied trying to think back.

'Yes, I couldn't wait for them to leave if it wasn't one thing, it was another if it wasn't one child, it was another. Phone call, after phone call, after phone call. I got tired of the phone calls and had to tell Miss O'Connor not to use my number unless one of my children was dying!' Jean said laughing.

'You did not Jean; I said eyes widening while still laughing.

'I had to!' she said quite matter-of-factly.

'She tried to say my Carly had special needs because she didn't like her teacher. Every minute she was calling me up telling me my Carly did this, Carly did that. I had to ask her; Miss O'Connor are you not qualified in managing primary aged children? She didn't like that one bit. I got sick of talking to her; I got sick of listening to her. I had to tell her straight, my Carly does not have special needs and will not be going on a special needs register!

I responded, 'apparently my son has social and emotional needs, can't make friends, or follow instructions, or get on with his work. Basically, my son who has been talking fluently before he was one, reading fluently since he was 3, everyone's favourite pupil because he is bright, has since coming to this school, gained special needs'.

'Don't let her bully you. At that school, they like to label the Black children. I don't know what Miss O'Connor's problem is. She tried hard to get my Carly. Don't trust her. She's evil!

I started to explain to Jean some of the issues I had been having since the boys started the school. I explained to her that I had observed Kwame and actually he was doing the things they had said he was doing. I told her all about the educational psychologist suggestion and that I didn't feel Miss O'Connor was being genuine. The conversation with Jean was a real eye opener, even though I'd been headstrong when dealing with the teachers up to this point. I had secretly at times began to question if I was simply being ignorant and assuming the world was against me when really it was conspiring to support me. Hearing Jean talk about similar issues she had had when her children had attended the school, reaffirmed to me that actually at times I needed to simply trust my own instincts because I knew my children. There was no other expert in who my children were or indeed are. I did not know everything, and granted I looked around at the other parents and I was notably one of the younger mums. So, what! What did that mean? Did it mean that people with more experience at parenting could push me around? Did it mean that when mature parents spoke to me, I should do as they say? Did my age and experience, make me incapable, in the eyes of everyone else.

My conversation with Jean was a turning point for my own personal development. Something I learned about myself, is that quite often I can be willing to take on the feedback of others, so much so, that I start doubting that which I know for sure. That conversation with Jean on that day was an absolute Godsend. I say this because I had no intention of sharing the details with her, I saw it as another hurdle I would have to cross even if I wasn't sure how. A conversation that may well have started and ended with 'hi how are you, very well thanks', had evolved allowing me to share how things really were and then gain insight which in turn could help support me in the challenge. I knew Jean was special, it was one of the reasons I initially wanted to be part of her team. That morning I appreciated her openness in sharing. Nonetheless there's something else I appreciated about Jean that day, something I appreciate about Jean today and will, forever more. That very special thing is, her ability and willingness to share. I don't know what she saw when she looked at me, and I can only assume that through her own wealth of experiences, personal and professional, she was able to understand or recognise when someone else might require that non-judgemental, empathetic truth that in essence results in a feeling of support and encouragement. Jeans conversation with me that day encouraged me and reminded me that I was enough.

As an added note, never underestimate the power of sharing. Your story can make the world of difference to someone else at a time when they need it most.

CHAPTER 15

Half term came, things in our lives reverted back to as they'd always been. Kwame and Cassius attended play-centre every day while I went to work. Low and behold I didn't have the complaints I'd had from school making it a relaxing break in so many ways. I could drop and collect the boys without the increased anxiety feeling as it approached collection time. Not once was I told about, social or emotional challenges. Not even the slight mention of the deviance that I'd been hearing of at school. It was a relief. I wished the boys didn't have to go back to school and I could continue sending them to the play centre.

I had met Delores on the first day. She was a nice lady. A mature woman, all the kids are play centre called her Miss Delores. I really appreciated her initiative to launch the play centre initiative within the church. It wasn't necessarily my thing, but I knew first-hand that places like this saved parents like me and GF, allowing us to continue working during school holidays. One of the evenings I collected the children, she spoke to me about a trip they were going on to a museum. All the boys wanted to go so GF and me how to sign the consent forms and packed the kids off ready to go. Kwame and Cassius were excited about going. Perhaps even more so about going on the coach then the actual trip to the museum.

I put the boys in their matching tracksuits and trainers. I had a tendency to buy them the same things when I did their clothes shopping. It avoided the whining of all the 'how comes I didn't get that one?' this way no one could complain. They both had exactly the same thing. There! Delores had mentioned in the letter that the children would be allowed to have spending money but no more than £5 each. I wasn't giving them £5 each. So, I had given them each £3 spending money. I mean what on earth would they be buying anyway a pen pencil or sharpener or something.

That evening when I collected them from play centre Delores shared with me that the boys had, had a fantastic time. I was still briefly talking to Dolores when Kwame ran over to me.

'Mummy mummy look what I got you, it's a present!' Kwame was excitedly waving a bag in front of me. I looked at him and a small bag in his hand what on Earth could he bought for me with his spending money at the museum.

I gave him a hug and a kiss, 'thank you very much baby'. Did you buy something for yourself as well?'

'No Mummy I didn't have any money left'

I rubbed the top of his hair.

'Awww Kwaams, you know you don't have to get anything for Mummy that money was for you to buy yourself something'

'Yes, mummy but look what I got you'

He pulled the gift from the bag it was a white mug that said I love you with a barcode. Even the memory of that moment still touches my heart because it was one of the most thoughtful gestures from such a small child.

'It's for your tea' he exclaimed proudly with his back straight as though he had just achieved something amazing.

I laughed.

'I love it baby!'

Noticing that I had arrived Cassius ran over waving his hands in the air.

'Mummmiieee

'Afternoon Cass', did you enjoy the museum?'

'Yes mummy'

He shoved his hand into his tracksuit pocket and pulled out £2.

'There mummy' he said handing me the two-pound coins.

'Where's the rest of your money baby?'

'Oh, I bought some sweets mummy'

'Oh okay, this is your change then? I asked still laughing.

'Yes mummy'

'Didn't you buy anything for mummy Cass?' Kwame asked with

big brother authority.

'No, I got sweeties!' Cassius replied dancing proudly.

Both Delores and I began to laugh. She was probably laughing at Cassius' excitement at having brought his sweeties just for himself, subsequently shovelling them down before his return to play centre.

Whereas I was a laughing because my sons were like chalk and cheese and it was absolutely hilarious to me. There was Kwame who used his entire £3 to buy me a mug. (A mug I still have to this day.) That did not surprise me. Kwame was thoughtful. He had always been a thoughtful child. These were the elements of his character that reminded me of myself, because Kwame would quite easily spend his £3 on me and have nothing for himself. Which sounds like the type of thing I have done, or better still I currently do at times with the people that mean the world to me.

Whereas Cass', he was very thoughtful but in a very different way to Kwame. Cassius would not spend his money if he didn't have to. He just didn't see the point. He didn't care much about actual material things. He was never overly excited about being able to buy things. I imagined he only bought the sweets because I had not given them any sweets in their lunch boxes. If I had packed them any sweets, I guarantee you, Cassius would have returned with £3. But nevertheless, I appreciated these two boys. I truly appreciated at that moment the diversity of their characters, and for the entire journey home that day that moment kept a smile on my face!

CHAPTER 16

I avoided engaging in conversations with Miss Reynolds and Miss O'Connor for as long as I could, once the boys returned to school. I felt like their time at play centre, had proven that there was nothing wrong with them. It made me feel even more determined to have my son's behaviour change at school. We had survived the entire half term without one complaint. There was no way I was being ignorant to something that was obviously there. If it were there, where had it gone for two weeks? I was keen to rectify whatever issues my son was having at school. I mean I needed to, I had to. I kept replaying the conversation I'd had with Jean over and over in my mind. Everything that she had shared with me sounded very much like us. If my son had any special needs or any learning difficulties, I would ensure he received adequate support. I would in no way prevent him from accessing that. But how often are children labelled with difficulties, issues, developmental challenges, that actually are not challenges, difficulties, or incapability's at all?

An example that sprung to mind was Cassius. As I mentioned before he was virtually a selective mute when he was younger, choosing when to speak and who to speak to. This coupled with not learning to speak fluently until he was well over three years old. Perhaps he too may have received some level of diagnosis if nurseries had been that much more overzealous regarding his developmental progress. For the record I admit I was slightly concerned initially. However, as a relatively new mum, all I had to compare him to was his older brother who if I was brutally honest, I felt learned to speak very early. Yet, who am I, to define very early? I remember learning from the boys' grandparents that their dad learned to speak very late, maybe four or five years old. I held on to that story, reminding myself each time, that there was nothing wrong with Cass' progress. Low and behold, if we fast-forward a few years, Cass' development may not have been in line with some of the best child development books. However, his individual development was in line with his character and personality. He has never been diagnosed with special needs despite possibly being one of the quietest students in his classroom, according to teachers. He is also one of the brightest young men you may encounter. Point being, whilst there are certainly some obvious determiners of unmet needs, I am of the opinion that if we view individuals as just that, individuals. Then we allow ourselves to be amazed, educated and enlightened by the developmental milestones that we each transcend through in our own time.

In Kwame's case, I didn't want to be overzealous just because his behaviour was unacceptable. Children behave in a variety of ways for a multitude of reasons. Some children just like attention, is that a deficit? My experience of Cassius' allegedly slow development coupled with the conversation that Jean had had with me prior, had contributed to my need to say no, to an educational psychologist observation for Kwame. I took into consideration the on-going complaints from school regarding social interaction, refusal to learn, or perhaps an 'inability' to learn as the school put it. Giving it much thought I discussed it with my mum and subsequently came to the conclusion that as it was the teachers who were struggling to manage my son's behaviour and teach him effectively. Then I would voluntarily come into school to support and assist with my son. How? When? No idea, but each night I lay my bed searching frantically for the answers on my bedroom ceiling, all I would come to, was the conclusion I needed to do it myself.

In addition, I also felt that Miss Reynolds needed to observe how to deal with my son by watching how I managed him. It was beyond me, why neither myself, nor any other close member of the family, had these issues with my son, just her. Behaviour management clearly was not her strong point. Yet without condoning my son's behaviour, I also knew that my smart kid would sense your inability to manage him. Trust me. You give him an inch; he will indeed take a yard, a mile, and any metric length you can think of. That is who he is. As a parent you have to be honest about who your children are. I believe once as parents, we are able to do this, it allows us, to not only advise others how best to deal with our children, but to understand our children and their actions. I knew who my son was. I know who my son is. For me looking at the way in which Miss Reynolds attempted to manage him and the way in which he responded, made perfect sense to me. The approach she was using was not appropriate to his needs. Maybe that was the approach she used for all the other children in the class and it worked phenomenally. Nevertheless, does one size really fit all in the classroom? No. Does all teaching reflect that? No. Therefore here is food for thought ... If we take into consideration cultural differences, learning styles, communication differences, and then individual characteristics, it can help us to understand how much work we need to do in the classroom to ensure that each of our children can best access their learning effectively. Miss Reynolds' softly-softly approach, was not working with Kwame. It simply wasn't the approach that best suited his character.

Furthermore, if a child believes he can get away with something with an adult, then they do! Wouldn't most children? More so, I felt that if I showed miss Reynolds some of the strategies I used at home, the tone of voice I used to show my son's I mean business, the countdown to three etc., she too could do the same and hopefully earn his respect. That way they could stop trying to talk to me about being so keen to label him or ship him off to an alternative school. I still hadn't quite come to the end of my first year at university as yet. My placement days were going well, now all I had to do was the written element, which wasn't difficult as such, but clearly, I had other priorities that were rapidly taking over. I knew I'd have the work completed by the deadline, but as usual I would have to pull some all-nighters and stock up on coffee. With regards to coming into school to help sort out Kwame, I was hard pushed to find free time in between university, placement and my part-time job, which I desperately needed to keep hold of, in order to make ends meet. So, after deliberating endlessly I decided to use all the free periods on my timetable to volunteer at the school. I also told myself that once my placement days were complete, I could also use those days to spend at the school, instead of overtime at work. I knew this meant we were gonna struggle financially, but I reminded myself it would only be for a time. I noticed that there was a gap starting to appear in Kwame's learning and I needed to close that quickly. When the boys started the school, both were at the top of their classes. Cassius was still up there, but Kwame was slipping. So, I needed to think fast.

Since ending up on my own with the boys, one of the devastating factors that always played on my mind was that of them not having a father as a role model. I knew it was not outright my fault, but I still felt that I had a responsibility. Naively I remember thinking that I could just be two parents. Believing that I would just give them whatever mum and dad would have given them. Yes, it would be hard but no it would not be impossible. Subsequently I had later read something somewhere, coming to the conclusion that whilst I could try to fill any gap in my children's life and give them the best of me, even trying to overcompensate for them not having their dad. The truth of the matter was that only a man could teach them to be a man. I unwillingly understood that I could teach them the qualities I feel a man should possess. I could teach them about expectations of a man's role, to himself, to his family. However, the true essence of manhood, I realise, is beyond me. Hard pill to swallow I must say. Particularly when I pride myself in being a woman who can do myself anything and more than a man has and can do for me. Why? Because for me, in order to admit that I cannot teach my sons something, leaves me with one of two options.

Either I'd be willing to accept that it would be something they do not learn (not a chance), or I would need to find a way for them to acquire it, obtain it, and learn it. So, what do you think I did? I started to do research. My experience within social services, my knowledge, and my other work experiences had provided me with quite an extensive awareness of support services available, external providers, and so on so forth. I started to look at provisions I had sought out when trying to meet the needs of young people I had supported. What initiatives did I believe in for young people, particularly young Black boys, similar to mine? What steps had I taken when supporting young people who needed additional services? All these questions when posed to myself over a course of sleepless nights and negative connotations, led me back to a mentoring organisation. Not one, which I had personally worked with, or had ever, referred a young person to, either. It was an organisation that had previously caught my eye one morning before school whilst watching GMTV. For those of you who don't know, GMTV is the name for what is now referred to as GMB with Suzanna, Kate etc. On ITV every morning starts at 6am. That particular show, well over a decade ago contributed to introducing me to the mentoring organisation that would change our lives. My sons and mine!

It was an ordinary morning I remember it like it was yesterday. I had switched the TV on and turned to GMTV, like I did every morning. Only difference being, that on this particular morning there were two young Black men on the sofa talking about raising the achievement black boys in Britain. Their presence had me fixated on the TV screen as I munched the words, one by one, directly from their mouths. The two men were inspiring. Articulate, Educated Black Men. Let me be very clear, all I have ever wanted is for my son's to be articulate educated and strong Black Men with sound knowledge of who they are. To be proud of where they came from, to be ambitious and to show themselves in their best possible light. As I watched these two Black men, I was mesmerised, proud of what they stood for. They talked about the disparity between opportunities and educational attainment for Black boys. I was glued, fixated on the screen. Everything they discussed, I too believed. They used statistical information to highlight how much more likely a Black boy was to be permanently excluded from school in comparison to White boys. I remember standing in front of the TV demanding that the children did not interrupt me because I needed to hear every last word.

At the time I recall feeling that they were speaking directly to me, that they somehow knew of my problems and had come on GMTV that morning in hope that I would see them. Much like the conversation that Jean had had with me previously, it felt like a Godsend, a sign, and a message. It sure wasn't luck. I don't believe in luck. I believe in signs, blessings, Godsends. Luck was not for me. I even remembered leaving home late that morning because I needed to know everything there was, about the organisation before leaving home to do my school run. I did not write any of the information down either; I simply remembered the organisation's name, which was to be fair I thought was quite memorable, and the name of the person who founded the organisation. I told myself that I would contact the organisation and ask to speak to the founder. I reassured myself on the basis of the interview, that he would probably be well versed in what I was experiencing with my son. At least he would understand the various ways in which Black boys are inappropriately managed at school, their behaviour criminalised as though they were responsible adults, perceptions widely differing. Hopefully I'd be able to gain mentors for both my sons.

Although my main issues stemmed from Miss Reynolds complaints pertaining to Kwame. I was also conscious that Cassius too deserved to benefit from a mentor. Men who would teach them about values, principles, and morals that were important to us. I had in my mind this notion that mentoring would help to fill the gap that I knew was there. A gap that may or may not be contributing to some of the difficulties my son was having at school. Either way a mentoring organisation, built on the fundamentals that this one was built on, was still an organisation that I wanted to support my sons. We needed more of these organisations that was a fact. We needed collectively to bridge the gap. I didn't wait long to contact the mentoring service. In fact, I decided to call them that very day before collecting boys from school. I made myself comfortable in the car and dialled the number I had managed to find on the Internet. I have no idea who I needed to speak to but remembered clearly the name of the founder sat on the GMTV sofa earlier that morning, Andre Lewis. When a voice answered the phone, I asked for Andre.

'Speaking' was the articulate response.

My mind went blank, all of a sudden. I just didn't know where to start. I had taken the details from the TV with all confidence, now I was speaking to the founder of that very service I didn't know where to start. I realised I had surprised myself and getting through to him that easily.

'Hi, I am Yolanda' would be a good way to begin, at least introduce myself.

'I have two sons aged five and seven and I would really like them to be assigned mentors.

'Okaaaa...y'

Andre's response was slow and deliberating, as though he was getting ready to decline.

'Where did you hear about the mentoring service Yolanda?' he sounded curious.

I started wondering if I had the wrong number and had contacted a different mentoring service.

'I saw you this morning on GMTV'.

It was intended as a statement, yet the added sprinkle of doubt resulted in it sounding more like an open-ended question.

'Oh right. Okay'

I got the impression I had dialled the right number. I had contacted the correct place, because Andre agreed that he had been on GMTV that morning…? Yet he still sounded doubtful.

'Can I clarify Yolanda, you're the parent of two boys age 5 and 7, you would like to register for our service?'

'Yes, I replied confidently. Believing that we were making progress.

'Firstly Yolanda, thank you for contacting us. Unfortunately, we only take referrals.

'Referrals'. I repeated as my heart sank into my stomach.

I had prematurely assumed I had found the answer, only to be told that my self-referral would not suffice.

'Yes, usually from school, social services, Youth Offending service so on'

'Okaaayyy' now it was my turn for the slow yeses.

'Andre, we don't have a social worker, my son's school would never contact your mentoring service, and I really can't afford to wait for my children to end up in any kind of trouble before we get the support of a service such as yours.'

I went on to explain to Andre our personal circumstances. I told him of the situation with the boys Dad, I told him about the old school and what had taken place since we had moved to this new school. I explained all about the school wanting to have an educational psychologist observe my son to diagnose him with needs they referred to as social and emotional, and my reluctance to do so. To cut a long story short, I poured my heart out to poor Andre while he sat there and listened to me for 40 minutes. By the time we had finished talking he had assured me that a mentor would be calling me shortly to arrange a registration for both my boys. RESULT.

I looked up at the sky and 'Gave Thanks'. I had to be grateful for the outcome of the conversation. I felt like I had been given an extra shot of confidence as I stepped out of the car to collect the boys from school that afternoon. Had I of been a cartoon character I would have had my hair blowing in the wind, slow motion' steps with sound effects to accentuate new found power, and a multitasking belt to hold all of mum's essentials. Like cocoa butter, Vaseline, snacks wipes, pen, paper and anything else you can think of. That was genuinely how I felt. Somehow, I had managed to evade both teachers so far but now I felt ready to approach them with some kind of resolution or strategy.

And today felt like as good a day as any.

CHAPTER 17

I strolled into the reception. School had not quite finished yet and I wanted to take the opportunity to speak to Miss O'Connor about what I had decided, before collecting the boys. I had to be honest and tell you that the Sun felt like it was shining. Yes, the air was cold, but the sun was out, that gave me an added sense of determination.

There was a parent was stood in the reception, I wondered if she too was waiting to see Miss O'Connor. Perhaps her son or daughter also has 'special needs' as they were intent on insinuating my son did. Who knows? She didn't look as fierce as I felt. Neither did she give the impression of a warrior woman, maybe more a country mouse if anything. No disrespect intended. I didn't want to appear as though I was pushing in front of the country mouse. So, after standing for a couple of minutes in the waiting area behind her, I decided to tap her shoulder and actually check if she was waiting to be seen. It turned out she had already been seen and she was now standing in the reception area waiting for the bell to ring so she could proceed to collect her children from their classrooms. Politely stepping in front of the 'country mouse' I approached the receptionist. I offered a courteous smile and addressed the receptionist. 'Good afternoon Miss, is Miss O'Connor available by any chance?'

'I'm not sure if she's available let me call through and check' she responded rather abruptly.

This should be interesting I thought. Let's see if the 'old battle axe' wants to see me. I watched as the receptionist pressed a couple of buttons on the telephone and waited for Miss O'Connor to respond.

'Sorry to bother you Miss O'Connor' she began somewhat apprehensively. 'I have Kwame and Cassius' mum here hoping to see you, if you are free?'

'That's great Catherine send her through for me please'

I raised my eyebrows slightly, why was the receptionist acting as though she was unsure of Miss O'Connor's Calendar. Heck this is a good start, I reminded myself leaving the previous thought in the waiting area.

As I walked through the door, I began scrutinising the dinghy photographs on the walls again. Photographs that looked like they had been fixed to the very wall since Tudor times. Specifically, the display wall leading to office comprised of a series of photos over the decades, perfectly positioned on the wall. Wow was my silent expression, as I realised that even the diversity of the children attending the school had changed within the last 20 years. Judging by the photos the school was obviously a predominantly White School. What I mean by that is that in the earlier whole school photographs, there was the occasional black face, but you had to really look with a keen eye, much like 'finding Wally' (if you're familiar), as opposed to now when there was clearly a more balanced cohort of children. Black children White children, Chinese children Asian children, biracial (I do hope that's the correct term) children. The predominant race was still White.

However, one could not ignore that there had been a clear shift in the intake over recent years. And if you looked at the photos spanning over 20 years, there was your evidence that this school had come a long way. It caused me to speculate about whether this was why Miss O'Connor felt the need to deal with the black children in her school in the way she did. Jean had already shared with me, the way her children were dealt with when they attended the school. It didn't seem very dissimilar from the way I felt mine, were being treated at present. I was of firm belief, both then and now of one thing in particular.

Racism is not necessarily as overt and blatant as it was when my parents came to this country. I know that from listening to their stories, history and observation. Yet, something else I know, is that racism can become embedded so deep within a person's psyche, that it becomes their norm. Therefore, they will insist they are not racist using irrelevant evidence to support their assertions, such as, 'my husband's Black' or my best friends 'Black'.

In a previous job I once supported a woman who referred to me as 'coloured'. To my face as well! Granted she was quite an old lady, one who I expect was born during a time when women who looked like me, were referred to as 'coloured'. She literally made the reference in conversation and continued talking as though it was fine. I corrected her immediately, explaining to her that coloured insinuated I was an array of colours such as Purple, Blue, orange, Green, Yellow etc., and politely explained to her, the correct term is Black and I was quite happy for her to refer to me as Black. She looked genuinely surprised by my correction. However, what I learned that day from the experience, confirmed that racism is taught. It is learned. Whether by reaffirming verbally or enabling through lack of, correction or silence. I had chosen not to remain silent with this woman, aggravated mentally, but smiling on the outside as though it wasn't important enough to warrant correction. I was incapable of doing as such. I instead opted for an opportunity to teach, an opportunity to raise awareness, for her to indeed learn something. You see, **racism can be a mind-set, and mind-set can be altered**. This old lady I had been sent to advocate for, had been raised during a time when racism was acceptable. Now that time had evolved, laws had changed. She had indeed grown older, but her beliefs had not changed. She had remained trapped in that very time warp. I felt it my duty to correct her on behalf of all Black people, believing that her poor use of terminology was due to a lack of education as opposed to anything else.

The other issue with racism is that racist practices can become the norm. They can become institutionalised. Thanks to Baroness Doreen Lawrence, who campaigned tirelessly after her son Stephen Lawrence was murdered in a racist, unprovoked, attack by white men in 1993. The enquiry that followed concluded that the Metropolitan Police Service was 'institutionally racist'. I don't know about you, but I recall the headlines like it were yesterday. It was at that time I had given birth to my first son and I will never forget, watching the news, reading the papers and shaking my head. Fearful of what would be awaiting my own son. I know I was not alone in the sadness I felt each time Baroness Lawrence appeared on the news. Each time I watched her, each time I listened to her speak, I prayed that God forbid, anything, anything whatsoever, should ever happen to my son, I would be as dignified in my approach as Baroness Lawrence was. Her resilience to this day remains vivid in my mind. Her perseverance, her determination, her tenacious pursuit for justice.... I can only imagine how difficult it was each day for her to face the world. Yet in the eyes of the world, this strong Black woman stood up for what was right. She fought tirelessly without physical weapons. She spoke articulately without losing her temper. She challenged MPs, government authorities, policies, and practices, without fear. All in the name of Justice for her son. I know I've mentioned it before but as far back as I can remember, I have recognised strong black women and the qualities I perceive to be that of a strong Black woman.

These have become my influences. The women I look up to. The current Sheroes of our time. The women who make us feel blessed to have existed during a lifetime when they had ventured. What a blessing it is to have lived through such a momentous era and witness such change. Therefore, with all of these influences, beginning with my Mum, to my Aunties, to people I didn't even know personally, I knew racism existed. I knew that sometimes it was embedded so deep a person may not recognise their actions as racist. I knew that meant I had to be willing to challenge those who overtly demonstrated racism. Worst of all I knew society did not welcome Black boys, who would eventually grow into Black men. Some might say big black scary men. I knew that black men were feared within our society, associated only with negative connotations such as aggression, violence and unemployment. I knew that due to institutionalised beliefs, policies and practices that Black boys would not be granted with the same opportunities as their non-black counterparts. I knew that at every hurdle, someone would be there to trip them up, shut them down, and raise the hurdle to a height considered unattainable. All of this before they could mature and evolve into their own greatness. This had been my greatest fear when I had found out I would have a son, on both occasions. I was marred with thoughts of joy but with thoughts of extreme worry. Worry that the authorities would abuse my sons, turn them into vengeful angry beings, and force them to give up on humanity. Surely not every mother of every race has this worry, so why then did I? What had I witnessed, observed and experienced, that differed to the thousands maybe millions of other mothers…?

Sensing that I had spent an inordinate amount of time looking at the history of the school I decided to proceed to the cave where 'the old battle axe' hid. The office door opened just as I was about to knock.

'Hello Yolanda, lovely to see you again, do you want to come in and take a seat' 'the old battle axe gestured to the empty chair in front of her old rickety desk. My obvious answer would be no, of course. But I had work to do, and I needed to let her know what work needed to be done.

'Thank you' I said as I sat semi-comfortably in the old wooden chair.

'How can I help Yolanda, have you given any more thought to what we discussed previously?'

'Yes, thank you Miss O'Connor I have'

'Oh, that's good news'

Miss O'Connor sounded excited. All that was left for her to do was to rub her hands together scheming like Meg, the witch from my childhood storybooks, Meg & Mog. Something told me she obviously assumed I was about to agree to the educational psychologist visit prematurely.

'Yes' I agreed with her before proceeding … 'I thought about it and decided that at this point I will not consent to the educational psychologist visit. I'm not convinced at present that we have exhausted all other options. What I'd like to suggest instead, if possible is that I'd like to come in and support Miss Reynolds in the class. I understand that Kwame is not doing his class work. However, I'm not convinced it is because he doesn't know how to. Rather I believe he is taking advantage of Miss Reynolds current approach. I'm not asking to be in the classroom on a daily basis, I would like to volunteer at specific times mutually agreed, and if it enables my son to access his learning better, fantastic. If not, I'll go back to the drawing board'

'I must say Yolanda; I do respect your decision. However ultimately the behaviours we are seeing from Kwame are synonymous with learning difficulties we are experienced in managing…'

'If this is the case' I interrupted Miss O'Connor. 'Why is it that Miss Reynolds is having such difficulty?'

I heard myself after I'd said it, realising my comment may well be misconstrued as being snarky. Although the question I was asking was a valid one, my intention was not to be sarcastic, it was a genuine question. I couldn't understand with all that experience, why did Miss Reynolds feel the need to complain about my son everyday as if she were unable to deal with him. If it were indeed a regular occurrence among students, why the need for the Educational psychologist.

'It is not that Miss Reynolds is incapable Yolanda. Ordinarily if we have a student with special needs in the class, we would also have a teaching assistant there to support the teacher and make sure that, that child can access their learning. Or a successful educational report that would recommend an alternative provision for the child.

'You mean a special school?' I said my tone sounding irritated.

'In this case Miss Reynolds does not have a teaching assistant assigned to her class, therefore the challenge for her is supporting all of the other students whilst also trying to meet the needs of Kwame. How it will work is, if Kwame is identified as having a special need, the school will receive funding and that funding will be used to pay for a person to be in class to support his needs, allowing miss Reynolds to continue teaching the rest of the class'.

'Like I said Miss O'Connor, I'm happy to give up some of my own time to come in and support'

'I don't want you to have to take time off work Yolanda, or university. I know you're studying'

This woman was very quickly becoming a damn nuisance! First, she compared her life to mine or herself to me. Now she was telling me that she doesn't want me to take time off work, and how the hell did she know I was at university??? I could feel my breathing pattern changing very quickly. I didn't like where this conversation seemed to be going.

'It's not a problem Miss O'Connor, I'm happy to do it!' I said refusing to engage in a conversation about my work or study.

'I think what I'll do next Yolanda, is have a word with Miss Reynolds and see what she thinks. I don't have a problem with you coming in to a few sessions and helping Kwame in the class. However long term, we do need to consider a more practical plan'.

'I agree,' I responded confidently, but this seems like a really good place to start I think!'

I knew she could hear the certainty in my voice. It was posed as a question, but I think we both knew it wasn't. She could speak to Miss Reynolds that was fine. No skin off my nose. But I was coming into the class, to see what exactly, my son was playing at!

CHAPTER 18

After seeing Miss O'Connor, I made the dreaded walk to Miss Reynolds class to collect Kwame.

Firstly, I desperately wanted to see my son after his day at school, yet the constant negativity that awaited me, heightened my anxiety every time the school day was over and was forced to face her. It wasn't her as such, even though her sheer appearance was beginning to rile me. Her oily hair, her heavy makeup and stupid blush coloured lipstick. She annoyed me just looking at her. Her dress sense reminded me of the meek teacher from Matilda. In fact, it was funny how both her and Miss O'Connor represented characters from Matilda. Miss Trenchbull and Miss Honey. Only thing is I quite like the character Miss Honey in the story. She was kind, empathetic. She even provided respite for Matilda. You have to love the teacher who went above and beyond in that way. Even in the story Matilda had encouraged her to stand up for herself because the Trenchbull had bullied her so long.

Miss Reynolds struck me like that. In slang terms she was a 'press button'. In simpler terms she had no mind of her own, she was almost one of Miss O'Connor's prized instruments. She humbly waited for her chords to be struck, so she could sing the right tune. I didn't think miss Reynolds was all bad, I just felt that she wasn't a woman who was willing to stand up for what was right, and I had to be honest about what that meant. Those conversations at the end of the school day that always left me feeling worse never better. That was just her way of doing what was expected of her. And in the midst of that, cultivated her inability to think outside of the box. Thus, resulting in her throwing her hands in the air when Kwame failed to comply, participate or engage. Frustrating I can imagine. However, I for one will not be beaten by a child. Therefore, the onus would fall on me to find another way forward. Another means to engage the pupil.

Nonetheless it felt to me that instead of searching for new strategies it was far easier to condemn my son. For that reason, the daily updates after school in the playground, were my least favourite part of the day. If I could lower a ladder from a helicopter above the playground for the boys to climb, trust me I would.

As I walked through the school, I bumped into some of the parents on my way. One of which I had become friends with since the boys had started the school, Jayde. She also had two sons about the same age as Kwame and Cassius. We'd got talking one day in the playground and exchanged numbers. Since then we spoke on the phone and had taken the kids out together on several occasions. She was unlike a number of the parents at the school, perhaps one of the reasons that she and I had formed a friendship in the way we had. She was younger than me by a couple of years, was married and lived at home with her husband and their two boys. Our relationship was refreshing to say the least. One of the things that became quite apparent quite quickly was her generous heart and hard-working approach to life. She came from a different background to me Jayde, her Mum was Black, and her Dad was White. When we had sat down in the past and talked about our childhoods it was clear that we were not raised in exactly the same way and possibly understandably so. Yet one of the things that impressed me about her was her morals and principles. Yes, I've probably said that before about someone else. I guess morals and principles are fundamental qualities for me in others. When it came down to her son's it was evident that they were her priority. Jayde was self-employed and worked hard to do her bit for her family. Her husband worked equally hard, often long shifts. He was originally from Jamaica, and it always brought a smile to my face to hear their interactions. She was ever so British, and he was ever so Jamaican. But they were a beautiful couple. To me they were a perfect blend of two worlds living harmoniously together. He would never tire from trying to teach her some of his Jamaican ways. Yet on the other hand he struggled to conform to any of her British ones. He couldn't eat the food; he could barely eat from anyone else. He made me laugh. As a Jamaican can I just say typical.

Above all that though, was something else I admired about Jayde. She saw her husband's fussiness, his bluntness, his pronunciation as hilarious. She was unoffended where even I may have been, had it of been my husband, talking to me. She was understanding when he needed it the most. But most importantly, she never ever stopped smiling. Jayde was a special kind of woman. The more I got to know her, the more I understood why he chose her for his wife. You can't pay for that kind of love and loyalty. I knew that, and I got the impression he did too. She even parented differently to the way I did. She was more lenient in one-way but then equally as firm as me, in most others. Like mine, her sons too, knew they had to respect her. They were polite, intelligent boys. They played, bickered, just as my boys did, and I watched Jayde manage them similarly to the way I did. I had even had the pleasure of meeting Jayde's mum dad and her Nan. They say one of the best ways to understand another person is to meet their family. This was true for Jayde. Her mum and Dad shared a level of respect that was a pleasure to see within your friends' parents. I could see how Jayde acquired the ability to love the way she did.

And then there was Nan. A beautiful kind, old woman, who Jayde absolutely doted on. Nan was amazing. She always made you feel welcome if you came to the house and she was there. She was the pinnacle of Jayde's family and would help Jayde out with the children at any opportunity. I was always happy to see Nan and called her just that. Nan.

'Hi J' I said extending a genuine smile.

Jayde smiled back showing her gold tooth as she greeted me.

'Hey Landa where you been man?'

'I've been here Jayde, but the boys have been at after school club too'

'Oh yeh, how's placement going, have you finished yet?'

'No not yet, but nearly' I replied crossing my fingers then waving them across her face so she could see.

'Wicked!' she replied with a famously huge grin.

We walked together making idle chitchat and talking about our boys. Jayde was telling me that her son had gotten into trouble the week before for calling somebody a 'prat'.

'When his teacher told me, I said ok. What I wanted to say was, that child is a prat anyway!'

I laughed as Jade gave her impression of the conversation. I could actually imagine her son calling the other child a prat. Yet what I found outstanding was that Jayde was unperturbed by the teacher having to speak to her about her son's behaviour. She could see the humour in her son's slight deviance. The teacher complaining or notifying her of her son's minor infringement bore no weight on her grand scheme of things. It was just one of those things. I needed to take a leaf out of Jayde's book. I needed to view the comments from the school, perhaps a bit more light-hearted, taken with a pinch of salt as opposed to a volcanic eruption that caused me to panic and fall to pieces. Jayde and I continued to laugh and share stories about some of the daft things our sons happened to do at school, and then came to the same conclusion we always did. Boys do daft things, without any thought of consequences. Whereas girls were a tad more strategic. That was our assertion anyhow.

When we arrived at the class, parents were still forming an orderly line outside the classroom.

'For f**k sake!' Jayde mumbled in frustration.

One of the parents spun round to look at Jayde

Clearly, she had overheard Jayde's mumble, and by the look on the parent's face, was totally horrified by her use of language. Noticing the look of horror on the parent's face. Jayde kissed her teeth and began tapping her right foot with impatience. I looked at the faces of the other parents, all of which were unequivocally unimpressed. It just so happened that Jayde was the only one expressing that impatience.

Good for you Jayde I thought. The queue outside the classroom was getting ridiculous. From outside we, the parents could hear Miss Reynolds reminding the children that they needed to listen and be silent when asked. Yes. I thought. They do need to do just as she said.

Subsequently, not at this time when I'm standing outside, and I still need to get my sons home and prepare dinner. Not to mention if the boys had homework! I decided that if Kwame did have any homework, I would explain to Miss Reynolds tomorrow it had not been done because we arrived home far too late. She needed to be more considerate to parents. Not all of us lived two minutes away.

After standing there for five minutes I decided to take the initiative and knock the door. Jayde saw me make the approach towards the door.

'I was just about to do that!' she said hands now on her hips.

I knocked the door and waited for Reynolds to turn around. I could feel holes in my back where the other parents were gazing at me eagerly awaiting the outcome of my knock. Perhaps for a moment they forgot we, the parents were collecting our children from primary school, not knocking at the door of the giant while he sang 'fee fi fo thumb'!

Miss Reynolds opened the door slightly, just enough to faintly whisper.

'Do you mind waiting behind so I can have a quick word with you Yolanda?'

For F**k Sake! I almost said out loud. Now it was my turn to use foul language. I was fed up of these conversations. What now Miss Reynolds?? Was what I wanted to say. What couldn't you manage today? Did Kwame sneak out of school and rob a bank?

She then opened the door, this time wide enough to address the other disgruntled parents, without waiting for my response.

'I am sorry for the delay mums and dads, unfortunately we've had a bit of an unsettling afternoon and I needed to speak to the whole class, to remind them of my expectations for behaviour as of tomorrow. If you could just bear with me, they will be dismissed in one minute.'

'Chuh' my thought was louder than I intended. One of the parents took the opportunity to lean over and said.

'I'm going to complain about this. I was late for work one evening last week because of this delay after school. It's just not on!'

She had a point. If this was Miss Reynolds' way of putting her foot down with regards to discipline, it wasn't working. Looking around at the angry displeased expressions worn by the other parents, she did not have our cooperation or support.

True to her word, the children were dismissed within a minute of Miss Reynolds addressing us, the parents. Well all the children except of course my son, for whom becoming 'the last Man standing' in his class was now becoming a habit.

Miss Reynolds invited me into the classroom and started to get ready to play the record.

'Unfortunately, Yolanda, we still haven't had a very good day. Today Kwame has again refused to do his work'.

She opened up his exercise book to show me. I could see where he had written the date using handwriting that I could only associate with someone who was writing with his or her toes. Looking closely, again I could see where Miss Reynolds had started to write the sentence for him and Kwame was expected to finish the sentence in his own words. Yet I could also see where he had not finished the sentence. Instead he had written two words and Miss Reynolds had finished the sentence for him and then written 'well done' 'good effort'. I could feel my eyebrows raising, blood boiling.

I'm sure I spoke to this woman about doing this already. This habit of setting the bar so low that my son need only slither underneath it on his belly like a snake, was going to make me blow a gasket! Let me see what she's going to tell me today now. I folded my arms looked her in the face expecting her to start speaking.

'Kwame became quite upset today...' she began. 'Insisting that he didn't understand how to do the work. Rather than continue to pressure or distress him, I let him go to his brother's class to help out the younger infants. He was excited about doing that and apparently his brother was really excited to see him'. She sounded pleased...chuffed with herself.

I looked up at Miss Reynolds trying to close my gaping mouth at the same time. She didn't stop there either. No, she was not done.

'I'm becoming increasingly concerned with Kwame. He doesn't want to play with the other children and when he does, tends to get upset quite easily. He does play with his brother and his brothers' friends at times. However, of course this is not always ideal as we would like to see him form positive friendships with his class peers. We have given Kwame a 'time out card' so that when he becomes distressed or upset, he's allowed to go to miss O'Connor's office to calm down...'.

Whoa whoa whoa! Let's just back up here! What did she just say? Helping out with the infants instead of doing his own work?? When he gets distressed? Time out card? I didn't know where to start. We were going from bad to worse and the strategies I was listening to Miss Reynolds describe to me were not my idea of strategies. That was not how you made progress with my son. That would not work! And who the hell said this was ok?!! Not me.

'I Beg Your Pardon. Hold on, let me just get this straight. Kwame is not doing his work; he is not being sanctioned. Instead he has been sent to a classroom of younger children to support the class, although he has not completed his own work. He is supporting others. Even though you say he has several pieces of unfinished class work'.

I realised I was tilting my head to the side, with a look of confusion as though demanding a sensible answer.

'And when he refuses to do his work, you are happy to do it for him, and then congratulate him? Not to mention wasting my time complaining it afterwards?'

'Yolanda what I think I must stress to you, is that these initiatives are here to support Kwame's learning. He finds it difficult to write and follow instructions.' Kwame is not bilingual; English is his first language. Define what you perceive his difficulty to be? Miss Reynolds', I said pronouncing my words so slow I could have spelt them out in the same length of time.

'I don't expect you to know this, but my son had immaculate handwriting prior to coming here. I seem to recall Miss O'Connor pointing that out to me when the boys first started.

How on Earth then, are you telling me he finds it difficult to write as though he is three years old!'

'Please don't get upset Yolanda'. Miss Reynolds sounded like she was pleading. 'Kwame's behaviour presents as quite challenging, particularly as I'm trying to manage and teach the rest of the class. Unfortunately, his behaviour is far too challenging for just one member of staff to manage. I am going purely by what he is demonstrating. I mean you saw, yourself, the other day' he does not engage' Miss Reynolds shrugged her shoulders as if to say he we're a lost cause or something. I was furious. I stood up, calling to Kwame to take my hand at the same time. He immediately did so.

'I'm afraid I have to go now Miss Reynolds; I need to collect Cassius I've already spent enough time here'

Miss Reynolds didn't bother to argue with me, as I headed for the classroom door.

'Ok thank you Yolanda, see you in the morning Kwame'. Now her shaky voice reminded me of my Granny's goats.

I kissed my teeth, storming out the class towards Cassius' classroom.

The anger was rising in my stomach, causing an involuntary build-up of tears.

'Are you okay mummy?' Kwame asked looking at me as though he too was feeling something.

'Yes baby' I could not muster more than that, because I knew I was already struggling to keep my angry tears under the surface, and whilst I was angry with Miss Reynolds, I was upset with Kwame too. I didn't know how long I could contain the tears, so I hastened my strides, forcing Kwame to hop skip and jump to catch up. When we arrived at Cassius' classroom, the class was empty. Great!

We walked back to where we had come from, heading towards the reception desk where Cassius was sat in the reception with his class teacher.

'Sorry Miss I was held up at Kwame's class'

'Oh, that's ok' Miss Franklin said handing Cassius over to me.

Cassius' face lit up as he threw his arms first around my legs and then around his brother's neck.

'You're strangling me' Cass', Kwame said, untangling his brother's arms from around his neck.

'Oh, mummy I thought you weren't coming to get me!' Cassius said still excited by our arrival.

'Of course, Mummy is coming to get you baby I was just talking to your brother's teacher'

'I know mummy' he replied cheerily, oblivious to everything, anything.

CHAPTER 19

In the car on the way home I purposely put on a CD with some of the boys' favourite songs. I needed the distraction. I couldn't talk to the boys yet. I had been choking down tears, since I left Miss O'Connor's office. Each time I glanced in the rear-view mirror to check on the boys. I could see the water filling my eyes like a fish tank. The boys continued to sing out loud to B2K, waving their arms and doing dance moves as much as they possibly could without being able to jump up and down. I felt a tear fall, and wiped it away quickly, before either of the boys could notice.

'Can you play that song again? Kwame asked

I put the song on repeat, still unable to speak due to the overflow of tears now flooding my throat. Traffic was terrible thanks to all the time we spent at the school, so by the time we got home, the choking tears had started the onset of a headache. I couldn't be asked to cook, so I took some food out of the freezer and put it in the oven for the boys to eat.

I turned the TV on and sat in the front room while the boys changed out of their uniforms. The news was on. I started to watch the headline and then decided I didn't need any more pain and misery this evening, switching quickly to the kids' channel, just as Kwame entered the living room.

'What are we having for dinner mummy?'

He was always hungry, always thinking about breakfast or lunch or snacks.

'Nuggets and curly chips' I managed to say without losing a tear.

'What happened at school today?' I asked him inquisitively. What was your teacher talking about when she said you couldn't write?

'I don't know mummy' he replied shrugging his shoulders.

'What do you mean you don't know Kwame; I saw your book. That's not how you write?'

'It was hard mummy I couldn't do it'

On one hand this would be a perfectly valid response to one parent perfectly valid question. However, this was not any hand, and this was not **any** parent, or even **any** child. This was me and **My Son**!

I didn't know what had flew up in his head to make him tell me he couldn't write, but I was going to get to the bottom of this.

'What did you find hard? I probed deeper sounding more irritated by the second.

'The work' he replied blasé, reaching for the remote control to turn the TV over.

I snatched the remote from his hands and turned the TV off.

'I need you to explain to me what you're finding hard, so I know what you need help with…'

'All of the work mummy' he shrugged his shoulders again

'But today when your teacher showed me your book, you didn't write anything. Your teacher has done the writing for you, and I know you can write! You have always had good handwriting'

'But Miss Reynolds said if I find it difficult, I don't have to do it, so I didn't do it mummy. She said I could go to Miss Franklin's class and help Miss Franklin and my brother 'Kwame, I don't send you to school to help Miss Franklin and your brother I send you to school to learn. Why is it when Miss Reynolds speaks to you, you're not listening?'

He shrugged his shoulders. I was now tired of the shoulder shrugging

'No Kwame', I shouted. 'I asked you a question do not shrug your shoulders when I'm speaking to you. Why are you behaving like this at school?' I was getting frustrated now, and my voice was bearing peak volume. There was no excuse and although I was asking a question, one part of me knew it was rhetorical, because what could he possibly say to explain and justify himself for his actions.

I was so fed up of the constant complaints at school, and now Kwame was sitting there talking absolute nonsense about finding things hard.

'I'm sorry mummy'

'I've told you both before, you cannot say sorry and keep doing the same thing you have to show you're sorry, not be sorry. Your teacher thinks you don't know how to write, and that you can't do the work, but that's not true…

'Okay I won't do it again mummy' he repeated hoping to put the conversation to bed.

'The other day I watched you in the classroom, all the children were doing the artwork and you were walking around. Why were you walking around Kwame?' I asked puzzled.

My voice was beginning to sound exasperated with frustration at the lack of explanation I was getting from Kwame. I wanted to remain calm but how could I?

I was starting to sound desperate; Kwame's behaviour just wasn't making any sense to me. I wanted answers; I had no answers. I needed answers, I wanted to understand. What do I need to do to fix this??? I resorted to having conversations with myself out loud.

'I don't know mummy; please can we go back to the old school so I can see my friends?'

That was it? He didn't like it at this school. Now it was making a bit more sense. He wanted to go back to the old school and play with the old friends. I got that. But I knew it wasn't going to happen. I felt like a shitty mum. My eyes were beginning to water. I couldn't contain them any longer. I wiped my cheek and attempted to finish the conversation.

'You're not going back to the old school Kwame. This is your school now. You need to work a bit harder, just like you used to in the old school so your teacher can see you can do the work.'

'Ok mummy, he said wrapping his arms around me. 'I will. Sorry mummy'

'It's okay baby…'

'Sorry for shouting'

'That's OK mummy'

I stood up to make my way to my bedroom passing Cass' in the doorway. I closed the door behind me and sat on my bed, taking a deep breath before bursting into silent tears. I did my utmost to keep my whimpers quiet enough that my sons would not hear me. It was a lot of tears; I had a lot of frustrations. I kept trying to take a deep breath in between tears to compose myself. My body jerked, in the way that hiccups takes control of you when you least want it, each time I tried to suppress more tears. I had believed I was taking the initiative to move my sons to this school thinking this was the best move for them. Only to hear my poor seven-year-old tell me he wanted to go back to his old school with his old friends.

I started to question my intentions for changing the boy's school. My decision had been based on a few factors. It was a private school and whilst the level of education at that school seemed to be great, I was paying for it, although the standard of learning was not proportionate to the price paid.

Then there was the fact that they forced the children to engage in an array of Christian and non-religious celebrations. However, they failed to acknowledge Black History Month. That you can imagine didn't go down too well but it was the response I received that spoke volumes to me. A call to the head teacher's office, to express that they had not intentionally ignored the fact October was widely celebrated as Black History month in the UK. But also, the kind request that I do not share this conversation or my thoughts regarding Black History month with any of the other parents. Hmmmm. What did he imagine I was going to do, or the other parents would do? Why was something as straightforward as a reminder that Black History Month existed, turning into a seemingly covert operation. Oh, let me not forget the offer for me to come in and talk to the infants about Black History Month…. I think you know; I did not pass up that opportunity. I loved every second of it.

If your children were lucky to be at that school at the same time as my children, you'll probably be the only year to ever have that experience!

Needless to say, I was of the opinion that if I was going to pay for it, I needed to make sure it was worth my hard-earned money. Especially when the money was as particularly hard to come by, as it was.

Their current school on the other hand was deemed to be academically of a very high standard and would cost me nothing, as it was a mainstream school. Yet ever since what was supposed to be a smooth transition into a very good school, was fast becoming a nightmare.

Kwame just hadn't seemed to settle in. He wasn't happy. He was acting up. Now today as I listened to him, I realised that slowly but surely, I felt like I was losing. I was losing in my battle to be a good Mum. I was losing in my battle to give my son's a happy childhood. My son was clearly unhappy, and I had no idea what to do. School were treating him like an imbecile, and he was too young to notice or understand.

My top was beginning to get wet with tears. I reached for my nightie, which was folded neatly at the foot of the bed where I'd left it that morning. I decided that it would serve as a tissue, handkerchief, and towel whatever I needed. All I did know is that I needed something to soak up the stream of tears that was now in full flow. I could hear the boys happily watching the TV, while I crumbled as quietly as I could. Alone, in my room. My nightie proved fit for purpose, helping me to muffle the whimpering sounds of me sobbing my life away. I inhaled for a minute in a bid to prematurely stop the tears falling. No joy. I was losing. I was losing dramatically. My nightie was soaked with tears. I needed real tissue now. I couldn't leave the room, through fear of the boys seeing that I'd been crying again. I sighed. I just couldn't get anything right.

I resorted to using every inch of the nightie to dry my face, I need to leave the room.

Maybe if I phone my Mum, I may feel better. I told myself confidently hopeful. I reached for my phone and dialled my mum. I didn't expect her to answer so soon.

'Hi Mum' I said trying to sound as normal as I possibly could, but realising I sounded even more unconvincing.

'You ok, is everything alright?' Mum asked sounding concerned.

I paused, swallowing a tear before answering.

'Yes Mum'

'Why do you sound like that?' she asked the concern still in her voice.

I swallowed again, and then proceeded to talk.

'Kwame's teacher spoke to me again today after school...'

'What's her problem now?' I could hear my mum was irritated, but still at work judging by her lowered voice.

'He's still not doing the work mum. His teacher is still doing his writing for him and then writing excellent or good effort, like he's stupid or something. Mum I don't know what else to do…' I erupted into tears on the phone. 'When I ask him why he doesn't do it he said he doesn't understand but Mum I know he understands. But then why is he doing it?' I sobbed some more.

'Don't start getting yourself all upset ok' Mum said reassuringly 'C'mon now' she was trying to console me I knew that.

I picked up my nightie again and wiped more tears from my eyes. I had reached the slight gasping and mild jerking, stage of my cry, sniffling heavily as I tried to regain some kind of emotional normality.

'Where are the boys now?' my mum asked

'They're inside the front room watching TV'.

'Have you all eaten already?'

'No Mum I've put some food in the oven for them to eat'. I said still sniffling.

'What are you going to eat? Mum sounded concerned again

'I'm going to find something in a moment Mum.' I said attempting to reassure her.

'Good, go and sort out the kids and I'll call you when I get home'

'Ok Mum, speak to you later'

'See you later, love you, and stop that crying, it'll be ok'.

I came off the phone and realised the tears had subsided. The heavy feeling was still there, the nightie now banished to the floor served as evidence that I had only but one moment ago been on the edge. But one small part of me felt better.

I left my room and walked to the bathroom to wash my face and clear any other evidence that I'd been crying.

When I came out of my room, the boys were still watching TV, impervious to the fact I was quietly having a minor breakdown. Cassius was pretending to be a Power Ranger, jumping and prancing in front of the TV. Whilst Kwame frantically manoeuvred his neck side-to-side, trying to see TV screen around him. I peeked at them thinking, this moment, this picture, was priceless all on its own. It looked like everything I wanted, we already had.

On the other hand, the picture didn't detail the bits in between, which tainted the ink gradually. My thoughts returned to our current problems. The issues at school hung over me like a rain cloud, making me feel more and more miserable. I entered the kitchen to check on dinner, surely, I had run out of tears.

CHAPTER 20

Over the course of the next few weeks placement was busy. I had also been doing some overtime at work to pay for a holiday I booked for myself and the boys to go to Jamaica. I was doing everything to make the holiday possible, and I couldn't wait to take the boys to see my grandparents. My oh my, how I couldn't wait to talk my granny into insanity. Flights were almost paid for. All that was left was to make sure the boys had all their bits and pieces they needed. It had been a tumultuous few months and I think we all deserved the holiday. My brother was coming too, with my Mum. It was set to be a good family holiday.

Not much had changed at school. The complaints were not coming as thick and as fast as they used to, but they kept coming. I had begun sanctioning Kwame for refusing to do his work or running out of the classroom. So far, I had confiscated toys, banned Television time, ice cream, cake and custard. Yes, even cake and custard. Because despite what you think, cake and custard is not the sustenance you need to survive, it's a privilege. And intent that my son was taking the absolute 'mick' at school. I had to hit him where it hurt. And with this son, cake, custard, ice cream. That hurt! Of course, I still gave him dinner, just no treats. No eating out, which he also loved.

Despite the old Trenchbull acting like she needed to consider my supporting Miss Reynolds. She contacted me afterwards to agree to a few times a week. During that time, I could come in and help Kwame in class. Grateful for the slight reprieve. That became the routine. I spent a combination of two mornings and two afternoons per week in Kwame's class so that he would get his work done. I'll never forget the first day I did it either. Of course, I didn't inform him that I'd be coming. I dropped the boys to school as normal, only to pop up 20 minutes later at the door of Kwame's classroom to help. If only you could have been a fly on the wall... I entered the class just as my son was running around the classroom. Yes, just running randomly while everyone was sat on the carpet. The funny part was ... Do you know what the funny part was?

As soon as he looked up and saw me, he stopped running, sauntered over to carpet, sat down and listened to the story! Still laughing...?

To save you re-reading my last line, I will say it again. As soon as he saw me, he stopped running, sauntered over to the carpet and sat down!

For once it was not my mouth that was wide open with surprise, it was Miss Reynolds! As she saw first-hand, how Kwame could demonstrate his ability to listen, and follow instructions now his mother was present. Had I not been feeling so smug, I would have been angry at Kwame for causing me to take time off, to sit through his class, even though we both knew that there was nothing the matter with him. I didn't even speak to him as I entered the room. I literally stood still at the door and looked at him. Just one look. I gave him that one look. Depending on your parenting you might be familiar with 'the look' and the effect that 'the look' had on you as a child or perhaps has on your children today. Come to think of it, much of our parenting was unspoken back then.

You got the look when an adult offered you food or drink, to let you know 'say no'. You got the look if your mum came to parents evening and the teacher told her of something negative you did at school, that may well mean would be receiving a 'hiding'.

And you got the look if you said something that you knew full well, you should not have said. Yes, come to think of it we were definitely raised on the look. In my case the look meant what the hell are you doing? But I guess if you had not been raised on the look, then what you saw that morning as I entered the classroom, would have surprised you as much as it surprised Miss Reynolds. I might I add, was not surprised. Far from thinking that the sun shined out of my son's ass. I simply knew that he was better than they thought he was. They both were. The problem was, for some reason, one of them wasn't showing it!

CHAPTER 21

I turned the music up loud in the car. I liked to have these moments before I collected the boys. Where I could sing out loud wave my hands around in the car to the beat of the music. It was my music therapy. It kept me sane. It was no wonder the boys knew all the latest songs. Music was my saviour. Different songs would have me feeling a different type of way. If I paid close attention the music, it would even have me driving differently. The likelihood was that I would continue on the same vibe once I collected the boys. But I still needed this time for myself, a little mummy time, a moment of music therapy. I sang along to songs happily; I was making good time to after school club. I had not a care in the world.

There had been no mention of the educational psychologist coming in.

Cassius' was doing well and had even been on a play date with one of his friends from class. Funny, the mother of the child did mention to me that my son asked for a knife and fork at dinner. She mentioned it to me because she had been so impressed as her son still eats with a spoon.

I smiled at the comment, if her expectation of my son was based on her own, I can see why she would have anticipated the same thing. Nonetheless it made me smile, that something that simple, which impressed her, was a basic standard for us. To this day my inability to eat without a knife and fork amazes some off my nearest and dearest. Thank you, Mum.

I pulled up outside school, parking the car half on the pavement. I was relieved that at least I didn't have to see Miss Reynolds today. I was collecting the boys from after school club, so today I had the added privilege and pleasure of seeing Sandra. As I entered the after-school club, I looked around the army of children scattered around. How have I not noticed that there were so many children after school club, maybe it was just today who knows? Hats off to the staff, because I don't know how they do it. As I stood there looking around trying to notice, no identify, my children, amongst the myriad of small people. I suddenly thought about how difficult it must be to hear yourself think with these many children around. I mean I always respected the staff here, particularly Sandra. Either way I suppose I will almost respect those who can have more children than me and still retain their sanity. This was a lot of children, a lot of screams, a lot of cries for attention, and an awful lot of mess. Nope not for me.

'You ok Yolanda' came the friendly voice from behind. It was Sandra.

'Hi Sandra, I'm good thanks. I was trying to spot the boys'

'Kwame is over there' she said pointing to the art corner, 'and Cassius s over there, she said directing me to the home corner where Cassius seemed to be engrossed in preparing a make-believe meal.

'Miss Reynolds has given me a letter to give you about a trip that the children have coming up at school'

She handed me an envelope. I thought it was strange that the school trip letter came in and envelope addressed directly to me as opposed to the teacher just handing the letter either to Kwame or Sandra to give me. I felt the envelope was perhaps a tad dramatic but let's face it, Miss Reynolds was often dramatic. I took the letter from Sandra and said thank you, just in time for Cassius to notice my arrival. And charge over with a pot filled with as much pretend food as he could find and waved it under my nose.

'I made you dinner mummy look!'

'Oh, thank you dumpling'

I looked into the metal pot, which Cassius was holding. Manufacturers must go through a great deal of trouble to make these pots look realistic; I was impressed. The ingredients, however. Well I had an amalgamation of bananas, bacon, tinned tomatoes, strawberries, hot dogs, cookies, circles and squares and a few coloured pencils. Definitely a hearty meal.

'This looks delicious baby' I said insuring the enthusiasm was present in my voice.

I looked in the pot again.

'I don't think I'll be able to eat all of this Cass'

'Ok mummy you can just have some of it, here you go' he said handing me a strawberry and a tin of tomatoes.

I pretended to munch the strawberry and tin of tomatoes while Sandra sniggered.

'Sutten sweet you?' I said to Sandra giving her a side-glance. She knew what I meant.

We both laughed.

'MUMMY!' Kwame shouted if you jumped in front of me to announce his presence.

'Hi Kwaams' I bent down to kiss him

'Yes mummy, I've got a letter for you, for a trip to the beach, but you will have to come with me, or I won't be able to go because of my behaviour'

There you go! There it was. The rain cloud all over again hovering over me. It seems that the school had found a new way to piss me off and this was it. Not satisfied with the fact that they hadn't seen me due to the boys being at the after-school club, now this.

'I think that's what the letter is about Yolanda' Sandra said probably sensing the accelerated decline in my mood. Sandra was not aware of the depths of the issues I was having. Nor was I in the mood to share them with anyone else. I decided therefore, just to try and play it down.

'Okay I'll read it when I get home' hoping to sound like it wasn't a big deal.

I waited for the boys to put their jackets on and get their bags. I didn't feel like talking to Sandra anymore. Actually, it wasn't that I didn't feel like talking to Sandra it was just that I didn't feel like talking. I wasn't going to let them mess with my mood this evening. For some reason Miss Reynolds had handed my son this letter and obviously said something to him, subsequently resulting in him giving me this long-winded explanation about its contents. Here was another thing I just didn't appreciate. If you give a child a letter for their parents then leave it at that do not say anything to that child except 'please ensure you give that to your parents'. Why was my son talking about himself as though he was a problem? 'Because of my behaviour'. I did not like that. To be honest it didn't matter to me, what had been said to my son. It mattered to me that something, had obviously been said, because my son a child was able to give me an explanation as to the requirements for this so-called trip before I had read any letter. And it mattered to me, because if something was going to be said to him, then I didn't see the need for a letter in a sealed envelope! I told myself not to open the letter until I got home and was feeling relaxed, but it was bugging me. I needed to know its contents, I needed to know what new misery the envelope contained. While waiting for the boys to put their seatbelts on I decided against my better judgement to open the letter before driving away from the school. Removing the letter from the envelope, the first thing I noticed was that it was not standard school trip letter. It was addressed to me specifically about Kwame.

Dear Yolanda,

As part of our current curriculum, we will be taking the children to Sussex to visit the Beach. The children will have the opportunity to explore, participate in learning walks and paddle in the water should they choose.

The trip forms an integral part of our curriculum and will allow the children to further apply their classroom learning. We would like Kwame to be able to participate in this trip. However due to concerns regarding his challenging behaviour, we are unable to authorise his attendance on the trip without additional assistance.

Therefore, we would like to advise you that we are willing to allow Kwame to attend the trip provided that either yourself or another member of your family 18 or over, is able to accompany Kwame on the trip.

Unfortunately, if this is not possible, we are unable to authorise Kwame's attendance on this trip.

Please will you confirm if a responsible adult is able to accompany Kwame on the trip, as we will need to confirm seating on the coach.

Yours sincerely

Mrs A O'Connor

I screwed the letter up and shoved it in the back, mumbling obscenities quite loud for a mumble. How was I supposed to go on this trip? I had to be at placement. What was wrong with these people? Who do they want me to send on the trip? My imaginary husband. What the f**k!!? I sat there wondering if they were trying to be funny. Was this a dig at me? Were they mocking my situation?

Furthermore, is this standard practice? Were they trying to tell me that all of their 'bruk bad' spoilt unruly kids, were also banned from school trips, if their parents were unable to attend??

I really didn't have the energy to talk to Miss Reynolds or Miss O'Connor about this. I just could not be bothered. As far as I was concerned, I didn't care if Kwame didn't go on the trip. I mean let's face it, England does not have any beaches. The kids would see a real beach when we got to Jamaica. I couldn't care less about this Sussex beach. I could imagine how filthy the water would be. For starters, Kwame would not be paddling in any water. God knows what would be inside there. Yes, I was scornful, even if I hadn't been. It was common knowledge that these so-called beaches England has, most of them to me, the water resembled the Thames. Hence why my son definitely wouldn't be entering the English over ground sewers. I started the engine and began to drive.

'So, mummy please can I go on the trip and please can you come with me'

'Kwaams, mummy has to go to work, I don't think I'll be able to'

I saw his face drop in my rear-view mirror.

'Please can you ask Grandma if she can come, or my uncle, or Goddie', referring to his Godmother.

'Grandma has work baby, Goddie' has work too, and your uncle has college'

On one hand I didn't want to burst his bubble. On the other hand, part of me felt like serves you're right. If you hadn't given the people the impression that you don't know how to behave, they wouldn't be able to use this against you! I looked in the mirror again at his face. He looked like he was ready to cry.

'Can I go with my brother mummy, to the beach?'

'I half chuckled. 'No baby, you go on your class trips and your brother goes on his. You have to be an adult to go with your brother'.

'But I am getting bigger mummy, I'm nearly an adult!'

I laughed some more.

'Yes Cass, but you're still not an adult yet'.

'Okay mummy'

Having now satisfied that conversation, my mind reverted back to the situation at hand. How was I going to make it possible for my son to attend this trip?

CHAPTER 22

University was becoming more challenging now. We, the students were all trying to finish off assignments, in a bid to be life or death deadlines. These were the final assignments for the year. Some people had put in overtime at their placements working additional days, meaning for some of them, placements were almost complete and only the written component was left. Unfortunately, I was not in that position. I still had days left to complete at placement, and my final unfinished assignment to accompany. On this particular day, I had been sat in the library for the last two hours drinking coffee and trying to find 4000+ words. I had managed a few hundred but not nearly as much as I needed in order to ensure I would not have to be up all night, the night before submission date. It was already 2 o'clock and I needed to leave shortly in order to make it to the school on time.

The library was busy, I assumed that like us students enrolled on other courses within the university were too rushing to meet their end of year deadlines. I looked beside me at the person using the neighbouring PC. He had a pile of computer science and technology books I gathered he was studying IT.

The woman opposite me seemed more engrossed in her phone then typing an assignment. Her keyboard was buried under a pile of law books. I always imagine that studying law must be really interesting but nevertheless really intricate. I mean the power in fluently knowing the law that intrigued me greatly. Particularly during a time when young people were being criminalised instead of guided, thus costing society it's valuable youth. I always imagine that if I were to be a lawyer, I would represent young people. Why? Because young people need a voice. They need someone to stand up for them and ask on their behalf for a second chance. They need someone to look at the context of which they are born into, providing ample and appropriate opportunities before judging them. They needed less judgement and more compassion and empathy to allow them to make mistakes and learn from them. I saw knowledge in the right hands as a power tool, and aside from the woman in front of me violently pressing buttons on her phone. Those who entered the profession with the intention to do such good, well good for them! Perhaps there was even more hope than we imagined for tomorrow.

The desk started to vibrate. It was my phone. I glanced at the phone knowing that I could not afford to be disturbed. This assignment was my priority. Placement would be a doddle in comparison to this, which requires me to use my words, my knowledge, and demonstrate that I had learned good practice. It was a private number. I wondered who it could be calling me at this time from a private number. Everyone who knew me knew I was at university today. Furthermore, if it was someone that knew me, why wasn't a name coming up instead of 'private number'. I pressed the button on my phone to connect, I waited to hear a voice before I said hello. I decided that if it was a prank call, I wouldn't give them the satisfaction of speaking.

'Hello, am I speaking to Yolande?' voice sounded official and definitely not familiar. To make matters worse the person on the other end was not pronouncing my name correctly. That really annoyed me. I never understood why a person would read all the letters I. The formation of my name and not get Yolanda. It wasn't like my mum had thrown a bunch of letters together and called it a name. My name was spelt exactly as it was pronounced. No disrespect to other people and the names they assign their children, but my name was not misspelt, it didn't have a silent A, or Y. It didn't have an unnecessary hyphen or three letters too many. It was simple, straightforward, and transparent, just like me. My name left nowhere to hide, and I knew it. When strangers remember my name after a first meeting, I'm always curious as to what caused them to remember. Knowing that most will call me a variation of names before they tire of my correction between clenched teeth.

'Who's calling please?' I asked using the same official tone that was greeting me.

'My name is Elsa, I'm a social worker from the Local Authority, calling from Kwame and Cassius School.'

My heart sank something had happened to one of the boys at school. And oh my God it must be bad, because a social worker was calling me from the school, not Miss Reynolds not Miss O'Connor!

'Is something wrong with my sons?' I asked my voice now involuntarily shaking'

The voice paused before an answer followed. The boys are ok Yolanda, unfortunately there's been a disclosure and I'm going to have to arrange a meeting with you. Are you able to come down to the school?

"Pardon me?' I looked at the phone again.

'There has been a disclosure Yolanda, and the school have contacted social services, I now need to meet with you quite urgently'

'Ok, I said' now beginning to feel the uneasiness in the pit of my stomach. 'I'll be there in half an hour'

'If you could just come straight to the office when you arrive, thank you'.

I put my phone down next to the keyboard in front of me, staring at the person opposite me. She was too engrossed in her phone she hadn't noticed the expression on my face, which I imagine looked like I'd seen a ghost. I half expected her to be looking at me, wasn't that conversation loud. Could she not hear the conversation I just had? The nature of the call that had disturbed me. It felt loud it felt like the voice was speaking to me through a tannoy.

I could still hear the voice repeating in my mind, 'there's been a disclosure' 'there's been a disclosure!' What did she mean by a disclosure? I knew what the word meant, but what would that mean for me? What did she mean exactly?? I started questioning myself, I had heard her correctly, she said the boys were okay. The boys were fine. But then what did she mean she needed to meet with me urgently? The school has contacted social services, why?? My mind was racing as I tried to gather my things together quickly, throwing them haphazardly into my bag. I logged out of the computer I was using and rushed down the three flights of stairs, to the campus exit. I knew I was in a hurry when I took the stairs. I never took the stairs even though I hated being in the lift with a barrage of people, breathing hot air in my neck back. Or sweating profusely and offensively. Despite this, even if I had to wait for five minutes for an empty lift. I would wait. Considering how impatient I am, I would rather wait for the lift then climb three flights of stairs. However today was different. This was an emergency. I didn't have five minutes to spare. I didn't even have half an hour. I needed to get to the school and see what was going on like yesterday!

I drove to school in silence. Music therapy was not going to help me today. I was nervous. My stomach was churning so much it was beginning to make me feel nauseated. I opened the window to let the fresh air blow in my face. Set my foot down on the gas pedal and began my race to the school. 'I need to get to the school! I needed to get to the school!' I was talking to myself out loud. Every traffic light changed to Red as I approached. I tooted my horn loudly with annoyance, at the car in front not going through the amber light. Even though the car was now stationary and the lights completely Red I continued tooting my horn shouting unnecessary insults. It wasn't the driver's fault. He didn't know what was going on, or that I was in a hurry. He didn't know I had to get to the school right now, to find out what was going on with my son's. He had no clue. To him I probably just looked like a crazy Black woman. Not a desperate Mum. Or a frantic mum. No just crazy. Plain old crazy.

I pulled up at outside the school and parked on the zigzag. I knew I shouldn't be parked here. But today was not an ordinary day. Today I did not have the time to search for the perfect parking space. I needed to get inside and see my boys. As I approached the reception, I noticed the receptionist pick up the phone and press a button. I couldn't hear what she said, but the position in which she held the phone to talk, told me that it was top secret. Most likely, definitely, about my arrival. I burst through the doors.

'I had a phone call...' I began to say just as Miss O'Connor emerged from her office.

'Do you want to come through Yolanda?'

I followed behind Miss O'Connor without acknowledging her. As I entered the office, I saw another woman. A younger woman, definitely younger than me, with curly ginger hair. She stood up as I entered the office.

'Thank you for coming so soon Yolanda I'm Elsa, I'm a social worker' she stretched her hand out to shake mine. I looked at her outstretched hand, and reluctantly shook it to be polite.

'Where are my son's?' my face wore no expression. I wanted to know where my sons were. I didn't want to talk about anything else before I knew where my sons were.

'They're fine Yolanda they're with Miss Reynolds in her classroom drawing pictures'

By this point the school day was now over.

'Do you mind taking a seat Yolanda?' Miss O'Connor spoke.

'What's wrong?' I demanded. It was clear that something was wrong. Otherwise why had I been summoned here?

''Unfortunately, Yolanda...' it was Elsa's turn to speak. 'Miss O'Connor has made a referral to social services, as the boys have made a disclosure of abuse'

My mouth dropped wide open as I looked over at Miss O'Connor, daggers in my eyes. What kind of abuse was she talking about? What did she mean abuse? Did she mean someone was abusing them and I didn't know? That was impossible. Who would do that? I didn't leave them with other people, they stayed at my mum's or at their other Nan and Granddads house. There was no way they were being abused. I would not allow it.

'What kind of abuse?' I demanded an answer.

'Well. She began, it has been alleged that you have chastised the boys'

'What!!!' my question was rhetorical.

'Have you ever slapped any of the boys?

I couldn't believe what I was hearing. This stranger was asking me to explain myself to her. This disclosure she mentioned on the phone was me slapping my kids? That was the abuse she was referring to!

'So, you're here because it's been alleged, I slap my kids?'

'Well yes and no'

'What do you mean yes and no? Is it yes or no?' now I was fuming. 'Furthermore, it's not against the law for me to slap my kids so what are you telling me, that in itself is a disclosure of abuse?'

'It's safeguarding Yolanda we have to investigate each disclosure'

'What exactly is the disclosure, what exactly is it that I've done?' I was waving my hands with each word becoming more and more impatient and infuriated.

'Well there have been several allegations over the course of a few weeks'

'I beg your pardon??'

What did she mean over the course of a few weeks? Most evenings I've found myself in this very office listening to them drone on about how terrible my son's behaviour was. No one mentioned anything about abuse then. I had been sat in Miss Reynolds' classroom several mornings and afternoons. No one mentioned anything to me about abuse. Come to think of it, in all of that constant niggling at me about an educational psychologist and Kwame's social and emotional needs. Why had Miss O'Connor and Miss Reynolds been acting as though they were trying to help me, when really, they'd been plotting against me for weeks! Why had this information resulted in the social worker being here today, if disclosures have been made over a period of time? It didn't make sense to me. I held my face in my hands for a minute and then sat up again.

'What has been said? I directed my question at Elsa.

'I am unable to share that with you at the moment Yolanda'

'So why are you here then?' my tone had transformed into one less composed, to one that was now confrontational.

'We have to follow certain procedures when a disclosure is made. An assessment will need to be carried out to decide what to do next'.

What does she mean to decide what to do next? What were the options? What was she referring to as next! And who would decide?

'I don't think I understand Elsa; you're telling me you can't discuss the disclosure with me, yet still you called me and asked me to come here. What is it you want to discuss with me?'

'There have been several disclosures made to Miss O'Connor and Miss Reynolds. So, first of all we need to make sure that the children are safe to go home with you'.

My eyes opened; I froze. My heart paused from beating. I looked over at Miss O'Connor who was sat comfortably behind the old rickety desk. Then I looked towards Elsa. I could not decipher the emotions I was currently feeling. All I knew was that my first instinct was to jump over the table and smash Miss O'Connor to pieces. All this time they had been complaining about my son, when really, they had been sitting down gathering Intel. And now. Now that they felt they had enough, they were trying to do what. Take me down. Confiscate my kids like chewing gum at school. I tried to think rationally.

'You cannot attack them Yolanda, you have to stay focused. They'll be expecting you to react don't react. Respond'. I knew that was my voice of wisdom, much like Jiminy cricket in Pinocchio. Yet just like Pinocchio I was finding it very hard to listen. The anger I was feeling was becoming unbearable to contain. My mind said attack, my Jiminy said no.

'What do you mean, safe to go home with me ELSA? I emphasised her name because by now I was ready to fight. I was ready to fight for these boys who they were telling me were being abused by me! And if Elsa wanted to take one for her team, so be it. I was willing to accommodate. 'I need to have a discussion with my manager Yolanda, to confirm what will happen next. Do you mind just waiting one moment while I make a call'?

'I want my son's'

I spoke calmly and clearly. I looked at Elsa and then turned towards Miss O'Connor. I didn't care which one responded all I knew was that somebody better bring my son's here to this office now! Miss O'Connor looked to Elsa as though asking permission.

'Did you hear what I said? I was now raising my voice. 'I said I want my sons!'

Elsa nodded nervously in Miss O'Connor's direction.

'I'll have Miss Reynolds bring them over right away'

I didn't respond to Miss O'Connor. I didn't have anything to say to her I just wanted my sons, in front of me. It was approximately two minutes before the boys appeared at the office door and I had assigned everybody present three minutes in my mind before someone better make my sons appear like magic. Elsa had left the room to make her phone call, I could hear her say something about the fact I was there in the school. The boys came through the door part way through me eavesdropping Elsa's conversation. Both boys ran over to me, wearing looks of worry on their faces. I bent down to hug and kiss them both and asked them if they were okay.

'Yes mummy' they choroused.

I didn't ask them anything about the disclosures I just held onto their hands tightly. I'd like to think my face was legible. It said 'you better kill me first if you think I'm letting go of my sons'. Elsa returned to the office to see both the boys standing either side of me.

'Ok, well, I've spoken to my manager. Do you want to let the children wait outside Yolanda?'

'No, they're staying with me!' I said wanting her to hear the anger and the tone of my voice. It was only fair that I made it totally clear to her that I was not that Mum. Don't mess with me today. I meant what I had said, in so many different ways and as I looked at Elsa, I knew that she knew what I meant. If she thought she was going to leave this building with my son's in tow, she made a BIG mistake!

'Ok well you can take the boys home for today and I'll be in touch with you'

What did she mean 'for today' like the boys returning home with me was temporary? 'What? Be in touch when? What did she want?'

'As part of our initial assessment, it's highly likely that both boys will need to be seen by a child protection medical expert'

I knew what that meant. Medical expert, child protection. That meant that you wanted to check my sons' bodies to see if I'd been abusing them. What the hell did they expect to find ... cigarette butt holes, cuts/bruises?

'YOU WHAT?? How dare you?' my eyebrows were knitted close together and I was talking through my teeth.

'You can take the boys Yolanda, and I will give you a call tomorrow' Elsa repeated trying not to engage with me further.

I tilted my head to the side and looked at Elsa. This was about the second or third time she had told me I can take the boys. Like it was up to her. Like she and I had them, not me. However, something said to me, leave it, so I said nothing. I kept hold of my sons' hands tightly and walked out of the school, to make my way home. The boys didn't say anything as we walked.

Once in the car, I looked in my rear-view mirror, their faces didn't look as worried as before, but both expressions were solemn.

'Did that woman at the school with the ginger hair talk to you to?'

I posed a question to both of them without looking back.

'Yes mummy' replied Kwame. 'She came to my class to talk to me'

'What did she say to you Kwaams'?

'She asked me if I was happy.

She asked me what makes me happy.

'And what did you say?'

I told her that I am happy but I'm not happy if my mummy tells me off and shouts at me'

'Okay, what else did she say?'

She asked me if you ever get angry with me.'

'I said sometimes if I'm naughty'

'Okay I said still listening as I pieced together the conversation in my mind.

'She asked me if you slap me and my brother, I said if we do naughty things'

'Okay I said'

'Was today the first time you've ever spoken to the lady?'

'Yes mummy'

'Are you sure...? She said something about lots of different things having been said to her have you said lots of different things?

The question was again posed to both of them.

'Well Miss Reynolds asks me when I come in sometimes, if I'm ok and how was my evening'

'Is it I said??' looking at Kwame in my rear-view mirror.

'Yes mummy, she told me I can tell her if I don't feel happy. So, I told her that last time, you didn't give me any cake and custard, but you gave my brother, I told her that that made me very sad'

I could barely remember the occasion that Kwame was referring to. Nevertheless, since he had been misbehaving, I had banned him from having treats so there had been occasions where he hadn't been given any cake and custard, but Cassius was.

'Anything else Kwame?' I asked, beginning to see how we had arrived at the phone call today.

'Ummmmm Kwame rubbed his chin. A habit he had picked up somewhere to demonstrate thinking time and exercised every time he needed more than two seconds to think about something.

'Yes mummy', she asked me about daddy.'

'WHAT ABOUT DADDY? I asked trying not to sound how I felt.

'I told her that daddy doesn't live with us Mummy'

'Why were you talking to Miss Reynolds? I asked Kwame, still picking sense from what he was explaining.

'Because she asked me mummy.

So that was it. This is was what had been going on behind my back. I started to recall the suggestion of time out cards and visits to Miss O'Connor's office to calm down. Why is it that Black children are often regarded as the pitied children? The ones who need saving from their own barbarianism. Why do authorities always seem to seek ways to rectify the inherent melanin within? I recalled the time in her office when she tried to insinuate that she knew how I felt. Or that she and I were the same or similar. Now the penny had dropped. It was all beginning to make sense.

Each day my son's attended school, they were prying into our lives, like burglars, searching for what was wrong with our family unit. I recollected the suggestion of an educational psychologist for Kwame's social and emotional needs... is that why they wanted him to see a psychologist, to confirm what they thought they already knew. Is this why they kept insisting he had emotional needs because of the secret conversations? Or because they believed they could uncover what was wrong with my parenting, fix the poor Black family. I looked at Cassius in the rear-view mirror.

'Cass', has anyone been speaking to you?'

'Miss O'Connor came to my classroom mummy at Golden Time, to see if I was ok. She was asking me if I was happy Mummy. Then she asked me about my brother'.

'What did she ask you about your brother?'

'She asked me if my brother was happy'

'What did you say Cass?'

'I didn't say anything I was crying mummy, I asked Miss Franklin to call you Mummy'

'Ok never mind its ok'. I said looking at both of them in the rear-view mirror.

'Are you ok Mummy?' Kwame asked.

'Yes.' I replied trying to force myself to smile to show sincerity. But I wasn't.

CHAPTER 23

I felt betrayed. There was no other way to describe the feeling of having your heart just ripped out. The worst thing was not being able to decipher who exactly I felt had betrayed me. Was it my boys, my sons who innocently spoke to these adults, answered questions, not knowing or being able to understand how that information was going to be used against us, or against me? I couldn't blame them for being children. I couldn't blame them for not having the mind-set of an adult. On one hand yes, I was angry, but was I angry with them? However, on the other hand, I knew that I couldn't be. I was angry at the situation. I was angry at my part in the situation because I hadn't seen this coming. Perhaps the betrayal came from, Miss O'Connor and Miss Reynolds, who had been systematically enquiring about our private life. Was it them who had betrayed me? No. They hadn't betrayed me. I didn't expect any better from them. I knew that they didn't care about me or my son's. In order for them to have betrayed me, I would first have to have trusted them, or to have expected more from them. You cannot be betrayed by those, which you never daren't trust. Those whom you believe will crush your existence at the first opportunity. I could not quite fathom what my sons may have said to warrant the social workers intervention, or what I had done exactly, specifically, to warrant this.

A child protection medical? A doctor of some kind, examining every part of my son's bodies. That in itself didn't sit well with me. Suppose they pick out an old chicken pox on Cassius and tried to insinuate it was something else. Suppose they identify scarring on

Kwame's skin from eczema, would that have been me too. My head was all over the place my mind running wild. All I was certain of, was that this weakened my heart. I felt destitute. Hopeless. I opened the front door, my eyes now overrun with tears. The boys didn't say anything, the mood was sombre. They silently knew something was wrong, heading straight to their room to take off their uniforms.

I kicked off my shoes without stopping, dragged myself lifelessly into my bedroom, closing the door behind me before falling to the ground and exploded into what can only be described as a fit of wailing. I wailed and wailed, surrendering on my hands and knees, as I crawled to the edge of my bed. I did not have the energy to stand on my two feet, nor the restraint to withhold my turmoil. This was it! I was not waking up from this I could feel my body giving way. I could no longer see out of my eyes clearly. Everything was blurry and distorted. Now I was somehow crying with my eyes closed, the tears still spilling from beneath my eyelids at warped speed. I couldn't silence my pain. It was too much. My chest was hurting, I started panicking that my hysterical wailing would in somehow cause the onset of a heart attack or stroke. I couldn't restrain myself. I was an emotional wreck. I couldn't even protect my son's from hearing me fall apart. I had lost all control of myself. My emotions had conquered my body, mind, and even now even my voice. As I repeated the words 'I can't do this anymore. I can't do this. I can't do this!' I didn't know who I was talking to I didn't know that anyone was listening. I wasn't even sure I wanted a response. I just knew I couldn't do this anymore. I was going to lose my sons. My Kwame and Cassius. Someone was going to take them away. I wouldn't see them again. They would no longer know me! What would happen to my son's? How would someone else know how to deal with them? How would they know that Kwame was intuitive, sensitive loving and kind? How would they know that Cassius, would say little if he didn't consider you family? How would they know that didn't mean there was something wrong with him that was just how he was? What would someone else know about my sons?

I couldn't take it. I wailed louder, and so hard, that my body ached. My chest was throbbing like crazy. I tried to take deep breaths to calm myself down, but it didn't work. I crawled onto my bed and tried to bury my wails of desperation in the pillow. Still the sounds of my pain surged through the pillow, like an electric current surges through circuits. My pillow was already soaked, and Cassius and Kwame were now knocking on my bedroom door, calling 'Mummy' having heard my distress from their room. I managed to slow my wailing down to a calmer cry, enough to assemble the words I'm ok, go and watch TV, I'm coming. Even talking to the boys made my mind do over time.

We would never have our moments again. We wouldn't have our token moments of ice cream or treats. Go to movie mornings at the cinema. What about our day-to-day schedules? How would someone else know what time they need to get my son's up? Or what their routine is. What if Cassius woke up in the night? Where would he go if he couldn't crawl into my bed? What if Kwame needed to talk about something? How would they know how to unravel things in order to truly enlighten him and dispel the extras? You had to almost know a child to really understand their conversations, when they're young. Supposing the family they sent them to were not even Black! Who will teach my sons who they are? Where they are coming from? What would happen to their culture? I knew what would happen. I'd seen it many times before. They would keep them until they grew big and scary and then they would feed them to the wolves. My sons. They wanted to feed my sons to the wolves. I squeezed my pillow and buried my face deeper to allow me to wail louder. I didn't know how to get this out my system I didn't know how to move from this point. I couldn't even control my emotions. These were my babies. They were mine. Through thick and thin, I had been the one. Me. When they were sick, I had been the one to hold them. Me. On the first day of school I had been the one to shed tears as they walked away heading to their classrooms on that first day. That was me! When they needed something and I didn't have the money, I was left to find it! They didn't come to help me! So why now would they rip my heart from my chest and leave me to bleed to death. I was crying out again. 'If they take my son's I have no reason to live. I have nothing left! Nothing Else matters! I cried and I cried, and I cried and then... I silently gave up. I gave in. I cried and I repeated I can't do this, I can't do this! My body was shaking vigorously as I tried to slow my tears down to a halt. I was inhaling with extra force causing more pain in my chest with each breath. This was it. I was done.

Over half an hour had passed. I found it hard to believe that I possessed the energy to cry consistently, with such force, and for so long.

By now I hoped I had run out of tears. Yet the tear-soaked pillow, duvet cover and the clothes I had worn to work that day, reminded me that this was not the case. Perhaps my body has entered into the reserve tank. Maybe that would explain the uncontrollable spillage. Whatever it was I clearly had not exhausted my supply. I pulled myself together enough to share the boys out their dinner and set the table so we could eat.

Cassius spoke first. 'Mummy why were you crying?' his innocence made my eyes start to well up with water again. I swallowed hoping that would make a difference to the tears.

'Sometimes Mummy just feels a bit sad'

Kwame saw the opportunity to probe further.

'Was it the woman at the school Mummy who made you sad"No baby' I said unable to stop the tear that had been waiting patiently to fall from the corner of my eye. Kwame wiped it away, just as Cassius came over and put his arm around my shoulder and kissed my forehead.

'It's ok Mummy, if you want you can play with one of my toys that might make you happy. That makes me and my brother really happy'.

I smiled and wiped away the tear. 'Love you Mummy' said Kwame kissing my cheek. 'Love you both baby' I said squeezing them both either side of me. These are my babies. I reminded myself. These are my son's. I had made a promise from the moment I gave birth to them that as long as I lived and breathed, I would be there for them. I had promised to do everything within my power to prevent them from becoming a statistic. I had promised to nurture them into being their Best Self! I had pledged to fight every battle with every inch of being The Almighty granted me. I had declared that these were my sons, and they were special! Come to think of it... this was one of those times. This was one of those battles. This was a fight! Mum taught us not to hit first. I didn't hit first. They hit me using my son's as weapons. This was a fight. A fight like one I had never known. A fight that would force me to fight using skills, I never knew I had acquired. This was a fight for my sons. My son's! And come to think of it, no one was taking them from me!

CHAPTER 24

Once the boys were tucked in that night, I closed my bedroom door picked up the phone and dialled my mum. I started at the beginning, explaining to her the phone call I received while I was in the library, and what the social worker had said. I told her all about what they had said about contemplating the children being allowed to be sent home with me due to safeguarding and safety. My mum was furious. It was hard to remember a time when I had last seen my mum in this mode. She had started cursing, accusing society of wanting to destroy her grandsons before they had a chance at life. She wanted to know the social workers name and contact details to ask her what the hell she was playing at!??

In hindsight bless my mum I believe now that she too was scared. Like me she probably was asking herself about all the unknowns. It didn't help that we didn't know what tomorrow held, we didn't know what was awaiting. Were they going to turn up in the middle of the night and try to take my children away when we least expected it? I didn't know. Yet every time I thought about it, I felt myself falling apart.

Having put the boys to bed I sat down and began planning. I needed to be strategic. One thing these people were showing me was that they would go to any lengths. What they were yet to understand about me, was that I would do the same. I knew they had the upper hand. Nobody would want to listen to me. And judging by the way they had spoken about the disclosures, neglecting to mention the questions that were posed to both my sons. Highlighted to me a clear agenda. I'd never experienced anything like this before. My knowledge was based on everything that I had learned in my line of work, study, life experiences, and the media. The media had shown me many times before what happened when these interventions went wrong.

When parents were accused of shaking babies to death, resulting in them being sent to prison to serve time for crimes that several years later would be deemed an error. I had seen those cases whereby several years later it was deemed that said baby died from sudden infant death syndrome and for whatever reason this had not been recognised at the time. I hated those stories; they broke my heart. To accuse a parent of killing their child, to criminalise them, isolate them from society, tarnish them with the stigma. To subsequently then later, admit that there was an error. Do you know what that does to families? Do you know what that does to the parents? I was not about to become one of those parents.

One of the most heart wrenching stories I ever read was about a family who took their six-week-old baby into hospital panic-stricken because the baby had fallen ill. Subsequently they were accused of abuse, the baby was removed from their care by social services. But that wasn't even the worst part. The worst part was that during a four-week trial the parents were cleared as a medical examiner was able to explain symptoms and conclude, it was a medical condition and deficiency that had caused the infant's death, not abuse that had caused the illness, or any scar. Unfortunately, by then the couple also notified that their baby had been adopted. I urge you to Google these topics and review the details because there are not one or two stories. There are way too many. The heavy-handed approach that parents can be subjected to is far from acceptable and can have long lasting effects on families.

I came off the phone to my mum, feeling empowered. I decided first thing in the morning I would contact Andre, from the mentoring service to follow up on the mentoring for my sons. If either of my son's had things, they needed to get off their chest, whilst I didn't want them speaking to strangers, I definitely didn't want them speaking to those devils at the school. I desperately needed them to be mentored, I desperately needed to unpick anything if at all, that may have been troubling them.

Losing them was not an option.

CHAPTER 25

I woke up extra early the following morning, there was no time for a lie-in or to oversleep, and absolutely no requirement for an alarm. The night had been long, and drawn out, each time I fell asleep I'd woken up, glanced at the time, only to see that it was 15 minutes later than I last checked. That lasted most of the night. That and the fact that I wasn't prepared to fall into any kind of deep relaxing sleep in case the door knocked, and they tried to take my son's, hoping I would be disorientated at that ungodly hour. No, I felt like I couldn't afford to sleep. I was on night watch. I made the boys breakfast, had a cup of tea and got ready as normal. I didn't want to take the boys to school I wanted to keep them at home with me. I wasn't even sure I should take them to school, just in case they stole my children while I was at work. My mind was still racing. If I didn't take my son's to school, they may assume that I had been abusing my son's and that's why I had not brought them back to school. I wouldn't give them the satisfaction. Why shouldn't my son's go to school? In fact, why shouldn't I take them? They were not abused. I was not an abuser and come to think of it, we were not about to hide. I didn't appreciate feeling like I was being backed into a corner when I hadn't done anything wrong. The more I thought about it, I decided the boys **were** going to school.

Once the boys had put on their last bits of uniform. I went into the kitchen and contacted Andre. I felt stronger this morning like I could take on the world.

'Morning please can I speak to Andre'

'Speaking'

'Hi Andre, it's Yolanda, we spoke the other day about my two sons Kwame and Cassius.'

Oh yes Yolanda has someone not contacted you as yet?'

No not yet Andre, and since then, more has happened'

'Oh,' Andre sounded confused.

I went on to explain. From the phone call at university to the social worker advising me that I was 'allowed' to take my son's home. Andre, I could hear was taking notes and saying things to me like 'don't worry Yolanda'. When I finished explaining, Andre went on.

'Ok Yolanda the first thing you're going to do is you are going to take the boys to school today, don't let them think that you're guilty, these are your son's, you take them to school as normal. Secondly will you be home this evening?

'Yes' I replied

'Ok Kevron is going to give you a call today and he will arrange a time to come down and speak with you and to meet the boys. You will need to fill out some paperwork Yolanda. But other than that, there's nothing that we need from you'

'What will I need to pay each week for the mentoring?' I asked knowing full well I was already financially stretched. On the other hand, it didn't matter how stretched I was I would pay anything for my sons to get what they needed. Andre gave me Kevron's number and advised me that if I didn't receive a call by 2pm. I was to call Kevron and explain who I was. I thanked Andre and came off the phone.

The boys were watching Power Rangers, probably glad I hadn't noticed the time.

'Let's go boys, we're gonna to be late!'

I helped them get into their jackets and grabbed the school bags. Just before we walked through the front door I stopped and turned around and looked at them.

'When you to go to school if the teacher asks you about anything to do with home tell them to ask your mum, Okay?'

'But what if she keeps asking?' Kwame said.

'She can ask you as many times as she likes baby, if she wants to know anything, they should ask me'

'Yes mummy' they both replied.

CHAPTER 26

After taking the boys to school I decided I wouldn't go in to university that day. I didn't want to take the time off, particularly so close to the end of the first year. But my head just wasn't in a good place. I was still feeling quite emotional about events from the day before. Although I had found the fight in me. I was still in a sensitive place. The fear of losing my son's still hovered over me. I had taken them to school despite how uneasy the thought had made me. I couldn't possibly go to university without knowing what was next. I told myself I would rather sit at home watching the phone waiting for the next step.

Andre had assured me that I would be seen today with regards to getting the boys a mentor. I realise to another, it may not seem like much, but for me it was a breakthrough, at a time when I felt like I just didn't know what my son's needs were, and how to meet them on my own with my current resources. I welcomed mentoring support for them. Something that would promote positive development and behaviour. The organisation in itself and everything it stood for, had appealed to me from the moment I had first sighted them on GMTV, so as bad as things seemed, that small detail gave me much hope. Let's face it at this point I really needed hope.

I was just getting ready to make a start on some lunch when the phone rang. It was private number again. It must be the social worker I told myself. My heart started racing I sat down in the sofa holding the still ringing phone in my hand as I made myself comfortable. I didn't know what I was about to hear, but I needed to prepare myself.

'Hello… I answered the phone as though I was asking a question.

'Hello Yolanda, its Elsa the social worker we met yesterday'

'Hello' I replied unsure of which tone to give her without knowing what she intended to say.

'Is this a good time to talk to you?'

'Yes, go ahead' I replied

'I've spoken with my manager and based on the disclosures from the boys. We will be conducting an assessment. The assessment will last 4-6 weeks and at the end of it, I will be able to tell you what further action will be taken. It could be a child in need plan, or child protection plan dependent on the outcome.

'Right…'I said sensing there was more.

'Due to the gravity of the disclosures, the boys will need to be seen for a child protection medical tomorrow morning'

'I beg your pardon'

'The children will need to be taken to the hospital to be seen by child protection medical examiner'

'What exactly is it you intend to find and what are they going to do with my sons'

'They will just check over their body and a report will be sent directly to us'.

'So just to clarify, I need to take them to hospital for someone to check they're not being abused'

'This is a requirement as part of our assessment Yolanda. If you want to, I could collect the boys and take them for the medical and then bring them back to school?'

'No that is fine if you give me the address, I will take them'

Even the thought of the social worker or any stranger taking them to have a medical examination made me feel uncomfortable. I needed to be there to make sure everything was above board. It's was not as though my children were unwell and having to be seen by a doctor. They were perfectly fine, yet someone was going to look over their body I didn't like it. My imagination ran wild again, as I told myself they may pretend there were scars and bruises if I were absent. No, I would definitely be taking them. I couldn't afford otherwise, not with so much at stake.

Elsa gave me the details, and I agreed to take the boys the following morning. One part of me felt relieved when I came off the phone. So, I would be collecting the boys from school today. They would be coming home. Elsa said herself that I needed to take them to the hospital, so obviously they were not being taken from me. I felt a sense of gratitude at the temporary reprieve. I wasn't grateful to Elsa, no. I was grateful to God. I was grateful because the situation in front of me forced me to sit up and take note. Despite the way I felt about all those involved, despite what I felt about their actions, the situation reminded me never to take your eye off the ball. I felt like I should have seen this coming, but I hadn't.

That afternoon when I collected the boys, Miss Reynolds didn't give me any feedback on Kwame's behaviour. I handed her the consent form for the Beach trip I'd signed that afternoon. Recent events highlighted the fact that I needed to keep an eye on my sons around certain people, because I just didn't know what conversations were being had. Perhaps by now they would be thinking twice about me attending the trip, but it was too late they had already insisted an adult accompany him, and that adult would be me. Miss Reynolds was courteous I did the same and collected Kwame from his classroom.

The story was pretty much the same when I collected Cassius from Miss Franklin. Unlike Miss Reynolds, Miss Franklin had made an effort to act as though she was not in the loop. Smiling, cheery, giving me a summary of Cassius' day. It was quite an exceptional effort on her behalf. As not to disappoint her, I mirrored her cheer and smile in the moment. It was the least I could do for her efforts.

I also asked the boys how their days had gone. Both said fine. I asked them if they'd had any visits or if anyone had removed them from class to talk to them.

They told me no. Based on what the social worker had said to me yesterday they probably had enough information to go on. They didn't need to interrogate my son's any further. Remembering that we would be having a visit from the mentor that evening. I thought it would be a good idea to mention it to the boys ahead of time.

'We've got someone coming to our house today to see you two.

'I don't want to see people's Cassius said.

'This is a mentor Cass'. He's coming to meet you and your brother. Mummy will be meeting with him too. After you meet him, you'll get to do different activities sometimes with him, and possibly other boys your age. Not at school. When you're not at school.' I added noticing the look of confusion on the boys' faces.

'We'll meet him today, you'll be able to ask questions, and then we can talk about it after he's gone'

'Okay mummy' replied Kwame.

The journey home was pretty normal after that. The boys chatted away to each other about their days, and I listened to the radio. I still had a lot on my mind, but I was determined to get on with it.

When we got home, I shared the boys their dinner that I'd cooked earlier while at home. I figured it would be a good idea to feed them before the mentor came. If by any chance I left them hungry and decided to feed them afterwards, the likelihood was the mentor would not get the best version of them. My children did not cooperate when they were hungry. In fact, we were all like that, my brother included. When we were hungry, trying to engage in conversation with us would be futile. At least if their bellies were full, they would participate somewhat enthusiastically.

The boys were engrossed in the TV when the door knocked. I peered through the spy hole. There were two people at the door. I opened the door and they introduced themselves on the doorstep, Kevron and James. Andre had sent them from the mentoring service. I invited both men in and directed them to the front room, where they sat the dining table. The boys hadn't watched from your front of the TV, so I turned the TV down and introduced them to our guests. The boys were reserved but greeted our guests. Kevron spoke first.

He was tall, built almost as though he used to train, with dark skin and a very low haircut. One might even refer to him as bald. He also wore glasses, which I noticed he took off when he sat at the dining table. My guess was that he was approximately 30.

James on the other hand, was slimmer in stature, wore a tidy afro, I would say was the same length all round. Whatever that's called. Both carried briefcase type bags. James, I noticed had removed am A4 sized notepad from his bag, together with a pen as he sat at the table. I realised that his removal of a notepad from his bag didn't at all make me feel threatened. Unaware of its purpose, still I felt hope as these two strangers sat at my dining table.

'Before we talk to the boys Yolanda if you don't mind can we have a chat with you first' Kevron said.

'Yes, that's fine I replied

I turned the TV back up and join the men at the table. Kevron asked what had prompted me to contact the mentoring service. I started by explaining how I came to hear of the mentoring service, then went on to explain the transition from the boy's old school to this school and what had taken place since. I didn't see the point of holding back on information, taking into consideration my intention and what I wanted to achieve for the boys. I started at the beginning and explained to Kevron and James our personal circumstances. Everything. This wasn't information I was willing to share with other professionals whether they were aware or not. But based on the work I believed Kevron and James were about to embark on with my boys, I felt I needed to be transparent. I noticed as both men listened attentively without interruption. James made a few notes and almost signalled to me as he wrote them, so I was aware of what was going on paper. Kevron continued to listen. When I felt that I had brought them up to speed on our current situation. I took a pause hoping either would say something.

'Thank you for being so open Yolanda'. James was first to speak. 'I appreciate your honesty and transparency. The one thing however I will say Yolanda, is that when you talked about the events that brought you up to this point, you talk about it with ownership perhaps even guilt if you don't mind me saying. The situation you've found yourself in is not your fault. It's unfortunate, but we will all have to take ownership for our own actions. It is not for you to assume responsibility for the actions of others. I can hear your passion in how you feel about your son's, but you can't blame yourself for everything that hasn't gone the way you anticipated. So far you done well to manage the situation, but you have our full support now. You are not alone.'

It was as though the Angels started singing in chorus. I had opened up myself to these two strangers and still they did not blame or judge me for all of this? For everything? I had revealed the most vulnerable areas of my life, laid it all out in front of me, like an exquisite banquet served as part of a celebration. Everything lay before me. The only difference was to me, there was nothing appetising. I didn't know how to respond. No one had ever told me that it wasn't my fault. At least I don't remember them using those words. I didn't know how to receive what James had said to me. Part of me wanted to believe him, to recognise that I couldn't be responsible for everything. But on the other hand, I kept thinking I made the choice to have these boys, my sons, so everything afterwards has got to be my fault because I brought them here. That was me. Anything they were exposed to, anything they were subjected to, was down to me. Perhaps sensing my descent into my thoughts. Kevron interjected.

'I agree with what James has said Yolanda. Unfortunately, there are many women who find themselves in positions similar to yours. We are human Yolanda. Sometimes as humans we have good intentions, sometimes they don't go as planned. It's part of the experience that builds us and builds our character. Listening to you, I will definitely say the experiences have built your character. It takes courage to stand up to professionals the way you have so far, simply through your belief in your son's and your passion for what you want for them. Don't sell yourself short. You're not perfect, and don't ever aim to be, it's an unrealistic aspiration. Perhaps the only one.'

I listened to Kevron and James as they went on to explain to me how the mentoring service would work. I would drop the boys off to the centre one afternoon a week for two hours. There they would take part in team activities, games, homework, sports etc. It sounded like a good place to start. What did we have to lose? If the boys really didn't like it I would have to go back to the drawing board. Simple! Kevron also explained to me that they also operated play centres during the school holidays, which the boys were also welcome to attend. My heart began to feel lighter.

'How much will this cost?'

I asked the question, but the truth was, whatever the cost I was going to have to find it. Whether that was by putting in overtime at work. I knew that the boys needed this.

'Don't worry about that at the moment Yolanda. When we get back to the office, we'll sit down with Andre and discuss further.

'Okay' I replied apprehensively.

I completed the necessary registration forms with our personal details and thanked James and Kevron. Once they had finished speaking to me, I went into the kitchen to allow Kevron and James to speak to the boy's 1:1. They introduced themselves, telling the boys about the activities they would be able to participate in, and what they would expect from the boys. To be respectful and courteous. Bless them both, the boys agreed that they would comply. Personally I think Kevron and James had them when they started talking about football. But either way the boys were excited. In return so was I.

CHAPTER 27

It was just passed 18:30 when Kevron and James left. My phone was ringing again, it was probably my mum phoning to see how the visit had gone. I was planning on calling her back, once I put the boys to bed and could talk to her properly. So, I picked up the phone expecting to hear the sound of my Mum's voice. It was Jean.

'Hi Yolanda. You okay my darling'

I was due to be at placement the following day, so I figured she was calling me to give me some information about one of my cases or ask me to undertake a visit before I got to work.

'Listen my darling social services have been in contact with us and your university. The university have asked us to suspend your placement pending further investigation'

'Huh!?'

I heard what Jean said, said but I was confused. Who had contacted them?

Suspended my placement?

'Pardon?'

It was a rhetorical question. I heard what she had said. Slowly it was starting to register.

'Whilst an assessment is being undertaken, the university and the board won't allow you to practice'

'But I'm not guilty of anything'. My voice sounded much like a plea.

'I know my darling, but it's not up to me, its procedure. It's safeguarding. You know how it is'

Jean was right, I did know how it is. But the difference was, this was me. I wasn't an unknown family that has just been brought to their attention. I wasn't the mother whose children repeatedly had unexplained cuts and bruises. We weren't even the family who were frequent visitors at A&E or the GP surgery. The only time my children even visited health services was for immunisations, or if something was visibly wrong or potentially serious. Aside from that there was nothing about our lives that should raise any questions. Or at least so I believed. I had worked within the team for almost three months now, supporting some of the most vulnerable young people. I had been praised for making progress with even those that were considered unreachable. How could I be told not to come back without any evidence?? My heart sank. I think I fell silent on the phone for some time. I just couldn't find the words. Was I really having this conversation, was this my imagination, yet again running away with me in tow?

'Jean, I don't understand. How can they do this if it hasn't been proven that I've done something wrong? The school have been questioning the boys and twisting their words. I haven't abused my son's'.

'Yes, my darling, and I know that better than most. But you know, the decision is not mine.'

I listened to Jean explain the process reassuring me that once everything had been sorted out, I could come back. Yet that wasn't enough. I had already been brandished a mother who abuses her children. That wouldn't alleviate what I was feeling in that moment. What about the job they had offered me over the summer? I suppose that too would be withdrawn. The prospect of a job doing what I was training to do, and for more money than I currently earned at my permanent job, which paid me okay to be honest. That was history now. The social worker had told me 4 to 6 weeks. By then the summer period would be over. How could this be happening to me? What had I done to deserve this?

'Yolanda hunny are you there?' Jean must have wondered where I'd got to because I was just sat there silently on the phone.

'I know this feels hard right now, but you'll be ok. It's ok, we can't wait to have you back on the team'.

Jean was trying desperately to reassure me, and be optimistic, but I sensed even she could feel that all hope was lost, as she broke the news to me. I had so much love and respect for this woman. Not just as my manager, but as a human being. She was a beautiful person, and I knew she was doing her job. Part of me felt bad, guilty, for the mere fact Jean was having to make that phone call to me. This was a woman who believed in me. Taught me everything she knew, not just about social work, but life, parenting. She had taken the time out to talk to me on occasions just because she wanted to. To share with me, with the intention that I would not feel alone, or disheartened by life's blows. She had seen hurt in my eyes on certain days and decided to spend her lunch break with me, just to make sure that I laughed. That wasn't her job that was her choice. I showed gratitude by ensuring I was the best student social worker I could be. I showed gratitude by returning to class and demonstrating the knowledge and excellent practice that Jean and solely Jean had taught me out of her desire to see me do well. Now she had been tasked with the unfortunate job of breaking the news to me. This woman who had become another of my Sheroes, had been sent to deliver the annihilating message that my dreams had been thrown into the rubbish chute, burnt until they disintegrated into nothing. Ashes. This poor woman had been sent to light the match, in an already simmering fire. I swallowed before I spoke.

'Jean its ok, you don't have to explain. I know its procedure. And I'm sorry for letting you down.'

'Listen here, don't you dare start talking like that. You have nothing to be sorry for and definitely have not let me down. You're a damn good social worker. You'll be even more amazing, once you get your qualification. This is just a bump in the road. You hear me? A bump in the road. Yolanda...??? Are you there...? Are you crying...?

I wasn't crying, I meant to say that. However, there's something about when someone asks you if you're crying, that instantly activates any awaiting tears on standby. I had been doing well up until that point, swallowing the onset of tears with all my might. Withstanding the pain, I was currently feeling in my chest due to the physiological pressure I was putting myself under. Yet that one question from Jean and the floodgates opened.

'I'm ok' I said sniffling.

I really didn't want to cry, I didn't want Jean to feel a way, and I knew she would if I did.

'Don't cry my darling it's not the end'

'It is I said talking through tears. 'It is the end. They're taking everything away from me, I'm gonna have nothing left. They're trying to take my son's, they're taking my job, they're taking everything Jean. Everything! They don't want me to have anything. It's too much Jean. It's just too much!'

I'm trying, I really am. All these years I've been here soldiering with my sons for this. When we may have benefited from support, no one cared. It feels like because I won't conform, I'm being punished that's not right Jean. It's just not fair!

'Listen here, since the day I met you you've been a strong, amazing mother. Everyone knows how you feel about your sons. Sometimes it feels like the worst day of your life but it's not. You will get through this. I haven't known you very long Yolanda, but I know you can do this. Once they complete their assessments, everything will return to normal. Just don't give up Yolanda, come on don't cry.'

I didn't respond for a moment, resting the phone so I could blow my nose loudly into tissues, I'd grabbed out of my pocket.

'I know', I responded still sniffling. 'I'm okay Jean honestly. I just need to get it out my system. This is me. I'll cry the emotions out of my system and then I'll get on with it. It's just everything at once I guess, it kinda takes its toll on you. Just when I think that I'm getting there. I get another blow. It's like target practice, the darts are holding me to the board. Each time I free one arm, another dart comes and puts that arm right back in place on the dartboard. It just feels like target practice on my life. I know I'll be ok. It just really doesn't feel like it right now.'

Jean sighed. 'I know but it will'

Jean attempted to console me for a while longer before I told her I needed to get the boys ready for bed. I thanked her for her time and kind words and told I was grateful for her, that she was an amazing manager and woman, and said bye. I knew I wouldn't contact her again, because based on protocol, if she continued speaking to me while I was being investigated, that could impact her role. I simply refused to drag her into this. I was grateful that she had been the one to make the call. I was grateful that she cared enough to talk to me. However, I understood policy and procedure. I had enough knowledge. I hoped our paths would cross again in the future, at a time when I would be able to smile and talk proudly of achievements both mine and my sons.

In the meantime, I was grateful that Jean had graced my path, because perhaps unknowingly to her, she had taught me so much. It had been another long stressful and emotional day. Nevertheless, despite yesterday's fears I was about to spend another night with my son's, and I was grateful. 'Tomorrow is another day' my mum taught me that. Translated that meant, we had another day of battle to get through, or at least I did. I seemed to be going through a roller coaster of emotions in such a short space of time. I had cried more tears then I knew I possessed. I cried until my head hurt, I cried until I had felt pain within my body, in places I never knew could be affected by emotions and not physical interaction. As much as I felt I had the power to get through this. I equally felt I didn't have enough strength. I hadn't been eating properly since the whole thing started. I was having my tea in the mornings, but that was about it. My appetite had deserted me. Probably left me for someone who would appreciate it more. That made sense. I wasn't really getting anything right at this moment. I felt like shit. The enthusiasm that Kevron and James had left me with, had also abandoned me. Now I was back to wondering what's the point. Why bother?

I let the boys sleep in my bed that night. Ordinarily this was not my preferred choice. Either way, I knew sleep was not going to be my best friend tonight regardless. It would renounce me just as hope had before him. So, I chose to sleep close to my son's that night. Sometimes I just needed them to know that I was near. I didn't know how to shield them from this, all I could do, was be there. Tomorrow is another day. The day of the Child Protection medical. Here we go.

CHAPTER 28

I woke up extra early the following morning and snuck out of the bed, careful not to wake Kwame and Cassius. I needed to get a moment of peace and reflection in, before the boys woke up. Each day it felt like I was placed in the town centre awaiting a barrage of stones and boulders to be hurled in my direction. I barely had time to rejuvenate myself. I shed tears, I dusted myself off, straightened my back, and then came the next blow. It was beginning to feel like a never-ending cycle. Repeating itself daily, like sunrise and sunset. Today I needed to try and keep my emotions in check. I needed to practice the kind of strength that meant that my sons didn't have to witness me in such turmoil. I didn't like it. That's wasn't their problem.

As a child, tears were one of the things that I never really saw from my Mum. Thinking back my mum just seem to fight and fight and fight. She dusted herself off yes, she got upset yes. But unlike my son's, my Brother and I never really had to witness my Mum in the state in which my sons had observed me. The more I thought about it, I convinced myself that I had done my sons a disservice. Exposed them unnecessarily to my despair.

As part of my studies we had looked at the different types of abuse according to legislation. Believe it or not under the category of neglect, things such as a parent being unable to manage their emotions, may will be deemed a concern to some professionals. I don't know how that sounds to you. For me it sounds like inequality. Why should a person who expresses themselves through tears raise concerns that should fall under the category of any kind of abuse? Does life not get the better of most of us at some point in our lifetime? Or perhaps it's just me. Perhaps I am the only parent in the UK who feels things. Who cries if her sons are sad? One who cries at the thought alone of losing all that she has, and we're not talking, job or career. In comparison, neither of those things means anything me, in relation to my sons. I understand that in order to raise children, you need to be emotionally stable. But do you mind if I ask, how many of us would be considered emotionally stable? Well I openly admit that I am not. I feel things, I always have, ever since I was a child. I not only feel the things that affect me directly, I feel the things that affect the ones that I love. I feel the things that affect strangers. I cry when I'm happy, I cry when I'm sad. I cry if you're happy, I cry if you're sad. I cry when I watch emotive films, TV programmes and documentaries. And then I cry when I hear amazing singers, poets. Crying is my thing.

The Bible said that Samson held his strength in his hair. My strength is in my tears. Tears allow me to release my emotions whatever they are. Frustration, anger, hurt, whatever. I never understood why weakness was associated with people who cry. The act of crying does not make you weak. The real onus is on what you do, once you stop crying. For me, I'm normally ready for the next battle after a bout of tears. It refuels me. Furthermore, do we not all go through stages in life when things get on top of us, causing our emotions to take over? I admit I didn't like that my sons had to see me like this, particularly as this was not my experience, as a child.

Can I also just add, there's something about allowing people to express themselves in the way they see fit, that promotes emotional well being.

A mother, a parent, in my opinion should not be made to feel incapable of parenting even if like me they are serial 'criers'. Parenting is like tenure; you are permanently a parent from the first moment your baby breathes life. However, there are no instructions, manuals or rulebooks on how to sustain life as a parent, only trial and error. In fact, if I am honest, I consider parenting one of the most challenging roles a person can be assigned, yet it often appears to be the first point of attack or judgement. Meaning, for each lapse either parent or child experiences, someone is there around the corner, judging, condemning, and questioning your ability to do said role. That's at least how I have been made to feel at various points of parenthood.

I sat at the dining table with my tea. I'd spoken to my Mum last night before I went to bed. She had offered to take the boys to the medical for me, but I had told her no. The situation was already too much of an inconvenience for us. I wasn't going to inconvenience Mum further. I picked up my phone and sent her a text message. I knew it was early, but this was my Mum, I knew she'd should be awake.

Firstly, my mum's sleeping pattern was even more bizarre than mine. In fact, she was probably where I got it from. Awake at the crack of dawn every day of her life. That must come from working all those jobs whilst I was young. I think Mum became accustomed to minimal sleep. Me on the other hand, I think it stemmed from the break of dawn almost being the time of day that brought me the most tranquillity. I savoured early morning moments, I have done since I was a child.

Secondly, I knew my mum well. With all that was going on with her grandsons, she would not be sleeping. She would be worrying but pretending to me as though she were not. I know my mum. Low and behold as I sent her a text, a reply immediately came back. She was indeed awake.

Mum: 'How did you sleep?'

Me: 'So so Mum'

Mum: 'how comes you're up? I texted back, even though I felt I knew the answer.

Me: 'I couldn't sleep much' she responded

Mum: 'we're ok you know Mum' I want you to her to know that we were ok. We would be ok.

Me: 'are you feeling ok about this morning do you want me to come with you?'

Mum: 'no Mum that's alright, I'll phone you as soon as we're finished'

'Okay'

I remained at the dining table for a while longer thinking about the day ahead. We had loads of time before the appointment. At least this morning we could leave home a little bit later due to our appointment time being 10:30am. It was pointless going to school first, so I let the boys have a lie-in, while I opened my textbook. Now that my family, were the family being assessed, my reading became a significant resource to what seemed to be our survival. There was the information I retained and recalled as part of my assignments, and reflective practice. Then there was the information I retained because my family, my son's, or future, depended on it. Although I was familiar with the name of the hospital that the social worker had sent us to. It was one I'd never visited before. It was not close to our home. Therefore, would never be my first choice in an emergency. It just so happened that the overall outlook of the hospital was also quite dismal. It looked like somewhere where bad things happened as opposed to somewhere where sick people got better. I knew it was just a building, a structure, but already negativity had brought us here today and the first impression of the building didn't make me feel hopeful. It looked like the kind of dreary place that killed hope, let alone people. Perhaps for some families it could have been the hope of their loved ones making a recovery. For me it just seemed to signify no hope of a positive outcome, irrespective of the truth. These people had the power to say anything they wanted to say. Insinuate anything they wanted to insinuate.

If Cassius' chicken pox scars were considered to be a mark of abuse, then that would be the final verdict. Nothing I would say would change that. As I held the boy's hands walking through the hospital entrance, I said out loud. God give me strength. That was my usual cry. Somehow, I believe that so long as I had strength, I could do anything in the world. Whenever I felt like something was bigger or more colossal than I could ever imagine. I asked God for strength and then I proceeded. I heard my Auntie Barbara do that several times throughout my lifetime and was sure it worked. I had to ask directions a few times before we could find the right department that dealt with child protection examinations.

To be fair I don't know what I expected to find, but it looked like any other room or department in the hospital. It wasn't signposted child protection. It didn't have images of abused children with relevant contact numbers underneath, on the off chance that someone visiting needed help or someone to speak to. The room was as dismal as the hospital itself. I gave their names to the only doctor that seem to be present, then told the boys to sit down while we waited. I didn't want to sit down. I had no intention of spending too much time there. I felt better just standing.

The boys hadn't said much as we entered the hospital. I got the impression that something was contributing to their feeling of discomfort. I explained to them it was just a check-up, yet all morning I sensed they hadn't viewed it as just a check-up. The same doctor came out and called us in. He was wearing a traditional whitish coat, and what I would refer to as Dr's shoes. I found it hard to believe that doctors could come to work with their coats in the condition that this particular doctors was in. It was a bit shabby, a bit like Lieutenant Columbo's rain mac. It didn't fit well, and it had what looked like a coffee, or tea stain on the sleeve. I started to question what type of place they had sent us to, for this examination. First the dark and eerie building, now the so-called examiner who much resembled the shabby detective we all loved from the TV. The examiner introduced himself to us and explained he would see the boys one at a time. He explained that I could, if I wish to, remain present for the examination. To which I advised him that I would. He talked to the boys about what he would be doing and told them that it would not hurt. I sat there listening thinking, please can we just get this over and done with.

He asked the boys who would like to go first, Cassius piped up.

'I do'.

'Okay Kassus, let's go'

'It's Cassius'. I said pronouncing his name slow enough that the doctor would be able to pronounce it correctly next time. I couldn't quite see how he looked at that name and didn't read it, Cassius. It was not a made-up name with a spelling that didn't make sense or a silent letter that served no purpose.

No. It was Cassius, like Muhammad Ali's birth name. Pretty simple I thought. I took Kwame by the hand, and we followed the doctor and Cassius into the examination room. The doctor asked Cassius to remove some of his clothes not his underwear, and slowly he looked around his whole-body making notes in a file as he saw fit. It didn't take long before the examination was over.

Next was Kwame. He followed the same procedure with Kwame, slowly looking over my son's body as though he were determined to find something. Before long that too was over. The doctor explained that the conclusion and results would be sent directly to the social worker. I asked if I would receive a copy of the report. He explained no but told me that the social worker would share the results with me. I felt uneasy about the process. Supposing the social worker lied, altered the results so they could take away my son's. Why couldn't I see it now, so that I knew, just in case they changed the details? I didn't need them to give me a copy, I just wanted to read the report written about my sons. I didn't pursue the request further I said thank you, took the boys by their hands and headed for the exit. I couldn't wait to get out of there anyway, it was depressing.

When we arrived back at school, I greeted the receptionist and explained that I had taken the boys to an appointment in the morning and needed to sign them in for school now. The receptionist didn't ask me any further questions. Perhaps you knew where we have been perhaps everybody did. Lunchtime was just about over, luckily, I brought the boys some lunch before dropping them to school, so that was okay. The boys appeared to had perked up since we left the hospital and were the usual jovial selves again. After signing them in, I kissed them both goodbye and told them out I'd see them after school. The boys ran off to enjoy the last few minutes of playtime, I smiled and turn to exit, coming face-to-face with Miss O'Connor.

'Afternoon' I said drastically changing my expression from a smile to a more formal one. I would no longer be smiling with this woman not even for appeasement.

'Good afternoon Yolanda,' Miss O'Connor replied sounding much more joyous than my greeting had been.

I walked past Miss O'Connor about to leave the building.

'Yolanda do you have a minute'

'I don't have a minute, no, Miss O'Connor'.

'I just wanted a quick word' she was pleading again

'Yes?'

My response was only three letters but broken down it could be interpreted to mean 'Speak fast I don't wanna chat to you'

'Have you thought anymore about the educational psychologist?'

'No, I haven't.' I kept my answers short, sharp and straight to the point.

'It's just Miss Reynolds and I were talking about Kwame's progress and we feel it would be very beneficial to him particularly now'.

I squinted my eyes, tilted my head, put my hands on my hips and looked at Miss O'Connor. 'Particularly now???' Let's see what response she has for me today, I started to tell myself. This woman had a way of talking to me that brought out the worst in me. It's like she didn't think before she spoke, she opened her mouth and projectile vomited out words uncontrollably. Now she was doing it again, I was going to wait for her answer my question. What was she referring to with her 'Particularly now'?

'Oh no, what I mean is whilst you're receiving support from the Local Authority'

You see this was what I was talking about. She just kept pushing, it was like she made a conscious effort to keep poking me with a pin. How was what we were receiving support? What was anyone doing for us? We'd been sent for a child protection medical. I'd been accused of abusing my children, to the point I felt I was going to have a nervous breakdown. Who was supporting me then huh? Who liaised with me to make sure that I didn't go home feeling suicidal and take my own life or worse still, that of my son's? No one. So as this Trenchbull woman stood in front of me using terminology like 'support' to describe what my son's and I were going through. My mouth took on a mind of its own'

'Let me tell you something Miss O'Connor, what we are receiving is not support that's the first thing. Rethink your definition of support!

Secondly, from here onwards, do not ask me again about an educational psychologist for my son do you understand me. Furthermore, don't even speak to me, unless my sons are involved in an accident or serious incident at school. You have anything to say, call the Local Authority and tell them because I am not interested!'

Miss O'Connor tried to call me back, I could hear her trying to reason with me as I kept walking. But it was too late. I was done talking to her. It was a sheer miracle that some of the words that had were resting in my mind had not woken and joined the conversation. She had been lucky! Perhaps it was my fault for not calling her out in the way I should have, that first day in the office when she had alluded, we were the same. Maybe I came across too nice or naive. Or maybe she had decided that I was a little girl who could be bullied by her. Who knows? What I knew that day, was that she was now clear that we would not be communicating unless we had to. I would no longer be courteous, and there would be no more little talks in her stupid dark dreary cave of an office. We were done here! I accidentally banged the door as I slung it open on my way out. To be fair it was an accident. I felt so worked up, I pulled the door without even understanding the force I'd used. Luckily all of the doors had doorstops behind them, which prevented me from causing any real damage. God forbid I should cause any damage I started thinking. The next call from the social worker would talk about how I tried to vandalise the school with the children and the staff inside. Safeguarding alert! I kissed my teeth as I sat in my car to make my way back home. There was no more placement after all. And certainly, no lectures to attend at university, because everybody should be finishing their placements ready to hand in their reflective assignments. I thought about going into university just to finish the assignment, but what was the point if they didn't want me back. It was an entire years' worth of work for nothing! Jean had suggested I submit my work according to the deadline. Clearly, she had higher hopes than me, of me miraculously being accepted back onto the course to finish my training.

Although I told myself that actually being awarded the credits maybe handy for something else, another degree perhaps. Although I knew I didn't want another degree I wanted this degree! This was the degree I had set out to obtain. The degree that allowed me to use my knowledge, my skill set, my experiences, all to make positive impact. And now I wasn't sure what path I would take. I considered finishing my assignment and then decided I didn't want to go to the university just to find out that my ID had been revoked and I wasn't even allowed on campus or something. Then I would really feel like a criminal. I'd definitely be humiliated by that. I could picture the two security guards in their black uniforms and stone faces, kindly explaining to me in their unintentionally loud baritone voices, that I was no longer allowed on the premises. No. I simply couldn't take the shame. After much deliberation I finally decided to finish the assignment at home. I had enough books to do the rest of my referencing. And this way I could remain at home in case I received a phone call that required me to get to the school swiftly, and get the work done.

I had been writing for about an hour and a half when I received an email notification. I stopped what I was doing telling myself it was GF sending me some humour from work. I appreciated her humorous emails when I was at work or university. I couldn't remember the amount of times whereby I had opened an email at work, and then caught myself laughing out loud with my colleagues started looking at me. So now I was practicing a poker face for when I saw emails from GF come up. I clicked on the email in desperate need of a reason to smile. It was from the University. The subject heading was private and confidential. I opened the email and started reading. It's interesting how words can take on a life of their own, depending on where you are presently and emotionally, not to mention wording and terminology within the communication. The email stated that they had been made aware that an assessment was being carried out on my family, a current investigation of abuse, and that for that reason they would have to suspend me from the course pending an investigation. The email went on to explain that at this point, I had not been withdrawn from the course, and that they would notify me when they had reached a decision. It went on to say that no information was required from me at this time. The final paragraph stipulated that I was encouraged to submit any outstanding work whilst the investigation was pending.

I pushed the chair away from the computer table and sat there staring at screen. I didn't feel like writing anymore of the assignment. I was upset with myself. I knew I shouldn't have bothered trying to finish the assignment. Clearly the powers that be had their minds made up. I just couldn't fathom how decisions like that could be made without evidence. Decisions that affected families and livelihoods. This was my life. These were my dreams, my ambitions. It was like no one cared about the individual at the centre, it was more about the process. Well that was the memo I had been receiving. No one considered, what if nothing becomes of this? It was apparent based on the combination of current actions, that my fate had been decided already. I didn't know what was worse, having 12 individuals, complete strangers presented with biased, carefully selected contextual information, subsequently entrusted with deciding another's guilt. Or rather this my current experience whereby everybody had been given the role of judge and jury to make a decision based on very little evidence. I had often felt that the current judicial system was in actual fact flawed. However, I hadn't quite come up with an alternative for the current system that didn't always make others feel as though justice had been served. We still had numerous cases recorded, whereby people had been found guilty, only to later be acquitted after serving several years behind bars. Whilst I am an advocate of the fact that we are all human, and therefore are privy to make mistakes. I still feel quite strongly that when a person's livelihood or life is on the line, we need to do as much as we can to ensure that the right decisions are made because that ultimately is about someone else's life. In some cases that may require advice. Not necessarily advice sought from reputable practitioners but from other human beings. Textbooks don't teach you everything, **sometimes a human approach or opinion is more valuable than the £2,000 a day practitioner that testifies incorrectly.** I read the email again, pressed forward and sent it to my mum. Mum called me almost immediately. She sounded exasperated. As though she too was beginning to reach the edge with everything that was taking place. She told me not to worry, to finish the work and submit it. Mum reminded me that I had come too far to not receive credit for the work I done thus far. I knew she was right. I even confessed to her I was in the middle of finishing the assignment when I received the email.

'Finish the work Yolanda, you've invested enough time into it, finish the work and submit it.'

'Yeah, I guess so' I replied still sounding demotivated

'Have you heard back from the social worker with regards to the medical?'

'No not yet Mum'

'Why don't you call her?'

'Because I feel like if I do call her, I look like I'm guilty, she might think that is why I am rushing'

'Surely she should understand how anxious this type of thing can make parents feel'.

What my mum was saying was not absurd, it's just that it wasn't realistic based on what we had experienced so far. I knew what she was doing she was trying to help. She had a way of saying sensible things as though she forgot sometimes that these people were not her, they don't think like her they don't share her intelligence. Unfortunately, life had already showed me that I couldn't judge everybody by my own standards. My expectations for other people could not be dependent on the person that I was, because they were not me and I was not them. Past experiences had told me not to assume people had the same kind of heart as me. Relationships in particular had taught me that. Ex-boyfriends who lie compulsively about absolute b*******, maybe cheat too. I was past expecting everybody to be as transparent as I often was. I liked it this way too, it allowed me to navigate the ugly, often dark, confusing, problematic society as best I could with my mental health still intact, and my son's either side of me where they belonged.

'She hasn't given me that impression so far, so I'll wait' I said concluding Mums idea. I didn't wish to call her, to be brutally honest. I didn't even wish to speak to her. I could wait this out, at least for a few more hours.

CHAPTER 29

I had just slipped the CD into player in my car, I was getting ready for some music therapy when the phone started to ring. Private number again. I assumed it was the social worker and answered the phone accordingly.

'Hello Yolanda, its Elsa. How are you?

'Fine.' I replied wishing she would get straight to the point. Speaking to her was simply antagonising. Her annoying voice, I just didn't want to speak to her or hear her or see her.

'I need to visit the boys and have a chat with you, I wondered if you'd be home this evening?'

'Home?'

Why did she need to come to our house? What did she need to speak about? What couldn't she speak to me on the phone?

'I'm not sure' I lied. I didn't want her to come to my house that was our sanctuary I didn't want her negative spirit or energy to cross our threshold.

'I do need to discuss with you the medical and what happens now'.

Crafty cow, I thought. She knows I don't wish to see her, she probably knows I don't want her in my house either, so now she was using the results of the medical to get me. She knew I wouldn't turn down the opportunity to get the results. She may not know a lot of things about me, but that, she had got that right.

'What time?' I said.

'Is 16:30 ok?

'Fine I'll see you then' I replied disconnecting the phone as I could hear her saying goodbye.

The phone call pissed me off. Now I was definitely going to need my music. I pressed play and started the engine. It took me about another five minutes before I drove off. I sat there asking, 'what next?' It was everything, all at once. My son's at school, social services, placement, University, there was nothing else left for them to add to an already growing Red and Orange inferno. Everywhere I turned felt like a barrier. All I had now was knowing that I was collecting my sons from school and bringing them home with me where they belonged. Everything else hung over me like a violent storm. A storm that randomly shot spheres of lightning ahead of my every move, turning the road ahead of me into a pile of rubble increasingly impossible to cross. I turned the music up louder, I needed to drown my thoughts. I needed just to think of nothing for a moment, just nothing.

I fed the boys and waited for Elsa's arrival. She arrived at 16:27. She was punctual. I watched her from the kitchen window searching for the door numbers before she entered our doorway, still waiting for her to knock before going to the front door. Reluctantly I let her in and guided her to the kitchen. The boys were playing with toys, so I left them to their own devices for a moment, so Elsa could speak to me.

'Thank you for agreeing to see me Yolanda' Elsa began.

I didn't respond, I just looked at her waiting for her to continue. Keeping my conversations with these people minimal was my way forward. They didn't care about me, they didn't care about my well-being, so if I didn't have to express myself, I decided I wouldn't. As I said when I mentioned the judicial system, I believed anything I said, could be used against me at a later date. So, I had no desire to speak to Elsa or anyone else.

My mum taught me that if you have nothing good to say, don't say anything. Although I didn't often take that advice, every so often I tried to. It just so happens that on this occasion I was successful, and very grateful of my own success.

'I have the medical results here' she said diving in her bag and pulling out a bunch of papers'

I watched her as she took the papers out of her bag and noticed what looked like paperwork for court proceedings. I could see my sons' names in bold, together with the Local Authority. I'd seen this kind of paperwork before. These were proceedings for an Interim Care Order! Social services were trying to remove my sons from my care. They were trying to take away my Kwaams' & Cass. My son's. My heart was racing. I swallowed, as I tried to digest what I had just seen. I was scared and I was angry. I wanted to throw Elsa out of my house. Literally. I wanted to shout and scream at her and ask her if she thought I was stupid.

On the other hand, if I did all of those things, then what would happen to my son's? If I lost it even for a second, they would use it against me. Part of me believed they were trying to make me lose it, trying to break down the core of who I was. I couldn't afford to. I would **not** allow myself to. I told Elsa I needed to use the bathroom and excused myself. I turned the tap on, flushed the toilet to give the illusion I was doing something and leaned on the bathroom sink staring at myself in the mirror. I took a deep breath. This wasn't getting any better, it was getting worse. They were trying to take my son's. MY sons. It wasn't my imagination. It wasn't paranoia. This was real! I picked up my flannel running it under the hot water tap and washed my face. I could see the tears congregating in the bottom of my eyelids. There was no way I was going to lose it now. I washed my face until I felt the water had disappeared from the section of my eyelids that had been keeping them safe. I Rubbed cocoa butter on my face then went back to the kitchen to deal with Elsa.

'You were saying about the medical results?' my voice was once again, more formal.

'Yes, she said going over the paperwork she was holding'. There were no concerns found in the results. Cassius had some scarring, but this was confirmed as a result of his chickenpox'

I was tempted again to say something, but remembered what Mum taught me.

'Based on the results, the Local Authority will not be pursuing that allegation. However, based on some of the information to do with Kwame and Cassius' development at school, we will continue with an assessment, as I discussed with you previously.'

I didn't need to ask what happened with the assessments I already knew. The school would submit reports my GP with submit reports, maybe even the Health Visitor responsible for the boy's immunisations.

Whilst they continue to contact me or make appointments to see me or the boys. I knew the process. Clearly what Elsa was omitting from her explanation, was that the type of investigation she was talking about would be referred to a section 47, which from a parent's perspective, meant they would gather selective contextual information and then decide whether or not they believed your children were suffering. Possibly resulting in your children being placed on a Child Protection register, or perhaps a child in need plan where 'support' would be put in place. Neither one of these plans appealed to me, definitely not the first. Also, I noticed the word support, was tossed around quite a bit, just not with the same connotation as mine.

'Was that it, Elsa?' I didn't care if she thought I was rude this was **my** house she was now on my territory. And to be honest it was time for her to go.

'Before I go Yolanda, I do need to just see the boys quickly and also have a look at their room.

'I beg your pardon' my poker face had flown out the window. I was frowning. 'What do you mean you need to see their room? See their rooms for what??'

'Yolanda, I assure you we do this with all of our families, we just need to look at the children's living space because for instance if you didn't have adequate space it would have to be something that we look into'.

Ok I thought, even though I didn't like it, I could accept that it did make sense. At least it explained to me how some people had been moved after their families had been subjected to an intervention. But I didn't need more space, I didn't need anything from them. I escorted her to the boy's room, stood in the centre of the room so I could observe where her eyes wandered, before I showed her out.

'Thank you, Yolanda,'

'You're welcome', I lied.

I was still thinking about the care order proceedings paperwork; I'd seen in Elsa's bag. As I followed Elsa back to the kitchen, against my better judgement, I decided to challenge her about the paperwork.

'Can I clarify something please Elsa... I understand the local authority are applying full care order proceedings with relation to my son's.'

Elsa's face said it all. Her complexion changed from its usual pale, to first gentle Rose blush, then beetroot Red. Clearly, I was not, to know of this.

'Sorry Yolanda?' Elsa was doing her utmost to make a rhetorical question sound as though she expected an answer.

'ICO Elsa, with relation to my son's...?

'The local authority are not pursuing care order proceedings at present'

'Really?' I said eerie sarcasm in my voice

'The local authority does not have substantial evidence to support an ICO being granted.'

'So basically Elsa, what you're saying is the judge has told you that you do not have enough evidence to warrant an ICO for my son's??' this was what Elsa was saying, it just seemed that she was trying not to say it.

'Yes Yolanda, Elsa's tone had changed now. She was sounding more submissive, as though she were the one who was being worn down, one judgement at a time. I figured she wasn't supposed to share that information with me, I was almost certain that I was not supposed to have seen the paperwork within the file she was carelessly carrying around in her bag.

However, that would teach her, I told myself!

'Let me get something clear, Elsa whilst I was attending the child protection medical with my son's, you were hoping your paperwork would be granted so you could remove them from me at the hospital...?

My blood was boiling again, I was trying to focus on what Mum had taught me, 'don't say anything, don't say anything, don't say anything'. But it was unsuccessful.

I said something.

'Let me tell you sutten Elsa' my language had changed I was in fight mode. 'YOU LOT AIN'T HAVING MY SONS! Do you hear me? Listen to me good. You think I don't know what you're trying to do?

YOU LOT AIN'T HAVIN MY SONS!'

Elsa tried to speak, 'Yola...'

'Do you need anything else today from me?' I demanded cutting her off.

'No Yolanda not at the moment, however I will need to come back and see you in about a week or so'

'Make sure you call me in advance before you come, don't turn up at my house Elsa because I will leave you outside'

'No problem Yolanda, thank you' Elsa replied packing her things into her bag and scurrying towards the door. I showed Elsa to the door and purposely slammed it behind her.

Good riddance.

CHAPTER 30

Without University lectures to attend and no placement days to complete. I had filled my free time with overtime at work. Every penny counted at this point. Kevron and James hadn't yet confirmed how much the mentorship the boys were receiving would cost me, so I undertook the additional shifts whilst I waited for them to confirm. At least this way I would at least have something to contribute to begin with. So far, the work they were doing with my son's was proving to be invaluable. I would drop the boys off once a week sometimes twice and when I collected them, they were bouncing off the walls with excitement. Both boys had formed friendships and look forward to seeing those friends when they arrived. Interestingly enough I hadn't heard anything about my Cassius being 'withdrawn' or not communicating much. I had yet to learn about Kwame struggling to follow instructions or sit still.

Nonetheless this didn't surprise me. Having observed the relationship that the mentors had with the boys who attended the club. It was obvious why such a program would work for our sons. On one occasion I had seen one boy sat at a table doing his homework from school. The young boy was about 8 years old, and he was trying every diversionary tactic he could think of to avoid doing the homework as if it were the plague. James calmly explained to him that he would not be able to play the game, until the homework was done and, to a high standard. He went on to explain to the boy that rushing through the work will not get him to the computer game any quicker. In fact, he explained, it would take far longer, because he will then be sent back to redo it again. Please can we take a second to give James a medal? I mean seriously 'all hail James'. Perhaps it is just me who sees this as remarkable. Perhaps my thinking is way too deep. But for me what I had observed that day between this man and this boy who will eventually, God willing become a man, was an expectation and a standard laid out before him. An expectation and a standard that this young boy should be carrying around as though it were a limb he could not live without. A standard that was set appropriately high enough for him to attain, as opposed to low enough that he could crawl to it. These were the standards and the expectations that all of our children required. The standard and expectation that says I will be the best version of myself. I will not succumb to a negative imposed, self-fulfilled prophecy. I will not compare myself to the worst in order to feel better about my accomplishments. I will strive for excellence not mediocrity. To the boy in question he probably thought that James was being unreasonable and asking him to do too much. Yet from where I stood in the doorway it was very clear to me, transparent even, that James was teaching him to aspire. He was teaching him not to settle, not to sell himself short. This was not only what I believed our children required, but more so, it was the power of our son's being able to receive that message, that inspiration, that encouragement, that promotion of striving for excellence, from a positive Black man. That was the 'icing on the cake' so to speak, for me. It saddens me that something that should simply be a standard for all of our children, can almost be referred to as a concession, an advantage of some kind, when in actual fact this is our children's entitlement, their birth right. We as parents, both **Mothers and Fathers, setting standards and expectations is part of our role. Just as feeding babies and changing nappies is an integral part of caring for new-borns.** For this reason, among many I knew I'd made the right choice in contacting this mentoring service for Cassius and Kwame.

I arrived at work half an hour early. What would normally take me up to 45 minutes somehow took me around 20 minutes. When I got there, my colleague Marcus was already packed up ready to go.

'Marcus you don't finish for another half an hour...? Why are you all packed up? I said teasing him.

'I watched you on the camera parking your car and started to get ready'

I laughed. Marcus was cool, we got on rather well. Once in a while he might just cause me to breathe a little bit of the fire out of my nostrils. But after breathing fire a couple of times, we understood each other better. Marcus was older than me. I didn't know his age, but my assumption was at least 8-10 years older. He was chubby, from Ghana and had a healthy relationship with food. Even more healthy than my relationship with food. This was his second job, he also had a full-time job, wife, and three young children.

'Suppose I planned on walking around the shops before I start my shift Marcus'

Marcus laughed a hefty loud laugh. His voice was enormous. Not usually the way you refer to the volume of a person's voice. Yet once you met Marcus, you would understand why his voice would be referred to as enormous. Even when he meant to speak quietly in my ear about one of the young people, the young person in question would end up saying 'Marcus I heard what you just said to Yolanda'. The man just could not help but speak very very loudly. You know like trumpet loud. You simply can't play a trumpet quietly. And don't get me started on the volume at which he laughed because that shook the entire building.

'Yes, my sister, but I know that you know I need to go home and deal with the babies before I go to my work'

Marcus had a habit of referring to me as his sister when he needed to leave early or was running late.

'Its fine you can go' I said rolling my eyes in jest.

'Let me just log off this PC, Marcus explained as he turned his back to me to do so. 'How's University going Yolanda?' he bellowed.

'It's ok'. I was glad he turned his back to me, because had he been facing me perhaps, I wouldn't have looked as convincing as I sounded. I've never really been a good liar, perhaps this is why I've resorted to be a person who wasn't embarrassed to speak their truth, because being caught out in a lie was even more embarrassing for me. Don't get me wrong I had told my mum lies when I was younger and boy did, I pay for it. And rightly so. But that was then. My mum was the law. Quite frankly no one else wore that title so who else was there for me to lie to?

'Have you finished your placement?'

I paused before I answered. I didn't want to have to explain what was going on to Marcus. I didn't discuss personal things with him. There was only one woman at work who I spoke to on that level, Carmen. If Carmen wasn't working then my conversations were fairly basic at work, nothing to do with my personal life.

'Uh yeh'

There. I told myself just two words and we're done. Yes, it was a lie. I admit that, but I refuse to tell a story and add more to that lie, so I assumed that the two words would be enough for Marcus, who remember, was in a rush to leave.

'Well done'

'Thanks' I replied ever so sheepishly.

My thanks was a lie, I didn't really deserve a well done of any kind. I was too embarrassed to tell him that despite my efforts, my parenting was clearly not as good as I would have liked it to be, or at least social services and the school didn't think so. Or how about that I had been thrown off my course, sacked from my job because I was considered someone who was abusing their children.

Can I make a confession... as I write that line, I still cringe. Because as a Mother. As a parent, being considered someone who does not have good intention for their children, someone who perhaps doesn't even love their children and perhaps has resentment in place of love. All of those considerations are demoralising disempowering, demotivating, criminalising, and ostracising. And what's worse is that the stigma follows you everywhere like a foul smell, even to bed at night. It crawls under your covers, snuggles close to you, wrapping arms of guilt around your waist breathing more guilt, fear and anxiety into your ears and the back of your neck. Stigma doesn't stop talking. It doesn't want you to omit its presence, so at every given opportunity, you'll hear that voice whispering, reminding you that you are failure. That you are not worthy, that you are guilty, that you are everything that it says you are. That is the power of stigma, it isolates you from everything and everyone, so you seemingly stick out like a sore thumb. **Stigma often sitting close to prejudice is one of society's most frequented weapons.** Regularly passed on like the baton in a relay race. And I Yolanda, had become its most revered target. I knew it had been following me around if I'm honest, it had been following me since the moment the school had begun calling me in, to advise me of concern after concern regarding my son's. In actual fact, come to think of it, stigma had been following me since the birth of my first son, when many believed I had made a huge mistake and was flushing my life down the toilet. At that point it didn't reside with me. It came, it whispered and then it left, off to the next project. However more recently stigma decided that he liked living with me, he liked following me around, maybe I was a willing participant. It was easy for him to penetrate me, I don't know. All I knew is that stigma made sure that I knew, that who I was, was in question.

CHAPTER 31

The day of Kwame's school trip to the beach had arrived. I'd woken up early to make packed lunch for the dreaded outing. Kwame was excited, he had been going on about it since the night before. Me on the other hand much less. I was going to be subjected to an entire day spent with Miss Reynolds. I barely spoke to her since the investigation had begun. I continued to keep it simple with her. Now, much to my dismay I was going to be sat on a coach with her, then I was going to have to communicate with her in order to understand what she required of me throughout the trip. I kept wanting to back out, spend the day doing absolutely anything else, but the truth was I had to go on this trip because I didn't want my son to be ostracised any longer than he was currently experiencing at school, with all this special consideration being given in class to the special little boy who doesn't understand how to sit still, and can't carry out handwriting tasks. It was also strange that since the investigation began, the complaints were few and far between with reference to Kwame and Cassius. Whether that was as a result of improvements where my sons were concerned or due to tensions between the school, and myself perhaps they didn't want to engage with me unless they really had too. Either way I didn't care. However, one could not ignore the drastic change of pattern.

The boys were enjoying their time at the mentoring service and had warmed to their mentors. For me I felt as though the work completed at the mentoring service would aid the development of my children at school. The sub-standards that teachers were trying to impose on my son's, the difficulties they were trying to impress upon my son's to convince them that they did not have the same capabilities as everyone else, was not going to work if our ideals as a family unit, our cultural ideals, our high expectations for our own individual success was consistently being reinforced. The mentoring service promoted Black boys into men. It celebrated their strengths it worked on their weaknesses and it encouraged them to dream big, turning those dreams into reality. For me this was going to be instrumental in bringing about the change that I needed to see with my son's at school. I will never lose sight of the saying, 'it takes a village to raise a child' because in my time of need, I went looking for my village.

We arrived at the school early, the weather was beautifully sunny, and the morning particularly bright, not necessarily warm but surprisingly bright, so the boys and I decided to go into the playground early so they could run around. I never took the time to do much of this, I didn't mind being in the playground a few minutes before the bell went. But not 10 minutes. Ten minutes or more to me encouraged all kinds of conversations and interactions that I wasn't that interested in having. Although I told myself Miss Reynolds might need to run through a few things with me in preparation of the trip. So at least if I was stood in the playground, she could see I was already at school and therefore available if she needed to run through anything with me. To be fair I reminded myself that my presence on the trip was not to support the trip but actually to support my son. As that had been the reasoning given to me as to why he needed an adult to attend. Come to think of it, Miss Reynolds shouldn't really have much to say to me because I wasn't a parent helper, I was a parent who had no choice but to attend the trip, to ensure my son would not be excluded from the trip.

The boys gave me their bags before running off around the playground chasing each other, tagging the odd child as part of some kind of game. I stood around watching the early morning activity in the playground. There were a number of parents engrossed in conversations. Some stood around holding their children's coats and ba͏͏ ͏king anxious as they waited for the bell to go. I greeted some ͏ ͏arents who had children in Kwame and Cassius' classes. ͏hem were going on the school trip. They were waiting ͏ ͏ wave their children off. One of the year 6 children entered the playground ringing the bell loudly walking into each corner of the playground to ensure that it could be heard by everyone present. Kwame and I walked Cassius to his class line, before making our way to the classroom where all the other children were excitedly sitting down attentively while Miss Reynolds addressed them.

I opened the classroom door and entered quietly, standing at the side while Kwame took a seat at his table. Miss Reynolds turned to look at me and smiled.

'Can we all say good morning to Kwame's Mummy, who will be coming on the trip with us today? I expect you all to show Kwame's Mummy how good a class you are and how well behaved you can all be'.

Had I not been in full view of the entire class I would have rolled my eyes at Miss Reynolds, but I was in front of the whole class and all the children would see, so I smiled politely and gave the children a small wave. Miss Reynolds went on to explain to the class the rules of the trip and then told them that they could speak to the person next to them quietly whilst we awaited confirmation of the coach's arrival. She walked over to me whilst the children were engaged in excited chatter.

'Thank you for coming Yolanda' Miss Reynolds started off with.

A thank you seemed hardly appropriate, if you tell me that my son can't attend a trip unless an adult comes with him, and he doesn't have the luxury of Mum or Dad, so inevitably it was going to be me. Hardly a thank you, I told myself. I chose not to respond as I already established, that my response was not going to be appropriate, so I smiled like I was mute.

'The coach should be here any second, then what will happen is, we'll make our way out with the children walking in pairs. I will be at the start of the line, if you Yolanda, wouldn't mind staying at the back of the line with Kwame'.

Interesting that I should be the one to stay at the back. Especially as I noticed there were other teachers who were also coming to support the trip. Why not place the teachers at the front of the line and the back of the line and then fill me in somewhere else, particularly as my role was not to support the trip, but to support my son. But I spared Miss Reynolds the alternative suggestion, and nodded my head, at the same time verbally accepting the direction.

'Once we arrive at the beach the children will be divided into groups, if you don't mind, I will give you perhaps three children to supervise?'

'No problem I responded.

After all I had nothing against the children, the children here, were not my problem it was the adults.

'Kwame will be with you throughout the day, he will not be put into one of the other groups.'

'Thank you' I said.

Another one of the teachers who was helping out with the trip came over.

'The coach is here Miss'

'Oh great!' Miss Reynolds said clapping her hands. 'Green class can I have your attention!' she exclaimed.

Sensing that this must mean they were ready to depart; Miss Reynolds was then welcomed by attentive smiley faces of small children shushing the person next to them so they could receive the exciting news. Well all except two. Kwame and the boy that was sat next to him. The boy next to him was standing up and doing some kind of dance possibly. But not only was he doing a dance as opposed to sitting down, he was bending over and waving his bum and the two were laughing hysterically. From where I stood, the behaviour looked absolutely ridiculous and unacceptable. By now, the class could also see what I could see, as the boy was singing a tune as he did so. Kwame had remained seated but was laughing loudly, hysterically. I couldn't see the joke.

I shot Kwame a look and he stopped laughing. Of course, the boy who was gyrating himself next to Kwame continued until Miss Reynolds spoke with him.

'Terry, take a seat please. Can I remind you that you will need to be on your best behaviour, otherwise you will need to go to Miss O'Connor's office!'

I wasn't sure if Terry cared much about Miss O'Connor's office, or if he just sat down because he really wanted to go on the trip. As for Kwame I couldn't wait to get a second to whisper in his ears. I wasn't sure about that friendship between him and Terry. **Some friendships, as with relationships, bring out the worst qualities within you,** and I've always believed that if that is the case, you should make an effort to distance yourself. Since Kwame was still young, I would make an effort to distance the two, because under no uncertain terms was Kwame going to behave in that fashion.

We finally boarded the Coach and set off for the English beach aka seaside. For some reason Kwame was sat next to Terry on the coach. Miss Reynolds had allowed it, so I told myself to sit on the side-lines allow Kwame to sit with Terry, but to sit behind them, in case Kwame started to adopt specific behaviours.

The coach was noisy. I had left home with my book and a notepad to keep me occupied on the coach and to isolate me from having to interact with the teachers. Kwame was sat right in front of me so I didn't need to look at him he was already within my peripheral vision and as for my hearing, well that was exceptionally astute, so I made myself comfortable having been given the advantage of not having to sit next to anyone, and buried myself in the beauty of my book. I could hear some of the children playing I spy type games and telling one another about some of the treasures they were going to find in the sand. It was nice to hear the excitement of children and be in the midst of that. I mean when I was a child, we got excited about playing outside or going to McDonald's. Although I do remember getting extra excited when I had to go on a coach trip to somewhere. Anywhere. It was irrelevant where the coach was taking me, it was just the whole fact of going on the coach and having packed lunch full of goodies. I'm sure that if the coach had pulled up at outside my house, I would still have been excited. I guess when you are a child the coach is exciting. Period.

It didn't take long for me to realise that Terry was quite excitable. Even among all the noise you could hear on the coach, Terry's voice still superseded the other children. What was also interesting was that at various points I noticed Terry was whispering to Kwame but then the two boys would erupt into fits of laughter. Something told me that wasn't a good sign the boys whispering, them bursting into laughter, but I chose to ignore it for the moment and continued reading my book.

We had been on the coach now for about 40 minutes when Miss Reynolds announced to the class that we would soon reach our destination.

Some of the children sang a chorus of yaaaay' Well almost all of the children. Whilst the children were shouting yay, Terry had decided to shout something else.

'yay poo-poo bum-bum willy'

I looked up from my book, eyebrows joining together as I looked at Terry. I knew Terry wasn't my child therefore I didn't expect him to respond to the look, but what came next still surprised me. Terry looked over at me and continued singing 'poo poo face bum bum willy' By now Kwame had noticed that I had been giving Terry the look and that Terry was not fazed by the look. He looked up at Terry and then started laughing loudly. This seemed to stir Terry on some more and he got louder. Other children started giggling slyly. Best part of all, Miss Reynolds wasn't doing anything, neither were any of the other teachers. I sat there, looked at Miss Reynolds, looked over at the two members of staff that were sat in the opposite aisles to me, and then back at Kwame and Terry.

Terry then turned to Kwame and said something along the lines of 'you've got a willy face'.

I opened my mouth to say something, then looked over at the other teacher who was looking at Terry and still had not said anything. I began thinking, this is the way you let the children speak at school. This was the language that these young children spoke before they even entered High School. I shook my head. Just as Kwame piped up.

'You are a willy and a bum-bum head…'

I flicked Kwame in the mouth. It was swift. So much so, that he didn't get to finish his sentence there was no need for him to finish that sentence. Immediately Terry stopped singing. Perhaps he feared that I would do the same to him, hardly likely might I add. Kwame had his hand over his mouth, I recognised the look on his face, he was embarrassed. And rightly so, because I was also embarrassed. Embarrassed that in my presence on this school trip, somehow Kwame thought he could behave in that fashion and I would ignore it. What on earth was my son thinking? It was not my problem if Terry's language was totally inappropriate at such a young age. It was not my problem if the school chose not to address Terry's behaviour and language, in the presence of other adults and children. But what was my business, was when my sons conducted themselves in a way, which was not how I raised my sons to conduct themselves. Kwame had foolishly started to imitate Terry's behaviour and now he was sat there with his hands on his mouth, tears in his eyes embarrassed in front of his friend.

I told Kwame to get up and come and sit next to me. It was going to be no more of him sitting next to Terry seeing as he was unable to behave in an acceptable manner when he was sat there. All of a sudden Miss Reynolds could get up from her seat and could speak.

'Terry if you continue to behave in this way you will not be allowed off the coach when we get to the beach'

All of a sudden Miss Reynolds could intervene, all of a sudden, she was willing to challenge Terry about his foul language and attitude. Why now, I told myself. Why had you not gotten up when he first started with the obscenities? We all know you can hear, because I'd even noticed the coach driver looking in his rear-view mirror to see who was using that verbatim. Terry sat down after Miss Reynolds spoke to him although he continued to laugh looking as though he felt quite amused with himself.

'Are you ok Kwame' Miss Reynolds asked, as if she didn't know that Kwame was in trouble. Kwame continued sniffling.

'He's fine thank you Miss'

The tone of my voice said challenge me if you dare. As far as I was concerned, Miss Reynolds had not intervened when the boys were acting inappropriately, and Terry was announcing nonsensical inappropriate words. However, it seems that as soon as I had decided to curtail Kwame's part in this, all of a sudden Miss Reynolds was out of her seat and making enquiries to my son about his well-being. Bitch sit back down. Is what I really wanted to say. Nonetheless, Miss Reynolds took the hint and sat down without me having to say a word.

Kwame was fine for the rest of the trip. When we arrived at the seaside, he went off exploring, he listened when the tour guide explained to them some of the things they might see or find. At lunchtime Terry had come to find Kwame and sit beside him. However, I noticed Kwame didn't say much to Terry. Besides the fact he was too engrossed in the goodies within his packed lunch box, I could see on Kwame's face that he didn't want to get himself in any more trouble by imitating the behaviour of Terry.

You see Kwame has never been stupid, he's always been an attuned, intelligent little boy. And he's not one for embarrassment, much like me. Now, after receiving the flick for losing himself, and forgetting his basic manners, Kwame was fine and had reverted back to his normal way of life using normal, appropriate, child friendly, language. Terry had noticed this and was slowly behaving a little bit more subdued than before. This made me question the interaction between these two ordinarily, when they were at school, and if one instigated the other to behave in the worst way possible.

Some of the children explored the sea while others remained on the sand. Kwame had asked me if he could go in the sea, just his toes. I told him no. The sea looked worse than I had imagined when I first read the outing letter. It was murky, there was rubbish in parts, and it was far from clear. The tour guide had mentioned that somebody cleaned the beach on a daily basis. This was not evident from where I stood. Hence why, Kwame was not allowed to go paddling in the sewer. I wondered if some of the other parents may have felt the same if they could see the water, they were allowing their children to venture into.

Or perhaps it was just me. Perhaps I was overprotective, overly scornful, overly whatever it was, as to why I felt that water was too filthy for my son. Or perhaps it was just a matter of preference. My expectation of water that my children could venture into meant I need to be able to see into the water. I need to be able to see what that water contains, at least under the immediate stream. Fair enough if I could not see as far as the bottom. But if at the top was surrounded by residue and brownish murk, my children could not venture into it, end of.

The end of the day came sooner than I thought and to be fair I was glad. I was glad that I'd been able to come on the trip with Kwame thus ensuring that he wasn't left out. As a result of recent events it wasn't as though I had anything better to do anyhow. When we got back to the school, I took Kwame and the two of us made our way to the car. School had finished some time ago, so I had asked Jayde to collect Cassius for me. Jayde didn't live far from the school, so we made my way to collect Cassius.

'Mummy' Kwame said 'I'm sorry for being silly today with Terry'

I pulled over the car for a minute and turned to face Kwame.

'Its okay son, please don't let me see you behaving like that again. I don't know Terry's parents and I don't know how they allow him to behave, but you know that you and Cass' are not allowed to behave like that or speak like that. That means that sometimes if you see other children doing those kinds of things you have to separate yourself from them, don't start following them because you know that your mum doesn't allow it'

'Yes Mummy'

I was proud of this boy. Proud of my son. Proud of his ability to reflect on his behaviour and understand where he went wrong. I knew he had gotten carried away on the coach. But he also needed to understand that once he started to behave like that, no one was talking about Terry. Chances are Terry's mum was never contacted to come and see Miss O'Connor. Yet still I had been, on multiple occasions. If my sons started to behave like the Terry's of the school, well you can imagine. I couldn't afford for my sons to fall into that. My mum used to say, 'puss and daarg don't have the same luck'. Again, she was right. We had to learn early that if we chose to do the same things as other people thinking we were going to be treated like those other people, well then, more fool us. If we did the same things as other people and expected to get the same results, again more fool us. The puss did not have the same luck as the dog, and it should never assume so either. I kissed Kwame, and then turned back around and continued to drive towards Jayde's house to get Cassius. We pulled up outside Jayde's house, just as I felt my phone vibrating in my bag. I've forgotten to turn the ring back on when we returned from the trip. Private caller.

I assumed was Elsa and answered the phone in my 'what now' tone of voice.

'Hello!'

'Hi Yolanda'

It was Elsa.

'As I mentioned before Yolanda, I will need to carry out a series of visits to both yourself and the boys during this investigation and I wanted to make another appointment to see you perhaps next week Thursday…?

'Time?'

'Can we do 5pm. this time, is that ok?

'Fine, see you then'

I kissed my teeth, put the phone back in my bag and knocked the door to collect Cass'.

CHAPTER 32

We were coming towards the end of term and I still hadn't received any information from the University. I was angry at them for having suspended my placement and my place on the course. It felt unfair. I felt as though my life was just hanging in the balance, we had a holiday booked for the summer holidays, but then what would happen in September when everyone was going back to university for the second year? What would I be doing? I hadn't contacted Jean, I knew that if she hadn't contacted me, she had no further information as to what may happen with my placement. Also, I didn't want in any way for her to feel as though I was expecting her to make allowances for me. I respected her too much for that. We had a visit coming up from Elsa, but I refused to ask Elsa. I felt like Elsa somehow might get a kick out of feeling that she was instrumental in my next steps. Or that I required something from her, even if it was merely information. No, I decided. I wouldn't give that pathetic little woman the satisfaction.

It was the day of Elsa's visit. I didn't have work, so I'd been at home most of the day finishing off my assignment. I was taking the time to catch up on my washing, cook dinner, and organise the boy's old toys for charity. It felt like I'd been doing it for only a couple of hours, when I looked at the clock and realised it is time for me to run and grab the boys from school. I made a quick dash around the house, and then left home racing down to the school. I chose not to mention that Elsa was coming today. I couldn't explain Elsa's role to the boys. Cassius had told me that she introduced herself as a social worker and told him she was there to 'keep children safe'. I hadn't appreciated that definition either. When speaking to a child as young as Cass', saying things like keep children safe can make a child's mind start to wonder and their imagination run riot. What did she mean by safe? Why wouldn't I be safe, may well be the first things that go through the child's mind. Leaving a child to potentially start to pick out elements of their life and deem them as unsafe. Because the imagination is a fun place to be, at the best of times even for adults. I did not like that definition, I don't know what would have been a more suitable or child appropriate definition, but I sure didn't like that one. Therefore, she was just Elsa, if the boys were older, I would have nicknamed her something less appropriate, but they weren't, so I did not.

The boys were out of their uniforms in record time. As we waited for the rice to finish cooking, I got them both started on their homework. Kwame had been given homework on materials, and Cassius on seasons. I went through the instructions for the homework with the boys, one by one, and then left them independently to work at the dining table, whilst I continued in the kitchen. As per usual, Elsa arrived on time. I guess she took pride in showing up on time to ruin family's lives. That was clearly a priority to her. The boys were still doing their homework when she arrived, so I let Elsa into the kitchen.

'How are you Yolanda?

'Great thanks. I knew I didn't sound convincing. In fact, I knew I sounded rather flat, for someone who was feeling great. But I didn't care. That was my answer and I was sticking to it. I didn't need to entertain small talk with her. The only reason I let her in was due to the circumstances, but no one could force me to be amicable, courteous or polite, if I did not wish to. Elsa seemed a bit nervous since our last visit. I put this down to her not being genuine or transparent. Had I not called her out on Interim Care Order paperwork, she would have omitted that detail from her visit. So now she felt nervous. Well then don't come to my house, I thought. Simple.

Elsa fumbled with her words before explaining that a Child Protection conference was being arranged for the boys. I let her explain the purpose of the CP conference as though I was oblivious, and then asked when it would take place. The sheer fact that she knew I had been suspended from university based on their investigation, she would also know, I was training to be a social worker and would probably be aware of the procedures she was describing to me. Nonetheless, still she felt the need to engage in more babble. So, I let her. Some people feel the need to demonstrate that they know some things to make themselves feel better, so why not let her recite from the textbook. Elsa went on to explain that a date had already been set, for three weeks from now. She gave me the date and I made a note of it in my diary. She had definitely been a busy bee. I resented the idea of a child protection conference but tried not to show it as she was talking. I explained to Elsa that once school resigned for the holidays, the boys and I would be going away for almost the entire summer. Elsa went on to explain that depending on the outcome of the conference, this might not be possible. I politely advised Elsa that this was a pre-booked holiday, and we would be going.

'Yolanda a child protection case is slightly different to a Child in Need case and so we would have to discuss these things.'

'As I said Elsa, that's absolutely fine I'm just letting you know that we are going on holiday, all three of us'

I realise that one of the things that kept getting my back up was when Elsa started to speak to me as though we were the parents from my son's not me. They had already tried to issue care proceedings and failed, so as far as I was concerned, I wasn't going to pretend that they were corporate parents for my children. They were not. There was no such thing in this case. We had all been looking forward to this holiday for months. I had been saving rigorously, and there was no way that these people were going to ground our holiday.

'Once the conference is over Yolanda, we will be able to discuss this in more detail. Also, if the children are placed on the child protection register you will be allocated a new social worker'.

Every time this woman came around to my house, I felt the innate urge to throw her ass out! It was as though she didn't know that you couldn't step into a woman's house and tell her what to do with her children. That was rule number 1, no?

'MUMMY' mummy, I don't know how to do this question.'

It was Kwame he had interrupted me, brought his homework book to me and was telling me he couldn't do it. I looked over the homework. The question was asking which materials were soluble. I turned my focus away from Elsa for a second without excusing myself.

'Look at the pictures Kwame, which of those materials are soluble?'

'I dunno' he replied shrugging his shoulders.

'What don't you know Kwame?'

'I don't know which of them are soluble Mummy'

'Think about it Kwame, look at the pictures what does soluble mean?'

'I don't know' he replied shrugging his shoulders again.

'What do you mean you don't know, you've been learning about materials at school, your teacher has sent you home with this homework, which means she's explained to you already, what soluble means?'

'I don't remember Mummy'

'Go and sit down and think about it. Try and remember'

The other thing about Kwame was that he could be lazy at times. With all his knowledge, if he decided he did not want to do something, he would not do it. He had a way of just switching off. I was always conscious when Kwame said things like I don't know, because that normally was the cop out, and it normally stood for I can't be bothered. So, sending him back to the dining table to think about it, guaranteed within a few minutes Kwame would be back, and he would tell me what soluble meant. But if he thought he didn't have to tell me, if he thought he could get away with not telling me, resulting in me telling him, then he would pretend that he just didn't know. That was my son. I was just grateful that I knew who he was. He was a child who liked to try his luck, you have to take your hat off to him for that. Kwame hung his head and went back to the dining table.

'Was there anything else Elsa?' I asked turning to face her again.

'Ummm just one more thing Yolanda. As part of our investigation in to making sure the children are safe, we take a historical look.

I turned the pot off and stood so that I was facing Elsa.

'I wondered if I could talk to you about your former partner'

My expression turned to one of confusion, former, meant past. Nothing to do with today, so what was Elsa talking about, what was she really asking me?

'You're losing me Elsa what do you want to know?'

'Everything is taken into consideration as part of the investigation.'

'Can I double check something please Elsa, who do you have on record as living in this house?'

'Yourself and the two boys Yolanda'

'Ok good, so just to be clear you're not confused about who lives in this house right? And we don't need to play games. I don't need to tell you anything that you have answers to. My only question is what is it, you want to know that pertains to this investigation?'

'My goal is just to gather information Yolanda, so I just thought it would be a good idea to ask you directly.'

'Ask me what directly Elsa, if secretly somebody else lives under the floorboards that you are not aware of? What on Earth are you asking me?'

'If you prefer not to go into it Yolanda then that's also fine'

'It is not a matter of if I don't wish to go into it Elsa, the question is what has it got to do with right here now, today, with these two boys?'

I saw Elsa take a deep breath as if she was fed up of me. Yet still she was stood in my kitchen, and not I stood in hers. She knew exactly where to find the front door should she need to use it.

'I understand if you don't want to talk about it Yolanda, so we can just move on.'

I was beginning to feel as though Elsa no longer wanted to probe.

'Actually, Elsa what you don't understand, is this is nothing to do with me not wanting to talk about it. This is more about me talking to you about what you need to know. Your goal is to gather information, relevant information, not just information that you merely want to know. This in my opinion falls under the category of what you want to know, because I cannot for the life of me, see the reference it bears to this situation, and for that reason we will not discuss that. End of. Perhaps if you can justify the relevance, I'd be more inclined'.

I didn't care if Elsa responded or not. I had said my last word on the subject.

'Ok Yolanda'

'Do you mind if I just have a word with the boys?' she asked changing the subject swiftly.

'How long do you need Elsa because they need to finish their homework?'

'It's just a well-being check Yolanda, to ask them how they're doing. 'Go ahead' I said to her, using my hand to gesture that she was allowed to enter the front room where the boys were working. Here we go again with the terminology I despised, 'well-being check'. I didn't like that it implied that they needed to be checked on to make sure they were still 'alive and well'. As if they would be anything other. As if I would allow someone to hurt my sons or worst still, I would, just for the sake of making their lives a misery. No, that was not within my DNA. I came from a family of women who taught their children with the best of intentions. Women who set the bar high enough that we would have to strive in order to reach out and touch it. Mothers who disciplined us when necessary, so that we knew how to conduct ourselves when we were out of their sight. You see the women who made me, those who contributed to the makings of me, refused to leave it to society to sanction us as they saw fit. Seemingly community inspired services that would beat and abuse us verbally, physically, and mentally, to the point of conformity, or worst death. The women who raised us, prepared us for the real world, setting high expectations at home, so we would not need to be broken, in order to assimilate to expectations that went against our morals and principles of life. In short, our parents prepared us for societal norms, so we would not have to receive harsh treatment shared out like leftovers in an orphanage. 'More please'. No thank you, I have enough of what I need to survive right here.

When Elsa entered the room both boys looked up from what they were doing.

'Hello Kwame and Cassius, I'm not sure if you remember me, I'm Elsa'

'Yes' Cassius said nodding.

I noticed she didn't put that in her notepad that Cassius could indeed speak. Instead she continued talking as if she hadn't noticed anything contrary to what she had been told prior. Instead she went on.

'How are you both today?'

'Fine thank you' both responded in harmony.

'That's great to hear'.

I walked back into the kitchen as not to give Elsa the impression that I was in some way influencing her communication with the boys.

I could hear her asking Cassius about his day and Kwame about his trip.

'At times I could hear them responding, other times they sounded less engaged in whatever topic Elsa attempted to entice them with.

From a distance it was a bit like watching the old woman enticing Hansel and Gretel to enter into a house made of sweets, cookies, and other goodies. Only this was not an old woman, and as for a disguise she wore a completely different one, armed with the authority to legally steal other people's children. I poured myself a drink and the boys a milkshake, leaving their cups on the side for when they were finished with Elsa, who was still painfully trying to spark some kind of fluid conversation with the boys. Elsa spent about 20 or so minutes speaking to the boys, before returning to the kitchen where I was stood sharing out their dinner. I asked Cassius to set the table, as I laid the plates on the table, together with the milkshakes that had been sat on the side. As the boys started to eat their dinner, I turned my attention back to Elsa.

'Was there anything else?' I asked her

'As part of my report I also need to ask you if there's any support you think you can benefit from with regards to Cassius and Kwame, and of course yourself.

'Mentoring'

I didn't need to think about it and yes that's what I wanted the boys to receive. If Elsa said they were trying to help well let's see, 'Please can you facilitate mentoring for my sons? I have found a service that I'm happy with, perhaps you can contact them and discuss it with them.

'The Local Authority has its own mentoring service that we provide so I'm not sure if this is something we can authorise'

'The boys have already started attending as I sourced them for myself, and personally I don't wish for them to receive mentoring from anywhere else'

'We have a great service in-house Yolanda, the mentors would visit the boys, take them out...'

'I'm not comfortable with that. Also tell me about the actual mentors. Are they male? Are they Black?'

'Unfortunately, I can't answer that Yolanda. However, they are experienced and have all been CRB (formally DBS) checked.'

'I didn't source this service by chance Elsa. I selected this service because they are culturally appropriate for my son's needs. I'm not looking for someone to take them out and use Socratic questioning to defame us a family. I want them to be in the company of positivity. Black male positivity and empowerment. Not someone to take them to the cinema and bring them home. I'm not comfortable with that. If the local authority will not authorise or commission it, I'll pay for it myself, don't worry Elsa.'

'I can discuss it with my manager when I'm back in the office, but I can't make that decision Yolanda'

'That's fine Elsa, like I said I'm happy to do it myself.'

'Was there anything else Yolanda?'

'Not at the moment' I replied feeling smug.

Elsa concluded by explaining that I would receive a letter confirming the date for the Child Protection Conference and that I was welcome to attend. I assured her I would be in attendance. There was no way a group of professional strangers were going to sit around a table and discuss my son's, without me present.

CHAPTER 33

The weeks were dragging on. Things stayed the same at school. Miss Reynolds had begun having her talks after school with me again, but they were much more concise than before. Whether that was because she was managing Kwame's behaviour much better, or because she didn't want to say too much to me, I couldn't really tell nor was I particularly bothered. Granted she had continued to send Kwame's unfinished tasks home at the end of each day. And I ensured that Kwame had it completed by the following day. I mean if he decided he wasn't going to work at school then he was going to work double hard at home, simple. As much as I felt the school had their motives, neither of my son's was going to go to school every single day and come home with an empty brain, I didn't believe in that. Correction. I don't believe in that. It cost money to send your child to school whether it be lunch, uniform, travel, school fees, whatever. As a parent I was not going to waste time and money, every single day, for my son to amount to nothing. Nothing was not an option. My strategy was clearly working because as the weeks had gone by, I noticed there were only a couple of days out of the week (as opposed to his previous record of five days), whereby Kwame had not completed all of his class work. It seemed my son had quickly cottoned on to the fact that the more work he had to do at home, the less Power Rangers he was going to watch. I was no longer going in and supporting the class in the mornings and afternoons as before. Apparently, the school had decided it was not be a good idea based on 'current circumstances. By then I didn't want to go in and support anymore. Whereas I had believed the school were trying to support at least a small positive shred of detail that was making the difference in the way my son was able to access his learning, it was quite apparent to me that this was not the case. I accepted it; it wasn't a big deal. They didn't owe my children anything. I would not allow myself to get caught up in the depths that these people would go to. As I saw it. The less time I spent with them, the staff, the better. I had already proven, Kwame's capabilities, now it was for Miss Reynolds to work out a way of asserting herself that promoted my son's learning.

The days were much warmer now, as one season ended, and a more optimistic one began. It was a good thing. It meant the boys and I could divert from our usual routine of school to home, or mentoring club, and were spending a bit more time at the park during the warmer evenings. Of course, this also added as an incentive for Kwame to maintain positive behaviour at school. As I sat on the bench in the park watching the boys play, I found my mind wandering back to earlier years. The years when the boys had been much younger, just babies. We'd come a long way since then. I certainly had. Judging by the current circumstances, I knew we had a lot more ground to cover, we were hardly out of the woods yet. But at least we were here now. Right here, in the park. Me with both my son's. You can't put a price on a moment. Especially not when we had to endure so much recently. Only several weeks earlier I thought there was a chance that I would lose them forever. I had firmly believed that this was possible. Despite the fact I wasn't prepared to go down without a fight. It was still quite a lot to deal with. Particularly as my experience had demonstrated to me the type of families that came to the attention of social services. Based on my perception of us, our family. I had to be honest in saying none of those families looked or sounded like us. This current situation that we were entwined in, was nothing I would ever have imagined for us. I could barely fathom how we could meet any criteria for abuse, yet my eyes were being prized open with metaphorical twigs, and my ability to see beyond what I thought I knew, was improving dramatically.

I had completed the assignment and submitted it. I didn't want to wait until after the child protection conference to submit. I wanted to have a clean slate after the conference. There was no reason why the boys would be placed on the CP register I was confident about that. So with the assignment complete, all that would be left for me to finish off, would be any remaining days at placement, which I knew would not exceed a week, and then a clean slate in September for year two. The communication from the University was quite specific, in that it did say that a final decision about my future on the course, would be made pending the outcome of this investigation. By investigation, that main conclusion of the CP conference I assumed. So basically, by the time we returned from our summer holiday, everything would go back to normal. Although we may well, bare the invisible yet mental scars as evidence of the experience, the rest of our lives would at least return to our own level of normality. Plus, I noticed that I'd been feeling a lot tenser than I used to. I was more impatient, intolerant. I found myself being short at times, with the boys and the people around me whom I loved and held dearly. I was isolating myself more. Ordinarily I love to spend time with myself, I am naturally reclusive, as much as I like to spend time with the people I love.

However, since this whole thing had started, I definitely preferred to spend even more time alone. This way I didn't have to feel the need to talk about it. I didn't want to talk, I just needed to survive. It was embarrassing to say the least. An otherwise private person, being subjected to what felt like, quite a public investigation for want of a better word, a flogging. I understood how government services worked, data protection, and information sharing. Nevertheless, all of it made me uncomfortable. Anything written in Black and White can appear completely distorted from what it might be if you look through a lens. That was how I saw what was happening to us. Hasty conclusions, judgements, pre-judgements. On what basis?

I am by way of virtue a hard mum. I'm tough on my son's. I don't think I know how to be anything else. If I didn't know better, I would tell you I'm not tough on them at all. But that would be dishonest. I am tough and I make no apologies for it. The way I see things my children are my responsibility, so I raise them in the way that I see fit. I do not want my son's criminalised I do not want them abused by authorities and legal professionals. My hope is, if I set the boundaries at home, strangers do not have to abuse my children in the name of the law, or justice. If I believe you do not wish my son's well, you will not chastise them!

Often in public, I noticed the approach of other parents in comparison to mine, young and old. I noticed boundaries if any. I noticed language and I noticed basic manners. I'm not saying I noticed these things because these were things I did better than anyone else. Quite the opposite. I simply happen to notice anything that was different from what we had been taught as children, what I had been taught as a child and what I believed in now as an adult. I can admit I understand and have always understood, that parents raise their children according to what they can cope with. And I think that's fine. I tried to impress basic manners upon all my children, because I can't cope with blatant rudeness.

Just to give you a tiny example, if either of my son's cough or sneeze, they are expected to cover their mouth, because in my opinion, it's disgusting not to. However, for some parents that's not a big deal, but for me it is. That is a vague example of what I'm talking about. To the person sat opposite me and my son's on the bus, perhaps I look like an unrealistic mum expecting the children to cover their mouths, or say 'excuse me' before interrupting me if I were speaking. Believe me when I say I have received stares when I address my children. However, what is my alternative? To raise my children in the way that they did on soaps such as EastEnders, Emmerdale and Coronation Street. No. You see I can't stress enough that parents, parent according to their own set of beliefs morals and principles. This does not include those who abuse their children. Rather I'm referring to parents who are very clear on their intentions for their child or children, and raise them according to those values. Having my son's and being clear about what they were being born into, and what I needed them to achieve from it all, I prioritised basic elements that they needed to possess in order to survive. Now that may differ from what the textbooks states. I may have my own hierarchy of needs that differ to those specified by Maslow. Nonetheless, I am entitled to. My voice may have more bass in it, than yours. Therefore, when I raise my voice to my children, maybe that startles you. Maybe the room shakes I don't know, I've never noticed.

However, I too am startled when I hear a child tell a parent 'I hate you or shut up!' I hope my point is clear. You see different strokes for different folks.

I remember watching soap operas on the TV, where children

222

would shout or scream at their parents and slam doors. Well I'm sorry. I'm not familiar with that line of parenting and there was no way my children, my son's, were going to be either. It was important to me that none of our family values were distorted with mixed messages. I didn't care if the teacher told everyone at school, they did not need to cover their mouth when they sneeze or cough. My sons were still expected to. It didn't matter if the little girl next door was allowed to come and knock for my children at 19:30 on a weeknight. That was not in my opinion appropriate for a child of my sons' ages, so I accepted that her parents gave her permission to do so. But Kwame and Cassius knew better, meaning unfortunately they would not be joining her. It just wasn't what we did. So as far as my parenting was concerned, I was definitely 'old school' by my own admission and that of others. The funniest thing was, that despite how others saw my parenting, I wasn't going to change to reflect anything other than my own upbringing, my own culture. I admit that in the immediate aftermath after the initial call I thought I was going to collapse and die. All of a sudden everything I thought I had, just seem to crumble and disappear and all I could see was my son's left amongst the rubble. But the fact was, that somehow, I was still here. I hadn't given up. I did have my moments. Many, many moments. But look, today was another day. The sun was shining, the boys were smiling, and we were here, together. I reminded myself how important it was to take a trip down my own memory lane to allow myself to express these moments of gratitude.

Despite the uncertainty of what tomorrow held. At least we had today. They may well continue to judge us, but I was in this for the long haul.

CHAPTER 34

I jumped out of bed. SHIT, we were late. I called to Cassius and Kwame as I rushed to the kitchen, tripping over my slippers and banging my toenail before gripping on to the worktop for dear life, sure I was about to end up with a concussion. But sure, enough the worktop had saved me from flying head first into the corner of the cupboard so I would live to tell the tale. With all the excitement of a near death experience, I decided to slow down slightly as I prepared breakfast for the boys.

It was the day of the child protection conference and my stomach was wreaking havoc on me. I was nervous as anything. I barely slept a wink the night before. I'd been on the phone to Gf, feeling quite sorry for myself before I eventually went to bed. Then I got up, had a glass of wine and tried to watch some TV. Still no joy. So next I decided to eat my dinner that I'd left in the microwave from earlier. I took a few mouthfuls and then put it back in the microwave, knowing I wouldn't eat it the following day. I just couldn't sleep. When I eventually fell asleep, I woke up approximately every hour after, until now, when surprisingly, I overslept. This was my worst nightmare. The whole point of me being present at the conference was to speak on behalf of my family and to listen and hear the views of the school and Elsa. I could not walk in there late, or worse still not at all. No. I was not afraid, and I would not give the impression that I was afraid. I was not in the wrong, and for that reason I would face Elsa, the Trenchbull, and her accomplice.

'Kwame, Cassius! C'mon we're late for school'

I was fretting about being late for the CP conference, but the truth is, before I could even make my way there, I first needed to get these boys to school, in record breaking time.

Having forgotten for a moment, my recent near-death experience I went back to racing around the kitchen like a headless chicken. Jumped in the shower whilst the boys were still eating breakfast and threw on a smart pair of trousers and a top. Luckily my clothes had been arranged from the night before, otherwise I'd be in trouble. I ironed clean shirts for the boys and helped them do the buttons to save time, in between combing my hair. Finally we were ready. It was almost inevitable that we were going to be late for school but at this rate, not more than 10 or 15 minutes. Besides, that 10 or 15 minutes would not be reflective of my arrival time to the conference, as it still gave me time to find parking and take a quick breather, before I entered the 'lion's den' free to be mauled by all.

James had called me the night before, to see how I was feeling about things. He explained to me that if I wanted them to attend, either him or Kevron would. I had thought about it for the moment but decided that I would attend on my own. We ended up having a good chat on the phone, James was positive. Having got to know the boys personally, both him and Kevron were finding it hard to understand what was going on at school that was causing this much concern, particularly after the initial disclosure of abuse had been unsubstantiated. He had also tried to reassure me that there was no evidence to support the children having to go on the child protection register. I knew he was right too. Nevertheless, the support from Kevron, James and Andre made such a huge difference to the boys and me. I made one last dash to the bathroom before we jumped in the car ready to start the day! I walked the boys into the reception area to sign them in as they were late. The receptionist was courteous, as she was most days. However, I didn't allow that to confuse me, she knew what was going on I think her role doubled up as Miss O'Connor's PA as well, so no doubt she had also been instrumental in facilitating communication between school and Local Authority. That wasn't much of a big deal to me though. I have a thing about balancing my expectations of other people. Like I said before, particularly those who I know don't have the same intentions for me or mine, as I do.

Cassius had been moaning in the car about being late for school.

Kwame on the other hand didn't seem to be perturbed at all. Neither were aware of the gravity of today. I preferred that. After all it wasn't their problem to worry about. I signed in the boys, wondering if Miss O'Connor and Miss Reynolds would both be at the conference. I knew there would be a representative from the school, and something told me Miss O'Connor would not pass up this opportunity. They probably didn't need Miss Reynolds to attend too, I mean why would she need her voice box if she was going to physically be there also. My thoughts were that Miss O'Connor didn't need Miss Reynolds for this bit. Miss Reynolds' had done as she was expected. Now the ball was firmly in Miss O Connor's court, all she had to do was bounce and aim. I mean serve. And no, I can't play tennis in case you couldn't tell.

I escorted both the boys to their classrooms and noticed both of their class teachers were present. That told me that the chances were, neither of these teachers would be attending the conference. Good.

Back in the car I selected my favourite dancehall cd, turned the volume to max and made my way to the conference. I knew I would have at least 10 minutes to reflect and prepare myself before walking in, so I decided to use the time to do anything but think about what lay ahead. I'd done enough of that during my insomnia infestation the previous night. If I was going to have the energy to fight, I needed my music therapy first. I managed to park my car on a side road, as it was the only spot where I could park for free for an hour, or more if worse came to the worst. Personally, the thought of being there for more than an hour made me feel nauseated. But the only thing I had to do was attend this meeting and collect my sons from school. Nevertheless, I prayed the meeting lasted an hour maximum.

I walked into the reception area and looked around at the other people sat on the chairs waiting. There were a number of women in the reception. A Somali woman who had what appeared to be a new-born baby in her arms. A young white couple, who every minute or so popped out for a cigarette. Even though they looked young to me, they were probably the same age as me. I imagined their story wasn't the same as mine though.

Nearest to me, a young black girl was sat, she looked about 20 and was sat by herself. She had been on the phone quite a bit, despite the signs asking visitors to refrain from speaking on their phone in the reception area. Her conversations had been loud, leaving me to piece together parts of her conversation, resulting in my knowledge that she was waiting for her social worker. She didn't seem that bothered about having a social worker, not like me I was very bothered. From what I gathered from her phone call, she had been making demands with regards to her new-born who had recently been removed, courtesy of an ICO I assumed, and as her social worker had not been returning her calls, she had turned up today, clearly not happy. A huge part of me felt really sorry for her. I wanted to talk to her, to say something, to offer some kind of compassion, but how could I. You don't just approach a person and expect them to start engaging in a conversation about their personal life. That was unheard of. Besides, I was hardly in a position to start offering compassion, empathy or even advice for that matter. Based heavily on the reasons I had found myself in that very reception area on this God given day, alongside this young lady. As I listened to her on the phone, I kept reminding myself that I could not offer advice to her. I couldn't go around offering advice to people without being asked.

Furthermore, how was I, in anyway qualified to do so? From where I was stood, I was hardly winning. Yet still I wanted to support her. I wanted to help her, to say something kind, offer some solace. I gathered she was speaking to her boyfriend, who sounded as though he was asking a great deal of questions, she was unable to answer. Subsequently leading to her raising her voice in frustration, to the point of tears. Now she was going to make me cry too. I reached in my bag and gave her a tissue, she said thanks and continued wiping her tears away. I didn't know the particulars of her situation, however I felt as though I could feel her pain. A gift, a curse, I'm not quite certain, but I'd like to go with the former. A gift. A gift I had harnessed ever since I was a young child. I had an inept way of feeling things. Perhaps it had something do with being in-tune with my emotions. If I read about something devastating, my mind would immediately venture to, 'what would I do if that were me' or 'how would I feel if that were me'. Either way, the result, was almost always, inescapable emotions. Possible tears, or at least, very watery eyes, sadness, change in mood etc. This is who I am. I know I am not alone, because we live in a time where the world experiences horrific tragedies and a nation cries with its victims and survivors. Think 9/11…. think Grenfell Tower. I know I was not the only person who shed a tear. It was almost impossible not to. On both occasions, we watched images on the news of human beings just like us, jumping to their fate in hope of an escape, knowing the risk was potentially no escape at all. Both pained my heart to watch. How could I not consider what may have gone through their minds during those last moments? How could I remain emotionally intact after hearing the screams on the news amidst the reporter's voice? Devastating does not even begin to describe. Hence why I am an advocate of support being offered to those that may have been affected by either tragedies, even if not directly impacted. Because I understand how emotions work, and I also understand that not all of us can thrive off logic. We cannot all be like Dr Spock. Some of us can share emotional connections with anything and anyone. As I write this, I realise it may sound like a curse. However, what may be a curse to some, has been a blessing to me. This has remained my driving force for supporting people who have experienced difficult challenges in their lives. I'd like to think that I am an individual, who knows what it is like to feel alone, hurt, unsupported, isolated, judged. Therefore, I endeavour to be that someone for someone else, wherever I can. Maybe that's Karma...? I don't pretend to have the answers. I only know that this is the way I have been, for as far back as I can recall.

I watched as the young lady appeared to eventually hang up on the boyfriend, who, from a third parties' perspective, was making her feel worse. She turned and smiled at me, so I took the opportunity to say something.

'Are you okay?' I asked offering a friendly smile.

'Yes thanks', she replied smiling back, and dabbing her eyes gently with the tissue I had given her.

'Yolanda, we're ready for you'

Elsa had come through to the reception to collect me. I looked over it the young lady beside me and smiled. A smile seemed appropriate, as we hadn't got as far as actual introductions. I really did hope that she would be ok, but I had to leave now. I had to go and tend with my own fate. I gave her a final wave, as I followed Elsa to the room where the conference would be held. I mouthed good luck to her, and she mouthed back, thanks. The look on her face made me feel better. No longer crying, or shouting through tears, she looked courageous now. Amazing what tears can do, I thought smiling to myself, for just a moment forgetting where I was heading.

CHAPTER 35

I entered the large boardroom, where a sturdy, but old table was permanently sat in the middle of the room. My eyes ran across the room quickly, counting approximately 10 individuals sat around the table. Most of which I didn't recall having seen or met before, aside from Elsa, Miss O'Connor and Mr Davis, who I believe was the Deputy Head teacher and also head of lower juniors at Kwame and Cassius' school. I didn't recognise the others, but immediately found my eyes drawn to the two uniforms sat at the table. I couldn't for the life of me figure out why the uniforms were in attendance. Even if they were invited, did we not have enough crime on our streets for them to contend with? They had been authorised time off work to attend our conference. Our non-criminal case. I wasn't sure this was the best use of public funds, nor could I comprehend why they had felt the need to attend, but hey I understand. It was a public flogging. Much like the old days, (before my time), when the entire town would come out to watch a beheading or a hanging. I guess this was a modern day humane, and more gracious form of such. Chairs, tables, formal clothing and uniforms alike. Oh yes this was much better than the old days. Elsa politely ushered me to a chair and indicated for me to sit down. I wasn't sure if it was intentional, but there were about three seats between myself and the Chair of the conference who was sat at the head of the table. Forgive my analogy in advance, because the seating arrangements reminded me of a painting that used to hang in one of my Auntie s houses'. It was a painting signifying The Last supper with Jesus and the Disciples. In the painting the table was laden with exquisite food, wine, goblets and the disciples were smiling and celebrating with Jesus. I couldn't help but think about how fitting the comparison was at this moment. According to the Bible, Jesus knew that he would be betrayed that night. That was pretty much how I felt. Looking around the table I knew that the representatives here, were not representing my family. I mean they were hardly traitors either, because I had never mistaken them for being friends or otherwise. Yet still, something about the entire set up, reminded me of the fateful painting.

I sat down and smiled courteously, not too much, just a slight curl either end of my mouth. I decided to take a closer look around the table. I still didn't recognise the faces. One of the women around the table had a jug of water nearby and was refilling her glass as though it had been especially filtered for her very existence. Slightly pompous. I turned my attention back to the chair of the meeting, a middle-aged White woman with a sort of musty brown coloured hair. I told myself she had been dying her hair, and this was an amalgamation of leftover colours as a result.

'Good morning Yolanda' the Chair of the meeting greeted me formally but smiled in what I believe was the friendliest smile she could locate at that moment. I returned her smile as pleasantly as I could and greeted her. She went on to explain the purpose of the conference and the order in which things would take place. She advised me that they would start with introductions, whereby everyone around the table would introduce themselves, along with their role, and purpose in terms of the conference, including me. After which Elsa would be required to explain why we were here, and then the chair would listen to reports from around the table. Reports about us, my family. They would read reports about us. They, that didn't know us. Lastly, she explained that I would be given an opportunity to speak, before each member of the conference would decide, whether they felt it was necessary for my son's to be placed on the child protection register, and if so, under which category. The categories at the time (as I am aware there have since been amendments):

Physical, Emotional, Sexual, Neglect. None of which I felt resonated with us, but nevertheless those were the categories they would have to select from. If a Child Protection plan was the case, it would be for an initial period of approximately three months before a review was held to determine if the situation had changed, either improved, or declined. If so, the boys would remain on the register this time with a review held after 6 months and so on. In my case, the alternative was that if there was no need for the children to be placed on the child protection register, then alternative support would be explored, for example a Children in Need (CIN) plan.

The Chair offered me a glass of water, or tea, which I politely declined, and the meeting commenced. The meeting commenced and the Chair began by introducing herself and suggested we go around the table clockwise. I listened attentively and jotted names down in my notepad that I never left home without, just in case. Present we had, the Chair, Elsa, Elsa's manager, a Police Officer, a Child Protection Police Officer, Miss O'Connor, Mr Davis, an Educational Psychologist and a minute taker. All of these people had taken time out of their day to show up for the flogging. Now it was my turn.

'I am Yolanda, Kwame and Cassius' mother'

I was sure to speak my words assertively. Making sure each word singularly made a statement. These boys we were here about to discuss were mine! My Son's.

I had carried them in my womb. That was all me. I could recall days when Kwame would kick vigorously within my stomach from the early hours of the morning. The immense feeling of gratitude I felt at being chosen for the part. This coupled with the memory of Cassius doing somersaults in my tightly crammed belly, giving onlookers the impression that there was some alien like thing moving within me. I remembered all of that. Just like I remembered the moment I went into labour with each of them. Each experience so far from the last. And yet, as I sat here, and reminisced, I could feel something again within my stomach. The fire, it was stirring again. I was uncomfortable about being subjected to this intrusion. I resented my life being discussed openly by strangers. Who granted them authority to judge me anyhow? What were their credentials? I would not succumb to this, this authoritative bullying. I didn't care how many of them I had to face, this was 'one for all and all for one'. In this case we were the Musketeers, all three of us. Me, Kwame and Cassius. These were my sons. And no one, but no one, was taking them!

CHAPTER 36

Elsa began by explaining the initial disclosure and how this and other concerns had led to a referral from the school. She explained about the child protection medical and the subsequent results that she had previously shared with me. When it got around to the uniforms. The police officer explained that he did not in actual fact have any information or intelligence on me. But went on to discuss concerns relating to my ex. I could feel my blood boiling, but I decided it best to let him finish, before I interrupted. He went on, in his most formal and matter-of-fact tone of voice before deciding his point had been made. The chair spoke.

'Do any of these details in any way relate to Yolanda, Kwame or Cassius?'

'No, not directly'

EXACTLY, was what I wanted to shout out loud. However, I smirked inside, and chose to say nothing. After all that was my sentiment exactly.

Nevertheless, I can't lie, I was irritated at the depths the uniform would go to. I wonder if his manager and or colleagues had a list of his exes. I would think it would be more prudent to learn who the uniforms exes were don't you think? Why did mine matter? If I had a high-flying CEO as my ex, would that be a point for discussion here and now? I doubt it. The uniforms comments, reiterated to me how selectively information can be used by those with authority or power, to discredit individuals. Again a bit like our current judicial system. Yes, I agree we need a judicial system. However, its reliability is at times questionable. A group of 12 strangers selected to judge are presented with carefully selected information aimed to prove guilt. Not innocence. Have you ever attended a court hearing? Ever heard a prosecutor bring up allegations that were later dropped or unsubstantiated? Relevant? Ever heard a prosecutor refer to associations of the accused in order to discredit character? What's the purpose of this? Better still is this empowering? Does it improve the future quality of life? How does the stigma impact the accused? All of these were valid questions to me. What was the intention of the uniform here today? Was this about my son's, me or a hidden agenda?

The Child protection Police officer spoke next. She explained that she had no record of any concerns relating to the boys. Our GP and health visitor had also been invited but unlike the others sat around the table, had other things, perhaps more significant and vital things, to do with their time. They had declined the invitation but forwarded reports. The health visitor mentioned that she had no concerns aside from the fact the boys had not yet received their most recent injections. This was true as I had been in two minds about the immunisations. Our GP said virtually the same, only added that although he had seen Cassius when he had caught chicken pox previously. Cassius was not in fact registered at the surgery. I was surprised by this comment, as Cassius was almost 5, meaning for 5 years they had neglected to tell me that. Even when I visited the GP for treatment of his chickenpox. That could easily be rendered I thought, I'll do that later.

Mr Davis chose to speak. He reported that Cassius' teacher had referred to him as very quiet, shy even. Although she admitted, he was very popular with the other children. Mr Davis added

'His reluctance to speak does concern us. We don't know if he's bottling up his emotions or otherwise'.

You what!

I looked at him, my eyebrows raised as though to question his addition to Miss Franklin comments. What on earth was this man talking about? How was he in a position to make assumptions like that? He had read the report, as had I, as we each had a copy during the conference. However, he'd decided to then add his own dim-witted opinion. Still I said nothing. I would not allow myself to be portrayed like I had no decorum, or self-control.

Then on to Miss O'Connor. Who had written a lengthy report on Kwame's behaviour in class, stipulating his inability to follow instructions and complete class work? Adding a generous helping of 'he tends to get quite upset at the smaller things'. Oh and of course, she had to add that despite his challenges at school, I had declined to authorise the Educational Psychologist to observe him, resulting in the school struggling to support him in class. She also mentioned that I had flicked Kwame on a recent school trip.

I added 'because he was not behaving appropriately and was using words I don't condone'.

'Thank you, Yolanda,' said the Chair as if to say, we've heard enough.

Miss O Connor also stated that she observed a difference in the way I treated the boys. This was a new one! She explained that I kiss one goodbye and wave the other goodbye. Not to mention that she had heard me tell Kwame off after school about his behaviour one day, and felt I was 'hard' on him. Oh, and for good measure, she added as a credit to me, that I had been voluntarily coming in and supporting the class up until the disclosure. I wanted to shout 'shut ya damn mouth!' Yet still, I sat there wondering why even bother to mention it. My question mentally rhetorical, as I already knew why she had mentioned it. A pathetic attempt to not appear biased. I noticed the added addendum about me treating the boys differently too. As she read her report, she looked up at me during intervals. I stared back at her, even when she looked away to continue reading. Still I said nothing.

There were other attendees who had been invited, who had also not been able to attend. Kwame and Cassius' old nursery Manager. Imagine. Their nursery. And Dolores from the play centre. Wow. They had certainly gone through a lot of trouble to find out about us, I wondered why they hadn't invited my hairdresser too.

As the two were not in attendance, Elsa read the reports from the nursery and Dolores. The report from the nursery I felt went straight to the point. The nursery had described the boy's characters, spoke positively of me and my relationship with them. That was about it. Nothing major. Delores' report was lengthier in content, although I hadn't had a chance to browse it prior to Elsa reading it out. Dolores explained that the boys had spent the holiday period at the play centre and had enjoyed it. Exactly, I thought smugly. Then she went on to say that she had observed that I treat the boys differently! She reported that after the boys attended a trip with the play centre, they had returned and Kwame had bought me a gift, a mug. Delores stated that I had thanked Kwame but hugged Cassius although he had not brought me a gift. I felt my jaw drop involuntarily. Delores had really said that. Why would she say that? What was she talking about? Yes, I remembered the mug, the trip ... but what of it. How did she come to the conclusion that I treated the boys differently? I was livid. So that's why she hadn't turned up. How could she look me in my face and say that? Coward. If she firmly believed that, why had she not contacted social services? Why be concerned after, a visit from Elsa? I started wondering if they were trying to drive a wedge between my sons. Divide and conquer.

I don't like people who are not upfront. I consider myself to be someone who speaks her truth. I do so because as I mentioned before, my Mum was the law when I was a child. So, my only fear was her. Therefore, expressing injustice was something I wasn't afraid to do. Standing up for myself, was something I was innately taught, and with it, the notion that my opinion on something, did not have to matter to someone else, but if it mattered to me. I would stand behind it. I couldn't understand all the whispering. I had no respect for Delores. The fire in my belly was in full blaze. I struggled to submerge the words, fighting for dear life to make their way to my widely opened mouth. I wanted to march out of the boardroom. I knew this was a flogging, but not even I, had anticipated all of this. What was really going on here? What questions did Elsa ask to initiate such information? Was it a mere coincidence that Delores had regurgitated the same blasphemous lie as Miss O'Connor? I found it hard to believe. I just about had enough when the Chair announced that they would now have to make a decision as to what whether the boys will be placed on the child protection register or an alternative Child in Need plan. The chair addressed Elsa and asked for her views, and whether she had any concerns relating to the boys and their need to be subject to a child protection plan. Elsa cleared her throat before responding.

'Yes' she started, I do feel the boys should be subject to a child protection plan.'

The Chair asked for her reasons.

'Because I feel Yolanda uses inappropriate language when

speaking to the boys'

'Inappropriate Language!' I exclaimed unable to prevent the words from escaping.

The Chair interjected. 'Can you elaborate?'

Elsa showed no hesitation before she started speaking again.

'I undertook a visit to the family home one evening' she stated the date. 'Kwame was doing his homework and asked Yolanda for the definition of the word soluble. Yolanda refused to explain the definition and I feel that was inappropriate language for her to expect a child of his age to know what that word meant'

I interrupted again.

'So, let me get this straight, because my expectation of my son, differs to your expectation of him, particularly as you are referring to a boy of his age and not him personally, that means the language I am using is inappropriate? Not taking into consideration that he had been learning about materials at school, and the definitions of these words. Therefore, when doing his homework, I expect him to know what that word means Elsa'.

I spoke calmly, trying hard to disguise my fury, and addressed Elsa, ignoring the panel of strangers sat at the table.

'The other problem Elsa is it you have a standard expectation of a boy my son's age, whereas my expectation is based solely on his capabilities. One size does not fit all, therefore I treat my son's not according to your standards but to ours.'

'Thank you, Yolanda,' The chair spoke as to finalise the debate that would soon be emerging between myself and Elsa and anyone else who felt the need to stick up for her. I didn't see why I should sit there and let her say such illiterate garbage, as a means for placing my sons on a child protection register. Under what category is expecting him to know the definition of a word abusive or harmful, or better yet 'inappropriate language?' An hour had already passed, we were not finished, and I was now fuming. I mean smoke coming from my ears. The Chair went around the table in turn and asked, each stranger to give their views on my family's fate. It was a resounding yes to the boys being placed on the child protection register, one by one. After the fiasco with Elsa, the chair didn't ask for reasoning. Why? Because she seemed to accept the strangers had good reason for their judgements. After all they were professionals. Now that the initial stones had been slung my way. The decision under which category the children would be placed on the child protection register, was in question. She went through the categories and asked for suggestions as to which category the strangers felt would fit their concerns better. They deliberated like I was invisible. I suppose I didn't expect any better. Obviously, it was pointless asking me which category because I didn't feel it was necessary in the first place. I listened on, as the strangers formally discussed my son's like children of the state. And by state, I mean children they had somehow legally adopted so had now formed some kind of responsibility for.

Elsa's manager suggested emotional abuse, as they hadn't been able to identify the cause of Kwame's behaviour. Miss O'Connor agreed, citing Cassius' unwillingness to talk freely to staff. Elsa piped up to refer to the initial disclosure in support of the added category of physical abuse, but it was decided the boys did not fall within the category. Shame!

It was decided that my sons would be placed on the register under the category of Emotional Abuse.

Attention turned back to me, as the chair asked if there was any support, I felt we could benefit from based as part of the plan. F******* cheek! I was tempted to say. What does it matter what I want? Didn't you just sit there and allow them to put forward one sided, biased unscrupulous argument and then make a decision against my favour anyway. She didn't need my input. No one cared about me, or us. The tears were now gathered in a puddle at the bottom of throat, much like a hole in the pavement filled with rain. I didn't speak. I didn't want to speak. There was no one around this table whom I wanted to communicate with. I wanted to say, none of you care about my sons. You'd rather me leave society to raise them. So, you could later chastise, beat and abuse them, until they were angry and unrecognisable, to the decent well-educated and positive black men I prayed they would be.

They wanted my son's to become statistics, to fall into the trap. I wasn't going to let that happen. I felt winded, like being soccer punched fight in the gut, I felt discomfort. I looked around at the faces that wore absolutely no concern for my sons. Perhaps the problem was not my son's. Perhaps the problem was with me. Maybe they believed I needed to be taught a lesson. Was this about my reluctance to conform and take orders? My reluctance to send Kwame to a Special School or authorise the Educational

Psychologist? Or was this merely about my reluctance to raise my children in the way that they felt was fit? Or was this because I was 25 with two young children. Two young boys. Was this about the predetermined unscrupulous future they foresaw for my son's based on their obsessive, internal, prejudice? Clearly there were disparities in the expectations for my sons. Elsa had made that clear, still insisting on puking up garbage for all to endure.

And what was that about not identifying the cause of Cassius' reluctance to engage in nonsensical conversations, or Kwame's behaviour in the classroom. Had it ever occurred to anybody that his behaviour was a result of something else?

There had been no mention of the boys having started a new school only still quite recently, no mention of the fact that neither one of the boys wanted to change school. No mention of potential difficulties with the transition. For some reason, as I listened to the strangers speak, one thing was intrinsically apparent. Each placed the onus on the home. External factors were only discussed in support of an implication of wrongdoing. That wasn't how you support a family.

If professionals felt a family was in need, is this the approach for support? Judgement and ridicule?

'I have already mentioned to Elsa that I'd like the boys to receive mentoring from a local mentoring service I have sourced'

Elsa's manager spoke up again.

'Elsa has discussed this with me, and I am aware that she explained to Yolanda we do have an in-house mentoring service'.

'And Elsa may not have told you, but I have said I do not want to use your in-house mentoring service, I would like a service that is culturally appropriate for my sons'.

'Please can I also request a social worker that is culturally appropriate for my family too?'

Elsa's manager spoke up again.

'Do you mean a Caribbean social worker Yolanda?'

What was wrong with this woman? Today had been the first day I met her, and already she was grating on me.

'No, I mean one that is culturally appropriate, African, or Caribbean descent I don't care. And it might be a good idea if she's a mum, someone with an actual understanding of day to day parenting, but please whatever you do. Do not send me a White social worker who has completely different values to me, because clearly the difference in beliefs, impacts the views on my family subsequently affecting the decisions you are making about me and my son's. This is not about race more than it is about what is appropriate, even suitable. Even I know, no matter how many books you read, it does not equip you for real-life parenting' Elsa's manager looked surprised. Maybe she was shocked by my request. I wasn't sure which bit surprised her most. That I made the request openly. Or that I was raising the issue of cultural difference, Race and their possible impact. Whatever it was, I had the right to make that request, so I was making it. They didn't have to honour it, but it would go down in the minutes that I made the request. As we were going to be here again in three months for a review, if it had not been done, I would mention it again, and again and Again! You get my drift right.

Elsa's manager sighed and pursed her lips tightly together in exasperation. Clearly, she wanted me to know she thought my request was unnecessary. Like I cared that she felt. Did anyone care about us? Did anyone give any thought to how this decision would impact me, about the impact now today when I then had to go home to those children, whom they said, were at risk? To be honest I felt that if they were so concerned maybe they should be concerned about how a crazy woman may react to such a harsh decision, such as the one that they had just imposed on me. However, I knew that wouldn't be the case. Their job here had been done. Fateful decision made, without a second thought.

'If you are not willing to commission the mentoring service I have found, I am not willing for my sons to attend mentoring', I told Elsa's manager, wanting to make it clear during the conference so we would not be revisiting the conversation again. There was nothing else they could do, they had already placed my sons on the child protection register, and I would never give the local authority cause or the satisfaction of removing my sons from my care. After discussion around various areas of support. The chair concluded the meeting, reports were collected, and strangers dismissed. I got up to leave and Elsa ran over to me.

'Oh, Yolanda, I probably won't see you again, because now you'll be allocated a new social worker'

'That's great news Elsa' I replied turning around to the leave the boardroom. If I never saw her again it would be too soon.

CHAPTER 37

Despite how I sounded, I left the meeting feeling disheartened. I knew what this decision meant for me. I had read up on it prior to the meeting and the last few nights leading up to. The child protection plan made me feel like I was being watched, observed. Like having a permanent camera on your life for all to see. If Kwame had an asthma attack and we had to go to hospital, social services would be notified. If Cassius fell over and injured himself, requiring any kind of medical attention, again they would be notified. If the boys for any reason had an incident at school, social services will be notified. The thought occurred to me that we did not have shared parental responsibility, yet all information about my son's was being shared. The thought alone, made me feel even worse, as I sat in my car, still unable to drive. On one hand, it felt like the battle had been won, yet I knew on the other hand this was just an on-going battle. I had succeeded yes, in keeping my son's, and I cannot express gratitude to the extent of which I felt it, for that mere fact alone. However, the decision that had just been made, didn't sit well with me. The child protection plans my children were about to be placed on, would mean our personal information would arrive at certain destinations, where summaries in the form of a report, would now precede or at least shadow us. This wasn't right. Now people wouldn't take us as they saw us, but they would look at the facts that supported what they would believe, they already knew. This was otherwise referred to as stigma. The stigma of a young, single mum, and two children subject to a child protection plan. Can we just imagine for a moment what it would look like, if I had to rush one of the children to A&E for an emergency and the database would show they were subject to child protection. Well I can tell you, the care we'd receive would likely be more thorough, because the report subsequently submitted would detail everything including whether or not the children were well kept or appeared malnourished. Luckily my children could never be accused of being malnourished, they had far too healthy a relationship with food for that. As for well kept, they were always well kept, that was not optional. Despite how I might have looked on some occasions, my sons were always well kept.

I stared out the window for some time, watching passers-by and looking at shoppers entering the neighbouring supermarket. It reminded me that I needed to get some bits for the house, but I wasn't in the mood to walk around the shops. Today we'll eat fast food, I wasn't in the mood to cook. Besides, now I had to start thinking about what I was going to do in September, because there was no way I was going to be allowed to finish my degree. I could wait for a decision, but by then it would be too late for me to do something else. Based on the premise that it was highly unlikely, they would welcome me back, I needed to start thinking about an alternative course. It was either that or full-time work. Although as quickly as the thought entered my mind, I pushed it aside, because full-time work would mean that an employer would require more of my time. Meaning I would have less time for my sons. I would then have the task of making sure someone was able to look after them, someone meaning grandparents or maybe my brother. But I didn't want to burden anybody. That was part of the reason why I had chosen to undertake part-time work. I wanted to be available for school runs, that was important to me. I didn't want to feel like a burden in the workplace, which is how I was often made to feel because I had childcare commitments. No, I wasn't quite ready for full-time work. I would rather work two part time jobs, with hours suited around my commitments. So back to square one. Now what was I to do?

I had only just started to seriously contemplate the question when a knock on the window made me jump.

It was the traffic warden telling me I had to move, otherwise he was giving me a ticket. I looked up at him, the look on his face showed intolerance. I wondered what the look on my face showed, because part of me was tempted to open the window and start shouting like a lunatic, but I caught myself. I had no reason to shout at the traffic warden knocking my window. Yes, he had frightened me, and that had inevitably tempted me to say something. However, the way I was feeling at that moment, had nothing to do with the traffic warden knocking my window and frightening me out of my skin. Nothing to do with the fact he was talking to me and looking at me with intolerance. It didn't even have anything to do with the fact that I wasn't ready to start driving, and he was giving me an ultimatum, which could be seen as a challenge. Nevertheless, I knew that my anger would have been misplaced with him. Some might even say, wasted on him. It was not he who had placed my children on the child protection register. It was not him who it said those negative things about the language I used, which was not even about language. No, it was not him. Therefore, my anger was not directed at him, it need not be directed at him. I realised needed to find somewhere to put my emotions, somewhere safe, private. My emotions were all that I had left at this point, that I could keep private. Every other area of my life was currently subject to an invasion. Work, study, home, no area had been left untouched. No holds barred when pulling punches. I kept thinking back to the comments made by the uniform. Why had he felt the need to bring up that stuff? In no way did it bare any relevance to anything, except to try and distort our family, my character. Bringing my children into something that did not involve, concern, or pose any risk to them, it made me even more distrustful of their agenda. What about the fact that Elsa need to dumb information down so that she would feel more comfortable about my son's learning? How dare she? She didn't even have children, Elsa. She probably wouldn't last a day in my life. Yet there she sat, telling me that inappropriate use of language meant raising the bar for my son. Fool. And as for the Chair, why didn't she correct her? Why didn't she stipulate that inappropriate language might be an example of me using profanities, not me refusing to give my son the answer to his homework? I couldn't get over it. I could tell this was going to sit with me for life. Never would I forget the depths that these people would go to, simply to discredit you, for their own ulterior motives. That they would clutch at whatever was within their reach if they felt it could be used to support their personal theories. Come to think of it, was this even something I really wanted to go into? So far, our experience of social services had been like a tornado, only there had been no aftercare, no emergency relief services. Just a tornado leaving behind devastation I was left to clear up. To rebuild. This isn't what social workers were supposed to do. Jean was nothing like that. Neither were her team. They actually cared about families and young people. I'd observed them on many occasions doing their utmost to support a young person, to prevent unborn or young children being removed from their care. They didn't go out of their way to destroy families or break the spirits of single mothers. I mean being a single mum was hard enough. I'm not alone, I'm sure, in the fact that we frequently give ourselves a beating about how terrible a mother we are. Or how little time we spend with our children, or how the time we do spend with them, we're too tired to do any activities or entertain lengthy conversations. I could go on; the list is endless. The fact is that the social workers that I'd been working alongside were nothing like Elsa or her manager. I couldn't come to terms with the power that was given unduly to others, it left a bad taste in my mouth. Even if I would be the only one in an entire team that was rooting for families trying to empower them, I would still be part of a larger organisation that didn't necessarily have the same motives as me. That was going to be a problem. I could foresee it.

With social workers in a bid not to be scapegoated, being overzealous with cases, overworked. Families probably wouldn't stand a chance. There would be nothing humane about investigations and interactions, it would become a tick box exercise, with only one logical outcome. That was not my idea of Social Work. Yes, I agree it is vital that we have services that protect the vulnerable be it young or old. But then does that mean we need a separate service aimed at keeping families together. A service whose sole purpose is to keep families together. The more I thought about it, I was beginning to think that social work was not something I wanted to be a part of. Perhaps I would be a part of something else. Something that empowered other parents when they were faced with challenges such as mine. A service that stood up for parents when the Elsa's of the world attempted to defame their characters. Yes, that was what I would do. Not now mind you, I still had work to do. But definitely later. Definitely later.

CHAPTER 38

I didn't get a chance to call my mum before she called me to find out what had happened. I spoke to her who had been there, what had been said by each of them. Mum kept saying 'SO WHAT DID THE CHAIR SAY?' In her mind the chair was impartial and so therefore would challenge any comments on information that was not pertinent to the case. I agreed with Mum but explained to her that was not how it went down.

'How are you feeling?'

I started to respond and burst into tears. Everything that I had been holding in since the meeting before the meeting, during the meeting, last night even, came pouring out. Mum didn't speak allowing me to compose myself. Impatiently I tried to talk through the tears, desperate to share what had taken place.

'What am I gonna do now? That's a year of hard work wasted. I don't even want to be a social worker anymore. I hate them all. Parasites, devils. All they wanna do is destroy people. That way they can take your kids and put them with foster carers, then, when they've had enough, they give up. Because why would carers be invested? Even if they were invested, what about the child? I hate them mum I hate them!'

My mum still didn't respond but I knew she was there. It wasn't unusual for her to allow me that silence. Sometimes she would sit on the other end of the phone and allow me to rant, and then when I decided that I was finished, she would say 'Okaaaay'. That was her way of saying we will talk about this, but when you are in a better frame of mind. That's my mum. Even though at times this irritated me I had to appreciate that knowing myself as well as I do, I can't have certain conversations until I'm ready, mentally, emotionally. In the same way that Miss Reynolds and Miss O'Connor's constant nagging daily, about Kwame began to wear on my spirit. Before I even had a chance to get back up, they were kicking me down again. I don't function at my best like that. Hence why my Mums silence on the phone not only helped me to compose myself eventually, but to realise that I didn't have time to wallow in my sorrows and self-pity. I needed to think strategic. I needed somehow to bounce back, dust myself off.

'Mum?'

'I'm here' she replied calmly, as though she had not just heard me having a minor breakdown on the phone.

'You okay now?' she asked but really we both knew that what she meant was, 'Have you finished now?'

'Yes mum' I said blowing my nose. I was slowly returning to a more rational state of mind.

'I'm not going to continue with my degree. I'll wait for my transcript and see if the credits can be awarded towards something else. That way I won't have to start from scratch'

'Are you sure you want to do that?'

'Yes mum, even if I could go back. The way they've treated us, the way they've judged me, I don't want to. This intervention has made me know, I don't wanna be part of something that does to families, what it's done to us. The whole intervention has been disturbing, even for the boys. No. I don't want it. They can keep their degree. I'd rather stand for something more positive. I still want to work with young people and vulnerable people, but I'll find an alternative way to do it.'

'Fair enough' mum replied using a tone that made it clear she was in support.

'Are the boys going after school club today?'

'Yeah, I need a minute before I get them, and that way I don't have to see the 'Trenchbull' and her 'apprentice'.'

'Alright, I'll call you when I get in'.

I came off the phone to my mum and realised something. Mum hadn't really said much to me about the details of my rant, yet I come off the phone feeling like 'Yolanda you got this!' I had one more phone call to make, to the boys' other grandparents. I wanted to call and let them know what happened in the meeting. I knew, their Nan in particular, would be waiting anxiously by the phone. They had both been so supportive. My boys loved their Nan and Granddad. Weekends spent there, were like the best thing since sliced bread as far as they were concerned. We were blessed to have them, through everything no matter what they had always been there for us, there for the boys. I could still remember calling to tell them about the disclosure in the beginning. They were horrified, angry, upset. Yet they never once questioned my parenting. They knew me well enough; it had been long enough. Their support was unrivalled. Never would they let it be said, that I didn't have my son's best interest at heart. I love them dearly and will forever cherish them for that.

Their Nan must have had the phone in her hand, because it barely rang twice before she answered.

'Hi Yolanda...?' she answered as though it was a question. 'What happened?'

I went on to explain to her, as I had Mum, all that had been said in the meeting and the infamous outcome. She was shocked.

'So, what does this mean now?'

I explained about information being shared about us, should the boys need to be seen by any other professionals, including education.

'But that doesn't sound fair' she said.

'No, it isn't, but that's what will happen now. And we'll get a new social worker who will see us once I think every two weeks sometimes, they make an appointment, sometimes she'll turn up unannounced'

'Why does she need to turn up unannounced what do they think she's going to catch you doing?'

'Perhaps boiling the boys in a stew for dinner' I responded my sarcasm directed at the process.

I told her about my request for a culturally appropriate social worker and about asking them to get in touch with the mentoring service.

'Yes good, because I can't believe this. Listen Yolanda, you're a good mum and we all think you're a good mum'

The kind words brought a tear to my eye. It was so hard to face, even the people I loved and the people that loved us the most, with such a dark cloud hanging over us. I almost felt ashamed that my children were subject to a social services intervention. It was embarrassing. The intervention alone carried a stigma that only the family affected will ever be conscious of. Those imposing policies and procedures may not be aware of the stigma. They may well be oblivious to the way in which professionals can begin to look at you when your child falls off his bike and breaks an ankle, and you subsequently take a trip to A&E for urgent care. As far as they are concerned, they were just doing a job. However, for a number of parents like me, the stigma was like a stench following you everywhere you went.

Look at Dolores. I couldn't imagine what caused her to have concerns. Yet I couldn't help thinking that when you ask certain questions, then a person is forced to start searching for something that may support your theory. Like the hypothesis of a science experiment where you are expected to collect data to support your hypothesis. Or how about when the news reports of a heinous crime naming the individual responsible. In the aftermath there will always be a series of interviews by people who perhaps taught that person when they were a child at school, or an ex-girlfriend who broke up with that person. All of a sudden, each individual can recall an event from their interaction with that person that's in some way indicates/supports that person's culpability for whatever their heinous crime. **Sometimes if you go searching for something in specific, everything can potentially support your view or direction.** I wonder if this in part or full, Law of Attraction? I wiped my eyes, smearing the remainder of my mascara across my face.

'Thank you' I replied through gentle tears. 'I am so grateful to you both, honestly' I sniffled some more.

'You know we're here for you and boys'

'I know,' I replied.

I came off the phone, exhaled and decided to make a snack. Cheese toastie would do, that and an episode of Frasier. I needed to laugh. Besides my appetite was returning and I needed to take advantage of that too.

CHAPTER 39

It had been about 2 weeks since the child protection conference. Surprisingly despite everything that had taken place, I somehow had managed to find some solace in the situation. I had been researching alternative universities and degrees that I could apply for in preparation for a September start. However, it was difficult without having the transcript from my 1st year of social work. My Hope was that any credits obtained there, would be transferable to a new degree. The only problem was, I still hadn't heard anything back from the University, including any information as to whether or not I would receive my transcript. I didn't like the idea of my life hanging in the balance, me sat, waiting for permission to continue or not. This wasn't me. I liked to plan things. I liked to have things in order, know exactly what I was doing and when. Each time I reflected on what had been snatched from underneath me, I felt disempowered. I resented the inhumane policies. I felt as though I didn't have enough control over my life to make necessary decisions. Searching for an alternative course wasn't as easy as I anticipated, because the fact was, I had been planning on obtaining this degree for the last few years. This is what I had dreamed of doing. This was how I was going to make a difference in the world.

I recalled doing my access course at college, and my tutor at college telling me quite matter-of-factly, that my choice of Access course, she didn't believe was suitable or appropriate enough for me to be awarded a place at university of social work. Make it worse when I applied to one of the top universities to undertake it, she basically urinated on my hopes. She had tried on several occasions to convince me to change my Access course to one, which she felt was more suitable. I listened courteously, and then explain to her that I would much rather continue with my current Access choice. Of course, she reiterated to me again that I would not be able to secure a place on a social work degree with my chosen Access, I smiled, said thank you for the advice. I understood where she was coming from. Her assertion stemmed probably, partly from her wealth of experience of never having a student select my specific choice of Access subject in order to undertake a degree in social work, and secondly because she probably thought I wasn't capable. Nevertheless, the fact was the Access course I had chosen to undertake was one which I felt was most appropriate to my future goals. That meant that I had to accept that my route may not make sense to others. However, the question was did it make sense to me? For as long as it made sense to me then that was all that mattered.

Can I mention that I do appreciate some people have a wealth of expertise in particular subjects and topics and I appreciate advice from those people. However quite often in life we do not require advice, we simply require a level of understanding, support, faith and encouragement. Although I did not require those things from my tutor at that time. There have been countless situations whereby my decisions have not necessarily made sense to other people and for that reason, perhaps support and encouragement were not offered. Subsequently, I have learnt to just do it anyway. You know, like Nike. When you have a vision for something in your life your vision should not depend on everybody else being able to see through an identical lens. You may come across, as I very often do, as hard headed and unwilling to listen or take advice, simply because you take a leap in faith, or live by purpose on purpose. Somehow, I've always preferred to be seen that way, rather than lead my life making choices that make everyone else feel more comfortable, but me uncomfortable, or seemingly make more sense. I'd much rather make choices that satisfy my soul's purpose. There was also no love lost between us, myself and Penny, my grey-haired tutor. She didn't think much of me and I didn't think much of her. We tolerated each other right up until I completed my Access course successfully, landed myself three University offers, two of which were at top universities that she did not believe I would be offered a place. On the last day of college our final conversation went something like this.

Me: 'I bet you'll be glad to see the back of me'

Penny: 'Yes'

I actually thought it was hilarious, I couldn't help myself at the time. I burst into laughter almost to the point of tears. I laughed, I laughed, and I laughed. And then guess what, I left college with slightly more respect for her. Why? The reason for this was quite simple. We were both adult enough to tolerate each other when we needed to, but we were also human, and it was clear that both of us were glad to see the back of each other. So, for me there was a mutual respect that came from that level of honesty. She was not attempting to hurt my feelings or be disrespectful, (least I don't believe that she was) she was just being honest. And to this day I truly respect her for it. I mean let's face it, I'm not everybody's cup of tea and that's ok. I respect honesty and with that I also understand that honesty doesn't necessarily have to be what you wish to hear at that time either. I consider myself to be rather thick skinned anyhow. That kind of Truth would never hurt my feelings. Not for long anyway.

Since the fateful decision at the CP conference, Elsa had not been in touch. Well I suppose she, wouldn't be in touch with us, the new social worker would. Still we have not heard anything about a new social worker. Although I was in no rush to meet one and hear more garbage. I was a bit annoyed that no one had got back to me about the mentoring for the boys. I wondered if that had anything to do with the fact that I had made it categorically clear that I did not wish to use the in-house mentoring service the Local Authority had offered. Either way I felt that someone should afford me the courtesy of getting back to me, particularly as I'd made the request. Even if the response was no, I didn't see why it would take a manager two weeks to make that decision. It just so happened that in that time, we had been offered a new house. Although I hated moving, I welcomed the new house. Not quite new beginnings, but we'd have more space, so the boys would definitely be happy. With our impending holiday drawing closer, my intention was to start getting packed up as soon as possible so that we could move, sooner rather than later. What I didn't realise, was that in London you can move across the road, or around the corner and fall under a completely different borough. What's wrong with that you may ask? What was wrong with that if we are moving houses, I not only had to notify the Local Authority. Well of course I didn't have to, but if I didn't, it wasn't as though they wouldn't be able to find us. Particularly with the boys being on the child protection register and the Big Brother eye following our every move. I had to notify the local authority, because in the same breath I wouldn't have them think that in some way I was trying to abscond or something. No, the new house fell under a different borough, so that would mean our case being transferred to new strangers. Interestingly still, our impending move had nothing to do with the local authority or social services. Despite all the offers of assistance and support, housing did not form part of their priorities. Which I admit did surprise me. Partly because I knew it was something that they could facilitate. Nonetheless we were moving, and it had nothing to do with them.

I wondered how long it would take before someone got in touch with us. Should I hold out and see. We could move houses and wait for them to look us up and locate us. Ha-ha! No that didn't seem worth it either. I didn't wish to play games with them. They already insisted on tainting my character, I couldn't willingly volunteer any further reason. I had Elsa's manager's name, I would contact her tomorrow and explain to her that we would be moving. While she was on the phone perhaps it would be useful for me to ask her about the mentoring for the boys also.

I went back to looking at university prospectuses. I had bent the corners of the prospectus of all the courses I was interested in. It wasn't many and the more I looked at them, I realised that the course was what either very similar with only a slight difference in Minor subject, or that they were along the same lines. One of the things I enjoyed about social work is learning so much about the law and rights, rights of the local authority, rights of parents. All of that experience coupled with the practical knowledge had boosted my confidence during our ordeal. Although at times I felt powerless, choking under the pressure. The little bit of knowledge that I did possess had served me well. I wanted to find a degree that would equally serve me well. One that would provide me with knowledge, not just applicable within my job role but also within society.

As a child, the adults around me would frequently say 'she's going to be a lawyer'. I'm not quite certain why exactly, I can only imagine it had something to do with my outspokenness and ability to pose a good argument. Whatever it was, I remember that as I got older, that seemed less likely to be my end goal. I loved the idea of defending people who I believed to be innocent, a career like that would, I confess bring me much joy. Yet the reality was that before you got to that point, there was so much in between that needed to be done. I didn't go to university when I was younger, fresh out of school or college. I had become a mum instead. That inevitably meant I had to limit my choices around what I could manage. When I finally decided to return to education, studying to be a lawyer would take more out of me then I had to give. I felt there was no way I could balance motherhood with the demands of initial training in law, and then studying the bar. But that was okay. Like I said, a lawyer was not my desired end goal, despite the good intention if I were to be blessed with such a role. Realistically though, there were other ways one could obtain knowledge of the law without training to be a lawyer, and still gain experience and qualifications that would lead to a well-paid career, or at least a very satisfying one. The two are not necessarily the same.

Eventually I decided upon a degree. Criminology. This would give me a fairground in on certain elements of the law whilst exploring socio dynamics of crime and punishment. The description intrigued me. I had long since had a passion about the injustice of our judicial system. I hated the way in which prisons locked away human beings treated them like animals and then released them back into society without preparation. Like releasing a tiger into the wild without first ensuring it understood that it could not eat people.

I'm a big Jurassic Park fan, and one of the things that springs to mind is the part of the movie where the man Indominous Rex escapes. And one of the cast goes on to explain that the dinosaur has been in captive and fed at set meal times. The animal knows nothing of how to conduct itself in the outside world, where humans reside. So, what do you think happens? Pandemonium! That was how I felt about prisons. I felt there wasn't enough onus on prisons to actually rehabilitate people. The government appeared to be under pressure, budget cuts, increase in violent crime etc. Prisons I felt were just holding grounds and then one day, the floodgates opened and Voilà! Have you ever looked at reoffending rates?

The other thing that intrigued me was also the opportunity to look into crime and punishment and how it impacted different people, different groups different cultures different races different areas, different social classes, all of which were matters dear to my heart. The more I thought about it, I would always be able to use that knowledge to support and work with young people and vulnerable people, so criminology seemed like the way forward. Besides, as with my time spent in social work, you never know when the knowledge will come in handy.

I've always had concerns about some of the challenges my son's may face as God Willing, they mature into black men. It was scary to say the least, scary on a daily basis. Worrying about them coming home from school, going out with their friends, wanting to keep them close so you can protect them. I often wonder how many other mothers of black son's feel the way I do. How many panic if they try to contact their sons at any given time and cannot reach them from more than five minutes, perhaps even less. Yes, it was scary, potentially crippling. Society was not going to take pity on my son's, and I knew that. Any amount of knowledge what would help to guide me in raising them, was going to be an added blessing. I needed everything I could get. So far, I had been stoned, placed in a furnace, and more, yet I was physically unscathed only physically. This experience was forcing me to recognise, I was going to need a lot more. Perhaps I needed to be more attuned, perhaps I needed to pay attention to signs. Whatever it was, there was no way I was going to survive unless I was able to grow. I went online and applied for a course immediately.

CHAPTER 40

I dropped the boys to school and started to make my way back home. Just as I was turning in the road, my phone started to ring from inside my bag. I couldn't reach it, to check who it was. I assumed it must have been GF. I would call her back in two minutes when I'd parked up and was inside. I heard when the phone stopped ringing, GF would probably leave a cheeky message on the voicemail, we had a habit of doing those kinds of things to each other. The phone started ringing again. If it was GF, she was obviously in a persistent mood. But then she knew that the chances are I would be at work today, so why would she keep calling. Either way I would definitely call her back when I got inside. I barely twisted the key in the lock before the phone started again. I was now slightly irritated. I fumbled frustratingly in the bag searching for where the vibration was coming from, snatched the phone out of the bag and looked at the screen with annoyance, before even reading the name.

It was a private caller. Great.

'Hello' I answered the phone as though I'd, been on hold for half an hour and someone was finally picking up.

'Oh morning, is that Yolanda'? The cheery voice sang

'Yes, speaking'

'Hi, I'm Robin, your new social worker'

'Hi' I decided to remain abrupt until I was able to distinguish the purpose of her call.

'I wanted to arrange a time to come around and meet with you and the boys'

'Ok when' I asked still disinterested.

'Well I can see you haven't been seen for a couple of weeks so the sooner the better, are you available this evening?'

'Yep, fine'

'OK shall I say 16:30?'

'That's fine',

'Thank you, Yolanda,'

There was no point in telling her about the house move on the phone, it made more sense to tell her when she visited. Even though I'd plan to call her and ask about the mentoring, no she had called me, I realised I had very little desire to communicate with her, or any of the others. Besides it would be better to ask her about the mentoring when she came, that way I could see in her face if she was trying to bullshit me.

Robin wasn't as punctual as Elsa. At 16:40, she still had not arrived. As much as I didn't think much of Elsa, at least she was punctual. I preferred it when they were punctual, that way they could come in, get it over and done with, then leave our home. The worse thing was that since Elsa came in and observed me doing homework with the boys subsequently making her ridiculous allegation of inappropriate language. I wasn't prepared to do anything but speak to the social worker when they arrived, and then got on with life when they left. That way I couldn't be accused of anything else. There would be no more facetious allegations of me using unsuitable language, because I refuse to dumb down language for my son. The bell rang. Twice.

'Give me a chance nuh' I shouted towards the door.

I had a feeling it was Robin, but I didn't care. She needed to know from now, that when she came to this house, you press the bell once, and wait patiently. In addition to that, she was late and ringing off the bell like uniforms. I don't think so.

As I opened the door, Robin looked as though she was about to press the bell one more time. I raised my eyebrows giving her a very serious glare. Some might say the death look. Hopefully my look spoke her language and she would know better than to do this again.

'Oh, sorry I wasn't sure if the bell was working'

'Well if you press it every three seconds, you can hardly expect much to change in that space of time. Speedy Gonzales doesn't live here.'

'I'm sorry you must be Youlander'

'No and I'm assuming you're Robin, I am Yolanda!'

'Oh, sorry it's such a... different name I've never heard it before'

I was tempted to reply, 'unlike Robin the silly little bird with a red chest'. But I didn't. Robin attempted to shake my hand. I pretended I hadn't noticed and instead opened the door wider to let her in, almost stepping on Kwame and Cassius who were now standing behind me, peering to see who was at the door.

'Oh, you must be Kwame and Cassius, Robin declared, sounding like Mary Poppins.

'Hello' replied Kwame from behind my legs.

Cassius just looked at her. Noticing, she tried again.

'Hello Cassius'

Cassius chose not to respond, and I decided not to force him, particularly after all the spew they had said about something being wrong with him, as a cause of his unwillingness to engage in their conversations.

One of the good things about Cassius as well, was that you didn't need to say anything to him, because he very rarely wanted to speak to other people anyway. So, you didn't have to say, 'look at her as though she's stupid'. Or 'don't answer any questions, just look at her as though you don't understand and make her start speaking even slower so that we can laugh at her expense', because he naturally did that anyway.

Without that you still had the image of this tiny little boy looking Robin dead in her face, and just not saying anything. Atta boy! I showed Robin into the front room and turned the TV down.

'It's nice to meet you, You... Yolanda'

I was hoping Robin was going to grasp my name very quickly, for her sake. I couldn't understand what was so difficult about pronouncing my name, there was no u in Yolanda.

'I need to advise you Robin that we will be moving to a new house within the next month'.

'Oh, that's nice' she replied.

'Yes, thank you. I'll write the address down for you so you can update your system'

'Oh, thank you Yolanda'

'Do you have the address already? Please may I have the postcode?'

I gave Robin the postcode.

'Oh, this falls under a different local authority Yolanda. Your case will have to be moved. You'll be allocated a new social worker from your new local authority.'

'Yes, I thought so'

'Also, Elsa mentioned that you were going on holiday with the boys over the summer?'

'Yes, we are'.

'I was wondering if you mind giving me the address where you'll be staying'

'Yes, I do mind, and no I will not give you the address. What do you think this is Robin? I'm going on holiday with my son's that has nothing to do with you.'

'As the children are subject to a child protection plan Yolanda, it is something we would usually ask for'

'That's nice but I'm not giving you my family's address. You don't have parental responsibility over my son's I do. That means I can take them wherever I like. I don't need permission.'

'That's not what I'm saying Yolanda, its fine. I'll have a word with my manager and get back to you'

'When will you get back to me, Elsa told me she would speak to her manager with regards to my son's accessing the mentoring service. To date I've had no response. And now I have a new social worker you, and still no response!'

'Elsa did mention it to me, and I am aware that she has discussed it with my manager. At present the Local Authority is unable to commission your chosen mentoring service. However, we are happy to provide each of the boys with a mentor from our in-house service.'

'Okay, perhaps it's best that we move on Robin, because I made myself very clear to your manager the last time we met. I understand if you are unable to commission the service. Nevertheless, I will not be using. No, better still, my son's will not be using your in-house service. I specifically requested a service that was culturally appropriate, no one is taking the time to demonstrate to me that your service is culturally appropriate, so that's okay. I will pay for my sons to receive that service myself.'

I always find it interesting that a number of services offered at no extra cost are never of any quality. However, parents who are unable to do better, are expected to settle for a substandard service out of desperation. I consider this to be a blatant demonstration of inequality. There are a number of services I have parted with my own money for, in order to ensure my sons, receive quality. That has been my choice. However, what does that mean for families who cannot afford to do the same, families who are otherwise forced to accept a substandard.

Totally unacceptable.

'Now that you will be relocating to another borough, you can make this request again within your new team and it can be reconsidered'

'Have you given any further thought to the educational psychologist?'

Huh. Now what made Robin just ask me about the educational psychologist. What made her any different to those that had posed the question before her?

'What about her Robin?'

'Have you thought about whether or not you might consider consenting to an observation? I had a chat with Miss O'Connor before I came here this evening. She expressed that both herself and Miss Reynolds were becoming increasingly concerned about Kwame's learning. We had a discussion, and we feel it would be a good idea to at least consent to the observation and then decide how you feel about the report?'

What did she mean they had had a discussion? How could they be discussing my sons, or what should happen with them? In fact, why was Robin contacting the school to discuss the boys? Why didn't she contact me? Miss O'Connor hadn't said anything to me. I mean I know I made it pretty difficult for her on a daily basis, but I didn't appreciate all of these whispers behind my back either. I was beginning to think that the conversation with Robin was a strategic move to put more pressure on me. I didn't believe that it was for the good of my son, so I was left with the alternative belief that they wanted the money for the school. And even if Robin didn't know it, I had already been giving the educational psychologist observation some thought. Since Kwame had started the school I wasn't happy with his progress, in fact I didn't think he was making appropriate progress.

When I thought about the situation by myself, I had given it some serious consideration. Perhaps the extra help in the classroom would enable him to work better and make better progress. I just hadn't mentioned it to the school because the truth was, our relationship was now strained. If I play devil's advocate and tell myself that the school were just doing their job, perhaps I could make an effort to return to the point at which I was, when the boys first transitioned to the school. This was the something I had been struggling with, because every time I replayed how things had unfolded, I couldn't help but feel that the school were not being transparent with me, either way. I still felt things could have gone differently.

I liaise and work with parents all the time and one of the things I pride myself on is trying to be as open and it's human as possible. That means, not believing I'm on a 'higher horse', but understanding various situations, various factors, and looking at how all of those things impact and contribute to families, to children. Miss Reynolds, Miss O'Connor, no matter how I looked at it, I couldn't see good intentions in their actions. What I could see was prejudgment and assumption.

I thought about the most recent assertion of the fact that I treated my boys differently. That offended me. It offended me that something they had seen, their own perception. They took that perception and brought it to a table full of professionals as though it was fact or truth. Yet never had that been mentioned to me. That was what I was talking about, the lack of transparency and partnership working. The comments never seemed to be based on fact, but more so on perception, hearsay or assumption. Therefore, how could I trust them? They didn't have any interest in my culture, race, upbringing, nothing in line with our socio dynamics.

I think what made it worse was that one of the first things we learnt in social work was around the Macro system, please Google it. The macro system looks at how a person's character and behaviour is shaped. It looks at the cultural environment from which the individual gains their ideals, where we live, ethnicity, school, family and so on. Exploring a person's macro system enables you to gain information that may only otherwise be obtained by asking direct questions. In fact, it can potentially prevent you from drawing unsubstantiated conclusions, making wrongful judgements, by offering insight that is not otherwise discernible to the eye. Come to think of it, this school, the teachers, the way in which they viewed our family in particular, was not in line with what I wanted for my boys. We had been at the school for less than a year, before all of this taking place. However, I also knew that they were not going to see the school through to year six. I simply couldn't. I couldn't be at school where we were constantly being watched, in anticipation of what could go wrong. This was not going to be the result a self-fulfilling prophecy, whereby labels were stuck fast to our being, until we eventually succumb and accept them, wearing the prejudice proudly like a birthday suit. I couldn't accept that. Sorry no. I wouldn't accept that. The school wasn't a good fit for my sons. By a good fit I mean, based on the characters that my sons were, and the school's ethos or beliefs, the two didn't go together. This was a good school but that doesn't mean it was a good school for everybody. If you know what I mean?

For example, the famous school, (I don't care to find the name) that politicians and other 'well to do' individuals send their children to. Without having visited it, is not a school for my sons, in my opinion. Why? Because their individual characteristics would struggle, I believe under those circumstances. If I did have a son or child I felt could thrive under the circumstances, I could do my utmost to try and get them into that school. That is the kind of parent I am. I understand that the best schools may not necessarily be the best fit for my son's, but that's just me. The problem was, or is, is that who I am, what I believe, doesn't appeal to everybody. It makes some people feel uncomfortable. I can't pretend to explain why. However, there are some things in life, that I'm very self-assured about, passionate even. I just don't pretend not to be. Again. Blame my mum.

Feeling like I'd been away with my thoughts for some time, I turned my attention back to Robin.

'Yes, I have given it some thought, I would like him to be observed by the educational psychologist'

'Oh, that's fantastic Yolanda'

In my opinion Robin was a little bit too gleeful over my decision. However, I decided to leave her to bask in it. I didn't feel it necessary to tell her I was also considering moving the boys to a better school for them. I didn't tell her that my thinking was, if my son for any reason was statemented and was entitled to additional support in the class, I would ensure he received that support, or the funding for that support. That funding would be awarded to the school I chose to send him to. Robin didn't know it at that point, but that chosen school was not the current school in question. First things first, let's get the educational psychologist in!

CHAPTER 41

Once I put the boys to bed, I decided to spend the rest of the evening looking for schools. James had given me the names of a few good schools that he was familiar with and considered to be good schools. I was grateful for his support. At least I knew when he was giving me the names of schools, he was considering the boys characters. By now both he and Kevron had gauged a good idea of their personalities and characteristics.

I discussed with James that I didn't want to separate the boys, however I would do so if I really had to. But that was only if I had to. I wanted to keep them together. That was important to me. Even before the boys started school, we had been through more than our fair share, yet we had remained together, intact. Faced with our current challenges, I realised we were back to where we had been before, trying to stay together. I wanted them to always be there for each other.

I didn't have a sibling a couple of years older or younger than me. Someone to walk to school with, go home with, check and ensure they're ok in school, vice versa. My cousins did, however. There were three of them. And at least at one point if not more, in their lives they attended the same schools. That meant they could defend each other; one could tell the story where the other one couldn't and so on. Some of you may not get my point. But what I'm referring to is that element of unity. We may not have recognised it then, but consequently that is what it was. With all the siblings being together, it meant unity. I suppose it was much like with my Mum and my auntie's. What we saw was that they were unified in the raising of us. Our upbringing. I now wonder why unity is not such a significant factor in most our lives, because we need each other. I don't have the answers, but it sure is food for thought. Either way I believe in unity. We were raised on it, and we will continue to raise our children on it.

My younger brother and I are nearly 10 years apart. Yet it holds no bearing in how unified we are. I believe in part, that this is down to my Mum, the way that she raised us. Of course, an element of that is down to the two of us, my brother and I. I genuinely see myself as his keeper. Without a second thought I also genuinely believe in my heart of hearts that my brother has my back 100%. You know like if I can't count on anyone else, I KNOW I can count on him. Like if I had a secret, I know he would take it to his grave, before breaking my trust. That was the way we were raised to view each other as siblings, and this was without my mum ever having to say it. Powerful right, that parents can in-still such meaningful values without any form of verbal insistence. I don't know, but maybe that's why my brother and I have the relationship that we do. Why our bond survives even the toughest of challenges. Perhaps all it boils down to is the way in which we value each other. That was the intention I was raising my children with. To rely on each other to trust each other before outsiders, and to always be there for each other. Particularly, after me. We had absolutely no room at the inn for outsiders. Not Elsa, Trenchbull, Miss Reynolds, Robin, uniforms, none of them. We were our unit, our island, our family. It was almost as though you had to pass an initiation before being deemed family. We couldn't just assume your intentions. That was the beauty of family. If my brother was troubled in any way, as was I, and vice versa.

In fact, a memory that springs to mind took place approximately 10 years ago. My brother and I attended a memorial event, where I sang. It was emotive day and during speeches, of course tears were falling gently from my eyes. I looked over at my brother and he too was wiping his eyes from across the room. Later when asked what was wrong with him. He replied, 'it was my sister man'. That was the beauty of sibling relationships that I'm talking about.

What I feel, you feel. When I cry, you cry. When I win, we win! Your children will be my children, as mine are yours.

My bedroom door creaked, then came a gentle knock.

'Mummy' came the small voice as the door opened wider to reveal

Kwame.

'What's wrong baby?' I looked over at the time, it was nearly 22:00. The boys had been in bed for almost two hours.

It didn't really come as a surprise that Kwame was still awake. He didn't care much for bedtimes, or sleep for that matter.

Cassius on the other hand, valued his sleep above everything, my guess was that whatever Kwame's reason for appearing at my door during this hour, Cassius was soundly counting sheep in the clouds.

'Please can I sleep in your bed?

Okay. Now I knew something was up. Kwame never asked to sleep in my bed. I think he was more accustomed to his own space. This was more Cassius, he liked to snuggle up, despite how terrible he slept.

'Yes baby, what's up? 'I opened a corner of the quilt to let Kwame into the bed, putting away the papers I had been sifting through and wrapping my arm around him.

'Mummy, did you get sacked from your job?'

'No baby I still work at my job'

'Not that one Mummy, your other job...'

I paused for a moment before responding what did this seven-year-old know about being sacked.

'Where did you hear that word baby? I asked genuinely intrigued.

'I'm not sure Mummy'

I knew Kwame was being less than honest with me, but I decided not to probe.

'I wasn't sacked baby, but I don't work there anymore'

'Was it because of me, Mummy?'

'Don't be silly baby, no. It's nothing to do with you.'

'Was it Elsa? Mummy? Did Elsa say you can't go back?'

'Not really baby, it wasn't Elsa'

'Is it because I told Elsa that you tell me off, but you don't tell off my brother?'

I sat up and looked at Kwame puzzled.

'Is that what you think Kwaams'?

'Kwame looked down and then said 'No Mummy, but Elsa asked me if you treated me and Cass' the same, so I said I get in trouble more that Cass. Then she asked me about the reasons I get in trouble. I told her I couldn't have cake and custard, but Cass was allowed'

My eyes filled with water as I listened to my seven-year-old riddled with some kind of guilt for no good reason. I was back to asking myself the question 'how did I do this? How did I miss this? So, let me get this straight, this little boy has been carrying all kinds of guilt about what had taken place. My job, everything. I gave him the biggest hug I could manage and kissed him on both cheeks before holding him again.

'I don't expect you to know this baby but, even if it seems like you get in more trouble that your brother, do I ever tell you off for something your brother has done?'

'No Mummy'

'When your brother does something wrong, do I tell him off?'

'Yes mummy' he replied

Do you think Mummy should tell Cass' off when you do something wrong?

'No Mummy'

'Shall I tell you off, when Cass' does something wrong?'

'No mummy, that's not fair'

'Exactly baby. That's what I think too. So, if you do something wrong, I will tell you off and if Cass' does something, I will tell him off too.

But it's not fair to tell both of you off, just because one of you has done something wrong. Does that make sense?'

'Yes Mummy'

'So never think I treat you differently. What it is, is that I don't treat you the same, because you're not the same. You're both so different. Cass' loves sleeping, you hate sleeping. Cass' like's cereal, you like cooked breakfast. Think about some of the other ways you are both different' I looked as Kwame stared at the ceiling in deep thought and smiled.

'I love you both with all my heart and I always will, equally. Don't ever forget that, no matter how much I shout, that has nothing to do with how much I love you. Mummy's human, sometimes I get upset just like you and Cass', but that doesn't mean I don't love you. It simply means I'm not happy at that moment.

Kwame smiled as though what I had just said had reassured any misinterpretations he had. I silently Gave Thanks knowing the battle I faced, was not only to ensure I kept my sons, but also that they knew, I had them. Not physically, but emotionally too. I needed them to know that we in fact, were united and always would be. I needed them. My battle, my pain, my journey was not with them. But FOR them.

I was beginning to understand more and more that my battle was not punishment, but part of the growth, as my journey to evolve into the best mother I could be. Not perfect, but imperfectly perfect. What I took from that moment lying here with my son was that he was sensitive to his environment, to my emotions, to his emotions, and most importantly, the part he played in those emotions. Part of my greater understanding was understanding that if I lost touch of those emotions, I could in fact lose him, perhaps even both. If at any point they were unsure of my intentions towards them, my feelings towards them ... then it was my responsibility to do something about that. Not a social worker not Miss O'Connor and not Miss Reynolds.

Me. I was responsible for making sure that they knew how I felt about them. I was responsible for making sure that they felt their safe place, was with me. And I was responsible for doing this, while still instilling the boundaries, which I knew would serve them well in life.

As I lay there with my arms still wrapped around Kwame, I deliberated with the task I had come to identify. I had always wanted to make sure they knew how I felt about them, tried to ensure they knew that we were one. However somewhere along the lines, perhaps my son had his doubts and because I had not noticed, those doubts had turned into his reality. For this reason, it wasn't a matter of me knowing, it was a matter of me doing. It was about a conscious effort not a subconscious one. It wasn't about what I knew, it was about what I needed to teach them, demonstrate to them, show them, and say to them. So far, I felt that had been what I was doing. But in a moment, that very moment, I had experienced a state of epiphany. My role was to make sure that they knew, not me, not anyone else, but themselves. I would not have my son's being led astray by children at school, so I most certainly wouldn't allow adults to infiltrate their minds either. If altering my actions, or my approach was necessary I would do so, as long as my intentions didn't change, we would be victorious. You see intention supersedes everything.

CHAPTER 42

It was a while before we were allocated a new social worker. I had contacted the Local Authority to find out what was taking so long, still anxious for them to have a conversation with Kevron or James from the mentoring service. Despite the lack of contact, Miss O'Connor had managed to arrange for the educational psychologist to come in over a series of days to observe Kwame and undertake other activities in order to identify any specific learning needs. She had made a particular effort however, to keep me in the loop, letting me know that I would have the opportunity to meet with the educational psychologist to discuss contents of the report prior to it being finalised. I put this down to her excitement at the possibility of achieving her own narrow-minded outcome for my son.

I read through the report and met with the educational psychologist. The report didn't please me, in fact in some ways it reignited the fire in my belly again, setting it ablaze. On paper the educational psychologist and given the impression that my son had a lack of understanding. She mentioned his defiance to engage, but only when using it to support her claim of him being unable to understand, as opposed to not doing what he was told. When referring to this behaviour, she often also referred to his emotional state, mentioning things like he tends to get very emotional or he tends to get quite upset over small things. I didn't like it. I didn't like the way it insinuated my son was some kind of nervous or emotional wreck. Perhaps it was me, but the report painted the image of my son rocking, as he sat singing and talking to himself. There was nothing positive within the content, just an insinuation of a possible mental difficulty. I wondered if they thought they were going to diagnose my son, subsequently prescribing medication to fix him. Medication that he would be required to take for life, perhaps with an increase in dosage when his behaviour deviated from their norm.

The situation caused my mind to run wild. I was tired of seeing Black men drugged to the point of recognition, injected to the point of obesity, and then surrender to self-imposed or premature death. There was something about how early the so-called system captured our sons, our men and then kept hold of them long enough for them to not, be considered a threat. I had seen it happen to boys at my school. The school would axe away at their being, use their reactions to support false claims of violence, intimidation, instability and then discard them like toxic waste. For those sons, every destination reached after their initial contact of school, sunk them further into contamination, until society shunned them at every opportunity, subsequently prohibiting them from elevation from their current circumstances. Often this would result in them undertaking further deviant behaviour, and or criminal activity whereby they would be incarcerated, caged like beasts and treated as such. Does that sound too much? Well not to me. For too long I have known this but abstained from saying too much due to not wanting to be accused of overthinking or receive the stares from others that believe I think too deeply. **The fact is that we can become so consumed with the images, the messages, the voices, that we altogether miss the hidden agendas of others.** Let's face it, some of us know more about celebrity parenting then we do about our own family, our own children. Why? Because the information is designed to be in your face, distracting you from even your own children...

As I re-joined the present, I reminded myself that although the report would follow him in some way, possibly throughout his time in education. Professionals working with him, would soon begin to decipher what he was unable to do, from what he decided not to do. I hope that they soon would identify him, based on what they saw before them, as opposed to what was written in Black and White. That was one of my main issues. The fact that Kwame's defiance was not merely seen as disobedience. Despite all the negatives, on the plus side I considered the fact that if Kwame were to be statemented,
ould be no good reason as to why I should not be able to see

progress over time. With added support there was no reason why Kwame's work would be at the standard that it had been. I had raised my concerns with the educational psychologist explaining to her my interpretation of what she had said. She went on to explain to me, that in order to ensure Kwame was eligible for maximum support, it was prudent that she emphasised what she felt his needs were. We agreed to disagree after some deliberation and Miss O'Connor intervening to diffuse things. I authorised for the report to be submitted and was advised that I would hear something hopefully sooner, rather than later.

In the interim Miss O'Connor had sourced additional help in Miss Reynolds class to support Kwame. I guess the excitement of extra funding, prompted her to do what I could only assume, she could have done from the beginning.

The holiday was fast approaching now, as was the end of the school term. I had managed to secure place at another University studying for an alternative degree. The only thing was I was unable to carry forward any credits from my previous course. This meant that I would have to start from the beginning and commit to a further three years of studying. More stressful evenings, more late evenings in the library, breaking down in front of the computer. More rushing from school to lecture and lecture to school. I don't know how I'd manage for the last year, but I certainly wasn't excited by a further three years of doing it. I was not best pleased by this. However, I had set my mind on completing the degree, and knew I would just have to put the last year of studying down to experience, and to be fair, an eye opener. If not for the whole intervention, I may have spent three years training to do a job that I may quickly have realised, was not for me. Perhaps this was a lucky break. The university hadn't even bothered to contact me, so there you go. I had accepted the offer and would start in September.

Elsa's manager had also called. Before she could explain why she was calling, I mentioned to her about the social worker she recently allocated us and asked her in her professional opinion did she feel that Robin was culturally appropriate to my family. She seemed taken aback by my question, asking pardon as though she expected my verbatim to change. I repeated myself for her for clarity, saying it slowly so we were both clear on what I was saying, before she went on to explain that she could only allocate social workers that she had available in her team. I told her that I understood that meant, her team was clearly not very diverse. She ignored my statement and went on to explain to me that she had spoken to her manager and they have no concerns about me taking the boys on holiday. I asked her if she expected me to say, 'thank you'. She went on to explain that a new social worker would be allocated to us shortly as she had been in touch with the other Local Authority and they were in the process of allocating our case.

This woman made me laugh. When she thought she could bully me she had so much to say. But when I had something to say, it was she who turned and ran away. I told her 'thank you' for the call before hanging up to continue what I was doing.

As for finding the boys a new school, I managed to find another school but there was only one snag. It was another Independent school. Which meant I had to return to the financial commitment of school fees, for both of them. I had done it before, and despite the strain, I saw no reason why I couldn't do it again. I knew I was going to feel the pressure; I knew I was going to have to increase my hours at work. Nonetheless I felt I had very little choice. Part of my epiphany meant that I had to be very mindful about the influences staff at the school were having on my son's emotions, and the impact that was having, particularly on Kwame's development. It was a high price to pay but it was worth it. I needed to help my sons regain an emotional balance. For this to happen I needed them to be an educational setting that I felt confident was building their characters instead of tearing them down or stifling them. A school that maintained a standard of boundaries, whereby Kwame could not categorically refuse to do his work and the teacher simply threw their hands in the air. And one that met the individual needs of both my sons, and did not fear their capabilities, instead encouraged and promoted them. I believed that the school I had set my sights on would do just that. I had an appointment to go and meet with the Head teacher in a couple of days. I looked forward to it, and hoped that the school did not disappoint, once I had actually visited and observed its practices.

CHAPTER 43

It was another beautiful morning, the sun was asserting its authority through the curtains hung at my bedroom window, demanding that I open my eyes and complement its beauty. I practically had to squint as I climbed out of bed before peering through the curtains. Still I felt good.

Today was the day I would get to meet with the head teacher at the new school I wanted to send the boys to. I was excited. I hadn't mentioned it to the boys yet. I didn't want to risk them mentioning it to one of their friends at school and Miss O'Connor or Miss Reynolds catching wind of my plans. Hopefully if they were offered a place for September, I would tell them over the summer, we would have a fantastic holiday and then they could have a fresh start.

I could hear the TV coming from the front room. Had I left the TV on last night? No way. I couldn't have. I never did things like that. I got out of bed and listened attentively as I opened the bedroom door, it was definitely the TV. I opened the front room door to find Cassius' sat in the sofa with his legs tucked in the chair, watching early morning cartoons.

'Morning Cass'

'Morning Mummy' he replied with his usual amount of early morning energy.

'What you doing in here?'

'Oh, I woke up mummy, and you and my brother were sleeping, so I watched the TV'

His innocence warmed my heart.

'So why didn't you wake your brother up, we've got school today'

'I did Mummy, but he told me to go away'

I laughed this time.

'Okay, will you tell him Mummy said it's time to get up?'

'Ok mummy, he said jumping off the chair like Tigger from Winnie the Pooh.

I really didn't know where this little boy got his energy from, first thing in the morning. Cassius returned holding the hand of a sleepy faced Kwame who was practically rubbing the skin off his eyelids as he entered the room.

'Morning Kwaams'

'Morning Mummy' Kwame replied miserably, as he sat on the sofa next to his brother.

'Go and wash your face Kwame, I'm gonna make breakfast'

'Okay Mummy' he mumbled.

We managed to leave home on time and as approached the school, the boys convinced me to park, even further away from school than usual, so they could get an even longer ride on the scooters to the school gates. Of course, this meant that I had to carry the scooters even further, back to the car. When we got to the school gate Miss O'Connor was doing her meet and greet duty. Saying good morning to all the parents and children as they entered. As we passed her at the gate, I made a point of looking at her and courteously saying good morning and kept it moving. The boys chorused 'good morning Miss O'Connor'. I noticed she greeted the boys individually citing both names. I wondered if she knew the names of all the children in the school. Ms O'Connor was still stood by the gate when I was leaving.

'Goodbye Yolanda' she said smiling.

'Bye Miss O'Connor'

I too had a lot to smile about this morning. I arrived at the new school ahead of my appointment. Although the school had a car park, I didn't want to be sat in the car park for a long period of time, as it might arouse suspicion or cause some concern. I didn't want my first interaction with them, to be someone questioning why I'd been sat outside the school for so long. I thought it best therefore, to park nearby on a side road, moving my car to the car park within 10 minutes of my appointment. This way I could also familiarise myself with the surroundings. I wasn't familiar with this area and it meant I would have to plan my travel once we moved into the new house.

The school was situated quite neatly off the main road. However, I imagined that during the school runs, traffic on that main road would prove to be an obstacle for parents trying to get to the school. There were a number of newsagents, a few hair salons and a post office on the main road too. I observed the footfall of people going in and out. I sat there until I had just over 5 minutes until my appointment time, then I drove back to the car park, and rang the main reception bell. The school looked quite sizeable for an Independent school. I began to wonder how many students they had. The receptionist answered the bell and I advised her of my appointment to meet with the Head teacher. She buzzed me in through the intercom and told me to follow the sign to reception. As I walked through the reception area, I slowed down to take a look at the pictures and names of all of the staff at the school. There were a number of black members of staff that was my first observation. I looked at whole school photos, noticing a number of black children but still children of other ethnicities. I read through the school's ethos in large bubble letters displayed on the wall. It said 'respect'. The school was quickly winning me over.

'Morning'

I jumped at the sound of the voice ahead of me.

'My apologies I didn't mean to frighten you'

'No that's fine I replied smiling courteously 'I was just reading the displays'

'We'll be updating those soon, it's time for a refresh'. You must be Yolanda'

'Yes, I am', I said extending my hand to shake hers.

'Lovely to meet you, I'm Mrs Asante, the Head teacher'

Stood before me was a grand but small stature of a woman. A woman who even without excessive, elongated height, stood tall and was well poised. Something about the woman who stood in front of me said pride. Though tempted to add proud, my point is merely that walking into a perspective school, being greeted by the head teacher who had the presence of authority and culture in one, was a welcomed change from my norm.

Mrs Asante's hair was wrapped up with an African printed headscarf that matched the print on her skirt. She had style. A conservative, but bold kind of style. I thought that said a lot about her character. She was a mature woman probably around 45, my guess from her name was that she was Ghanaian. Slender, but in no way skinny, she looked as though she had the ability to beat me in a 100m race hands down. Maybe even with her hands behind her back.

'Good morning' I replied almost starting again.

'I thought we'd take a look around the school first and then we can go back to my office and have a chat and you can ask me any questions'

'Great' I replied following Mrs Asante through a set of double doors.

I followed Mrs Asante as she introduced me to each of the classes, allowing me to enter the room for a few minutes to also observe the teaching. When Mrs Asante walked into the classroom all of the students stopped what they were doing and stood up, until she told them they could now be seated. In one of the classes there was a child sat on a table by himself. Mrs Asante quietly asked the teacher why that was. The teacher explained that the student had been disruptive and when she separated him, he had no one to talk to and therefore would engage in his class work. I thought of Kwame and wondered why this teacher couldn't show Miss Reynolds how to use this practice.

The school provided lunch which was strictly vegetarian. Students were free to bring packed lunch but those that did could not bring items that contained meat or fish. I hadn't heard anything like this at a school before, but there was a first time for everything. The school had a provision that continued up to 16 years. Although Kwame and Cassius were nowhere near that age, Mrs Asante still showed me the high school classes. I liked the look of the teaching, the few minutes I spent in each classroom, I felt like I was leaving with even more knowledge than I had prior to entering the classrooms. The classes were not disruptive, the children were sat quietly, they put their hands up to ask questions, each child had on an identical uniform. I was impressed. Small things, basics even. Yet do you know this is not considered basic for everyone. By the time we had arrived at Miss Asante's office, I wanted to ask 'Where do I need to sign? Pass me a pen.' Miss Asante went through with me, the provision at the school, explaining what was covered in the fees and what was exempt. She spoke to me about class sizes explaining to me that the boys would not have more than 15 students in their class, and in most cases, less than that. I tried to contain my excitement at the information Mrs Asante was giving me. Everything so far sounded good. Mrs Asante explain to me that she had founded the school and told me the story behind it. I admired her, her courage, yes courage again. I admired her courage for bringing the school to this point. On the wall in her office she had newspaper clippings of features of when the school first opened. Wow, I thought to myself. That must have been some journey. Listening to her, I was happy to give her whatever money I could accumulate to pay the fees. If it meant continuing to support the work that was being done here at the school, then I would be happy to help. Mrs Asante confirmed the boys' ages, then explained that at present they had a place for Kwame but did not have a place for Cassius. My heart sank. What would I do now? I needed to move both the boys.

'Yolanda we will however have a place by October half term for Cassius'

'Is that a definite Mrs Asante?' I asked clinging desperately to hope.

'Yes'

'Okay' I breathed a slight sigh of relief.

'Did you have any other questions Yolanda?'

'Actually, not a question. I wanted to advise you that Kwame and Cassius are currently on the child protection register. Therefore, the school will receive a call from a social worker once the boys start attending. Unfortunately, I can't give you a name at present, because we are currently waiting to be allocated a new social worker as we're moving to a new Local Authority'.

There I said it. I didn't want to tell Mrs Asante; I mean who knows what she was going to think of me now. I didn't know if she was going to turn out to be like all of the other professionals that believed that perhaps I didn't deserve to have my son's, or that I was a terrible mother. Or worse still I didn't know if she was going to turn out to be another Dolores, smiling kindly with me like Judas Iscariot, exchanging pleasantries, only to fabricate lies about my sons and me. I honestly just didn't know. Yet in that moment I had felt the urge to share this with Mrs Asante. Quite frankly, I would rather her hear it from me first, than anyone else. I like transparency. To me you have to respect someone who is open about what it is. Despite how things may well end up as a result, I knew if she read about us on paper, we would sound a hundred times worst. Perhaps she probably wouldn't offer the boys a place at her school.

'What category have they placed the children on the register under?' Mrs Asante was straight faced, but not in a manner that gave you the impression she was making a judgement about you. I explained to her and told her about the disclosure and the medical.

'I don't see why they didn't give them a Child in Need plan, why child protection?'

I went on to explain to her some of the reports that were read during the conference and what the school had to say, in particular with regards to the boys and their development. Mrs Asante nodded her head as I spoke. 'Okay Yolanda thank you for letting me know. I'll wait to hear from them'.

Was that it? Wasn't Mrs Asante going to say anything else? Wasn't she going to change her mind about the offer of a school place? Her facial expression remained the same. Boy did she have the perfect poker face, I couldn't tell what she was thinking. Did this mean the boys would still have a place at the school? Although she hadn't said anything otherwise. I was almost half surprised, half uncomfortable with her not saying much. I had told her everything, even that which had been said about us that I considered an absurd lie. Although the more I confused myself with questioning, I couldn't come up with what I thought she should say.

Mrs Asante handed me an envelope with some paperwork for me to complete and sign. I told her I would have it completed and returned to her with a deposit as soon as possible. Mrs Asante introduced me to the receptionist whom I had somehow missed as I entered the building, the deputy head teacher and both Cassius and Kwame's perspective teachers. All of which were warm and welcoming, telling me they looked forward to meeting the boys. I felt like I'd been here before, looking at a new school meeting the head teacher who welcomed my son's, along with other teaching staff. Nonetheless I knew something about this was different. I couldn't put my finger on it, but I felt like I was making the right decision. After all, all I could do was try. If I had the right intention, I had to have faith that the rest would follow.

CHAPTER 44

The sound of light rainfall landing on the pavement outside my bedroom window did not have its usual impact of sinking me further into the crevice of my mattress, buried by the snug feel of my old, yet reliable duvet. Soon I would be experiencing the seasons from another window, a different room, a new home. Before now, I had not given much thought to us relocating. Of course, I had been caught up slightly with so many other things that also needed to be dealt with. However now our move was firmly on the horizon, I was surprisingly anticipating it with a silent enthusiasm. The anticipation was clearly having a positive effect, because the miserable weather had failed in its pursuit to force me into hiding, as it had done frequently in the past. No not today. Today I welcomed the obscure weather with open arms, so what if it was supposed to be summer, so what if I hated rain, so what if it meant I had to wear more sensible shoes, instead of my open toed sandals. Today I would embrace whatever, I would remain in control of my own mind. As I prized my eyes wide open, I decided there would be no adverse weather conditions in my mind today, no hurricanes, no tornadoes, no storms welcome.

Since having visited the new school I had been giving serious thought to whether I would change both my sons once a place became available for Cassius or if it was worth allowing Kwame to start the new school and Cassius join later when the place became available. The decision-making had me going back and forward in my mind, a battle of tug of war with no one ever winning. Just a series of ties. I have never had to make the conscious decision to place my son's in different provisions, or to separate them. Well not if the provision was age appropriate for both of them anyway. Once I found any provision that was suitable for both, I would send both. Most things were done in twos, in other words, most things my sons did together.

My other worry was that I had no idea what my new timetable at university would look like, and instinctively how I would juggle the school runs with this new timetable. I had only just managed to get through my first year previously, that varied between after school clubs, occasional breakfast club, and assistance from my mum or me racing down the A40 trying to make it to the school within the small window that was allocated. It was pressure, I can't pretend that it wasn't pressure. Yes, I made an effort to attend all my lectures, and when attending, to attend punctually yet often, I would still arrive at lectures and slump into the seat, flustered from my race from the car or my race from the school. Even when I managed to park less than 10 minutes from the University, I had still found myself sweating like a pig when I arrived at the university entrance. Removing layers that I had no intention of removing when I got dressed that morning. That was my norm, my routine. I guess that helped to explain why I tended to fall asleep shortly after I put the boys to bed. It was because by then, the day had caught up with my body and physically mentally I was exhausted. It was likely that now instead of two more years until completion I had three. That inevitably meant three more years of running, racing, sweating, all while trying to find some balance to family life. I could continue to make use of after school club, as this was still an option, but the option only applied while the boys were at their current school. Once I move them to the new school, unfortunately the new school did not have an after-school provision, which inevitably posed a huge problem to me as I knew that they were going to be times whereby my classes would finish later then the school. I had no idea how I was going to combat that; I simply knew I had to find a way, but which way only God he knew.

As I laid still, exploring these options before the start of my day, I began to question if trying to establish a career for myself at the present moment was a good idea. We were still going through quite a bit as a family. I was still trying to make the extra effort to maintain control of my children. To maintain a sense of unity that not only I knew about, but one that my sons understood as best as a five-year-old and seven-year-old could. I was still trying to keep them in a protective bubble. I wanted them to remain unscathed when we finally were able to exit this. I could wait a few more years and perhaps do it when they were at High School, but I wanted to be there for them when they started high School. When they may begin to become tempted by deviant behaviour, possibly getting in with the wrong crowds, hanging around, getting into negative situations, growing pains. I wanted to be on hand for all of that. It wasn't that I knew my children would get into situations at High School, it was that I was realistic in my expectations. I looked at my own childhood I looked at some of the challenges, we were faced with as young people. Lucky for us we didn't have the Internet back then, now young people have an array of challenges, peer pressure is at another level to what we experienced, it is worse.

Like I've mentioned before, I've always been a very hands-on mum, a very open mum. I've never wanted anyone else to raise my children, to act as the primary caregiver, it would not sit well with me to have someone else raise my children. That is just my personal preference. So each time I was presented with an opportunity, I've always had to measure how much of me, that opportunity will require, how much headspace, how much time, how much energy, because if it takes away from my son's, I have to think twice and reconsider its true value according to us. My thoughts had turned into a full-blown conversation with myself. The dialogue had turned from elevating to one which was slowly submerging me. I realised I've been here before with this line of questioning myself, I had already had a conversation similar to this before I undertook the social work degree. So, I decided to give the same response, 'no I can't wait to obtain this degree I've waited long enough, now my boys are of school age I needed to create some stability for myself, more importantly for us. I've made choices and those choices in part, are what had brought me to this point with both of my son's.

However, I am not going to be a victim of circumstance, I would define and achieve my own success based on that which I felt was important'. I spoke to myself with certainty, so much so, that by the time I finished talking, I felt in charge again, I felt in control of my life, my destiny. I had shut myself up! I had struggled to feel this recently, with all that had taken place, and it was nice to regain some kind of empowerment just from understanding my own self, from learning how I needed to communicate with myself in order to feed my own soul. If nothing else, at least that was something I could take away from the recent turmoil. **Learning to speak to myself kinder.** The clouds began to disappear instead of turning grey, instead of continuing to grow darker, they got lighter until they disappeared altogether, blending into white skies making it impossible to decipher. This was what I needed. I needed not to be governed by the weather forecast but to create my own season, a season of spiritual wealth, because this is what I understand fuels my existence.

I called to the boys who were already in the front room bouncing around on the sofas making contact sounds like, 'gotcha' and 'my turn'. I had no idea what they were doing in that room, or if they were at risk of breaking something important to me, but this morning I was not concerned. The boys came charging into my bedroom, Cassius first wearing his pyjamas like a costume with his pyjama top tied around his tiny waist and his dressing gown hood on his head. Kwame on the other hand was dressed in his pyjamas, yet he had gone the extra mile and added his Peter Pan hat from an old World Book Day costume, together with the matching Green cut off shorts over his pyjama's bottoms. As I sat up in my bed looking at them, part of me was crying with laughter inside. I looked at my sons in their makeshift outfits and laughed. The boys looked puzzled; not once did it occur to them that I was laughing at how ridiculous they looked. Perhaps that was because that was not the type of thing mums did, perhaps mums don't laugh at their children...? I doubt it and if I am wrong, then I'll be the first to admit that I laugh at my children all the time. In fact, I wish I laughed at them much more, because it ignites me.

That being said I would happily have them create these preposterous costumes, if it meant I could start my morning off with this type of roll around on the floor laughter. I wonder if that makes me a terrible mum. My sons were not at risk or being harmed in any way by my laughter. In fact, as they stood in the doorway wondering what I found so funny. They both burst out laughing. I had no idea why they were laughing; they had no idea why I was laughing, but we were all laughing.

What more could I ask for. The landline started ringing, both boys raced to answer it shouting, 'I'll get it!' Kwame clearly beat Cassius to the mark because he was the first to announce Goddie's on the phone. And by Goddie, he meant GF. I looked up at the time, she was up pretty early for a Saturday. Kwame brought the phone to me.

'MORNING Girlfriend, what are you and the boys doing today?'

'We don't really have any plans; the weather doesn't look too great so we might just stay home and watch movies'

'Ok well, we'll come and join you. I'm going to get ready now, then we should be with you by about midday'

'Yes GF' I replied sarcastically, knowing that my best friend had no sense of time. She would arrive alright, but she was not going to be here at midday. Midday was far too early for her. She would probably be with us by 13:30 or so. I came off the phone and realised the boys were dancing around with excitement, after figuring out that Goddie was coming down, or more importantly, singing because Kymani, GF's son, would be coming to 'their' house to play. The jokes were no end with the two boys this morning. The boys hadn't seen Kymani for a couple of weeks, and I could hear Kwame talking about which movies he was going to show Kymani and which Power ranger move he was going to teach him. Cassius interjected to tell his brother that he could already do that move because it was easy. As the argument ensued both boys preceded to have what looks like a 'kick off', similar to a dance off but the aim of this was who could kick the highest. I watched as they kicked so high, they fell onto the floor, onto the sofas, and then on to each other. I could see this was going to be a funny day, hilarious in fact. I walked to the kitchen to start making breakfast. I noticed the mail on the floor. Picking it up, I checked the time again, noticing the postman was surprisingly early for a Saturday. I hoped when we moved into the new house, our new postman came at a regular time, preferably in the morning. As a child our postman always came in the morning. In fact, he used to come before I left the house to go to school, and back then my school started at 8:30am. The postman around here definitely didn't operate like this.

I gave the boys something to eat and then started to filter through the mail, leaving out the bills and the debts till last. I didn't see the point of adding a level of stress to the morning that I just didn't need. And that was inevitably what the bills or the debts were going to do, so that could wait I told myself. I started to open the other letters, one of which was a large A4 sized envelope. Hmmmm, I read the stamp, it was from the University. Not the one I was planning on attending in September, but the old one who had told me not to come back, while they investigated. I stood there staring down at the envelope in my hands, for some reason that I couldn't put my finger on, I felt nervous about opening the envelope. Obviously, the university would be aware that my children were now on the child protection register, which in itself would obviously lead to some kind of decision or the other on their part. But why was I nervous, what exactly was I nervous about? Hadn't I been awaiting notification from the University? I mean I had been anticipating notification from the University. I knew they were going to contact me, and I wanted them to contact me. So why on Earth was I stood still staring at the envelope as though this was a huge surprise? The envelope was definitely bigger than the small brown envelope I expected to receive my decision letter in. However, l hoped the transcript of my first year's credits was also enclosed.

As I started to peel away at the corners of the envelope I began to panic. What if this is my transcript enclosed but I haven't passed due to everything that had taken place in my personal life. If they had not awarded me the credits for my assignments, and the work I had completed so far, I didn't even want to see what was in the envelope. I knew I had worked my ass off, if they were not going to award me my credits, I was willing to burn the envelope right then and there. Speaking to myself I could hear the surety in my voice. However, there was that niggling feeling, my Jiminy Cricket, reminding me that I wasn't making perfect sense. For starters I would not be burning anything. I'm sure I would possibly feel like burning it, but that was not my reality. Besides where would I burn it. It wasn't as though I owned a house with a huge open fireplace.

My reality was that even though I felt like I had come so far in making a decision not to return, failing in what I had undertaken, failing in what I had made every effort to succeed in, would probably put me over the edge and I knew it. In life sometimes you just need to be honest with yourself. Being honest in who you know yourself to be. One of the things I know about myself is that having made the decision, would not alter how I felt, if for some reason I had not fulfilled my part. Or in other words had not succeeded in what I had actually done.

The suspense was killing me, so I gave up trying to open the envelope in a dainty manner and began tearing of shreds of the envelope flap in order to yank the contents from inside. My transcript was enclosed. I had gained all of my credits! Each and every one. I had been graded highly on my course work, in assignments including my assignment on my professional practice, which was part of the placement. I couldn't believe it. Of course, I knew I had worked hard, I knew that I should have been awarded every single one of these credits that I was staring at. Yet for some reason I was speechless. For some reason there's a difference between what you know you deserve and being awarded or recognised for what you deserve. I wonder if that has anything to do with injustice and discrimination in the world, why often people work hard for an end goal, achieve that end goal and then have to stop themselves from falling to pieces in disbelief. What on Earth is that about? I couldn't make sense of my inability to fathom what was in front of me. I read through the document slowly looking at each assignment and the percentage of credits awarded. I knew I could do this. I knew I had something to offer. I knew that I knew what I was talking about. And this right here before my eyes was proof. I tried to remember where I put my phone so that I could phone my mum and share the good news with her.

'Please can one of you pass mummy's phone!' I called out to the boys.

'Actually, never mind

I changed my mind quite quickly, realising I was celebrating, as though I was going to return to the university, and complete my further two years, but this wasn't the case.

'Here you go Mummy' Cassius handed me my phone.

I wanted to tell him it's ok now mummy doesn't need it after all, but the speed at which he moved to bring me the phone, I didn't want to disappoint him. I decided I wasn't going to call my mum. Of course, I would speak to her later, and I would mention it to her, but I was beginning to feel that by celebrating the transcript, I was going against my decision, and the thought process that lead to that decision.

I glanced over at the paperwork one last time and then placed it back into the envelope. I looked at the other debts and bills, selecting the envelopes one by one to see who needed to be paid first. I opened one of the envelopes realising I didn't recognise the sender and pulled the letter out. It was from the University, again my old University, not the one I had intended to begin in September. I sat down before I began reading the letter.

Dear Yolanda....'

The letter stipulated that they had liaised with the Local Authority which I'm assuming they meant Elsa and Elsa's manager, and have been made aware that both my sons had been placed on the child protection register. However, the university had decided that I was able to return to university and complete my course. The letter advised that they would just ask of me to keep them informed if there were any changes. I assumed by changes they meant if the children were removed or perhaps any kind of abuse was ever substantiated. I looked away from the letter and instead turned my focus to look out the kitchen window for a moment. The weather that had failed to drown me only moments earlier, was beginning to toy with my feelings. I could feel that my momentum was tainted. However, I couldn't make sense of why.

Firstly, the university had awarded me my credits. Secondly, they had told me that I was welcome to come back and complete my course, as they had concluded their investigation. What was going on here, what was really happening? Was someone looking at me and playing a game of chess with my life? A game of cards with my family? I was pleased, yet on the other hand, I was not pleased. On one hand I wondered why all the rash and immediate decisions surrounding my livelihood, only to turn around and tell me that everything is ok, we're satisfied now. I was grateful but were they aware of what I'd been through recently. What my family had had to go through? How can you turn someone's life upside down, and then say oopsie-daisy you can continue as normal now? You can't do that. How do you humiliate an individual in such a manner, only to say it's okay, we're satisfied that you haven't done anything wrong? I found myself again considering people who were wrongly convicted only to serve 10 years, 15 years, any amount of years really, before later having that conviction overturned. I can't imagine how that must feel. Because I had not lost my children, I had not been thrown into the barbarism of prison. And yet I was sat there thinking, is that it? Is that all they have to say for themselves?

CHAPTER 45

Finally, we were ready to move into the new house. We still hadn't been allocated a new social worker either, which indirectly annoyed me, because to hear the way in which social workers referred to my family, then to balance that with the level of concern they seem to show it was disproportionate. I'd already told myself that social services are clearly quite choosey when selecting the families, they wanted to intervene with. I was past believing that it was all about concern. I had taken the boys to school already and was scheduled to start moving things into the house. I had managed to enlist a couple of friends, and my brother to help shift as much as we could. The larger items would be transported via a van. As I put the key in the front door of the new house, I exhaled a sigh of relief. This would be our new home. This is where we would settle, for now at least. I began by unpacking items that could go in the kitchen and gave the house another once over. I had informed the social worker that we would be in the new house within next two days, meaning Friday. They had reiterated to me that the new Local Authority had our case and would be contacting us. I spent the day at the new house, I wanted it to be comfortable for when the boys and I spent our first night there the upcoming weekend. I also wanted to familiarise myself with the area, the neighbours, and sounds. You know every house has its sounds. It's the difference between us knowing when they might be an intruder in our homes, or if the fridge is singing gently, or the next-door neighbour slamming a door in their house. I learned about sounds when I was a child, and it's something that I bear in mind as an adult. Different places have different sounds, good sounds, bad sounds, indifferent sounds. Sirens were the most prominent sound where our current, soon-to-be old house was, and the new house, I quickly established aeroplanes were the prominent sound. Absolutely perfect for me. Well unless I was trying to watch something on TV.

I decided to leave the new house just in time to collect the boys from school. There was no after school club, meaning I was collecting them directly from school, meaning I would not be able to avoid seeing certain members of staff today. I parked the car and rushed to the gates of the school, a couple minutes late. As I walked through the door, the Trenchbull was stood in reception. I said hello courteously and kept walking.

'Oh Yolanda' can you just wait there a moment'

'Yes Miss O'Connor' I replied in a manner which sounded as though I was exasperated.

'Will you come with me please?'

'What is it Miss O'Connor?'

I didn't have time for her nonsense today. We were moving on with things. She was soon to become the past, along with her prejudice staff, prejudice school, culture-less school, culture-less values, dilapidated cave of an office, and moron sidekick with no moral servitude. Did Miss O'Connor really want to hear about it today?

'The boys are in my office Yolanda'.

'Why are my son's in your office Miss O'Connor?' my tone of voice was a dead giveaway. It was the tone of someone who had decided enough was enough. The tone of someone who was tired of being battered from pillar to post, and then back again. The tone of someone who had been pushed to the very edge of existence, and had to resurrect themselves, against the plethora of digs, kicks, judgements. This tone was different to the tones I had given Miss O'Connor before. This tone was a finale. I was tired of her feeling like she was in charge of my family, tired of her waiting until things were seemingly ok, and then over turning the table on us, leaving us to scramble around on the floor trying to piece our lives back together again. No. No more!

'Please Yolanda if you will, can you just follow me?

I followed Miss O'Connor to the office walked in and stood by the door. I wasn't staying and did not need to sit down. The boys were sat in the office, next to a man and a woman I didn't recognise, but assumed they were uniforms because I noticed walkie-talkies, protective footwear, and standard stonewash jeans.

'You two stand here, I said to the boys' calling them over to where I was stood near the door.

'Do you mind sitting down Yolanda'

'Yes, I do mind, and no I will not. What do you want to talk about?' I demanded.

Sensing something was wrong Cassius who had stood beside me when I called to the boys, started to cry. There was a knock at the door, and I moved out of the way to allow it to open. A woman walked in with a phone in her hand.

'Oh hello, you must be Yolande'

'No I am Yo-lan-da!'

'Oh, my apologies, my name is Marianne, I'm a duty social worker'

'And...?' I replied

'The school have contacted us today, as one of the boys has stated that he doesn't feel safe to go home'

'I beg your pardon! That doesn't make sense. Why would one of my son's feel that they don't feel safe coming home? What have you asked them for them to tell you that? Furthermore, is there an allegation, is there a disclosure, as to why they are not feeling safe to come home?'

'No Yolanda there has not been a disclosure, however we have to take these concerns seriously and make sure the children are safe to go home?'

'Or what Marianne? Or what will you do, are you removing them?'

'Yolanda if you can just sit down for a moment, I'm simply here just to establish that everything is ok'

'OK HOW? What is it, you want to see?

One of the uniforms decided to speak.

'Yolanda we're not here to judge you were just following procedure'

'I'm sorry officer, did I ask you anything? Better still, are you taking my sons?

'No Yolanda that is not why I'm here'

'GOOD. Kwame, Cassius', let's go. I grabbed the boys by their hands, turning to leave the room.

'Please wait Yolanda' Marianne squeaked.

I stopped and looked at Marion the uniforms and the Trenchbull.

'Do you know what gets to me about you lot, you have barely contacted me since the CP conference, yet still you turn up here today with my sons in an office, you've got my son crying for no reason because you keep putting my kids through this s***! You see if you don't have the power to remove my son's, stay away from them, because I need you to know that I've had enough of this and I will not accept any of your b******* any longer. Furthermore, if you're that concerned make sure the next time you call me into this office, you've got paperwork to support whatever you're saying!'

I slammed the door and stormed to my car, pulling the boys alongside me. I didn't talk the in the car, my mind was racing. My day has gone well up until this point, we were finally ready for the move, the boys were not going to stay at that school, definitely not after today. Nonetheless I was fuming. Each time another situation arose, I felt targeted. I was tired of feeling that way. More regard needed to be given to parents. The array of judgements was like bashing someone and expecting them to grow and change and evolve and blossom. That was impossible. That wasn't how you nurture or support change. Ever tried sowing a seed, depriving it of basic sustenance, then beating away at its roots as it sprouts? I couldn't help but think that some of the judgements were based on my race, age and external factors, which had nothing to do with anything. I was tired of complaining on the phone to my Mum, about feeling discriminated against. I was tired of crying my eyes out because my best was not good enough, and I was tired of these people feeling as though they had the right to be judge and jury in my life. I wondered if they even had children of their own. If they even knew the struggle it was for parents to be the best that they could be for their children amidst the turmoil of life.

I mean why is it that mothers, tend to face so much judgement, when anything is called into question. Why is it that nonfatal mistakes are not considered part of the learning experience? Are there even any roles in life in which humans do not make errors along their journey to becoming the expert? Why should parenting be any different? Without a second thought I found myself driving towards the local authority's main office. I already had all the contact details, and I knew which team was dealing with our case. I drove to the office and asked the reception to call the team manager. The receptionist was helpful, and it wasn't long before the team manager was downstairs meeting with me in one of the meeting rooms attached to the reception area.

The manager, Janet, who came to see me, was not Robins manager, it was someone who held a higher position than that, and what was interesting is that she was familiar with us before I had turned up.

I sat down in the room with both the boys, as did Janet.

'What can I do for you today Yolanda? Janet's voice was pleasant. I didn't notice a hint of judgement, sarcasm or a patronising tone.

'I have just left my sons school Janet…'

I explained to Janet what happened when I got to the school. I told her how angry I was at the way I felt I was being judged, and my children would be being used by adults. I told her about the recent child protection conference where the social worker had accused me of using inappropriate language because I expect my son to know what the word soluble means. I mean I told her everything. I even went on to tell her, that I decided not to pursue a career in social work based on our experience of the recent intervention and told her how judgemental and unsupportive I felt their practice was. Although Janet was a black woman, I told her how disappointing it was that it wasn't best practice to allocate social workers that are culturally appropriate, based on some of the barriers that even she, should be aware are face within different cultural backgrounds. I offloaded in its entirety to Janet, and when I felt I said enough, I asked her if she felt she had a carer that would be best placed to raise my son's in place of me.

'No Yolanda that is not the case'.

'Well now that we've cleared that up, my request is that your social workers refrain from scare mongering and judgemental practice, as I've explained today to Marianne, I will not allow you to put me and my son's through this any longer. I fully understand the parameters of the child protection plan and so far, have adhered to that. However, it does need to be made clear that the child protection plan does not mean we are sharing parental responsibility'. I stood up knowing that I had said so much and opened up so much that my next step was tears, and I needed not to be sat in this dingy meeting room, when the waterworks began.

'Thank you for your time Janet, because another manager would have sent a message explaining they were too busy, I'm sure'

'You're welcome Yolanda, and for the record I'm not judging you, I can see that you care about your son's and I can see that they feel the same. Thank you for being honest with me about the way you feel.'

I was still upset about the uniforms speaking to me, and the school contacting them, even though there were no allegations. However so far, this was about the most humane conversation I had with one of the professionals. And although I was upset on one hand, I had to Give Thanks with the other, because this was the point, I had been trying to make all along. Treat families like humans, this is not a case study featured in a textbook. This is a real family, and the family consists of more than the outline, what about the colourful elements that bring that family to life. In the midst of my ranting that was basically what I was saying. I wiped away the tears as the boys and I walked back to the car. I held their hands tightly and bent down and kissed both of them on the cheek. The nightmare just seemed to be never-ending.

CHAPTER 46

It was our first weekend in the new house. I had cooked breakfast for the boys instead of cereal, so that we could sit down and eat together, marking a new beginning. The boys were excited about the new room, and bed, and had been asking since the night before to play in the garden. After they were both washed and dressed, I let them play in the garden and watched from the window, as they run around wildly enjoying the new space. As I watched them, I decided it was time for me to draft a letter to Miss O'Connor to advise her that Kwame would not be returning after the summer period. I explained in the letter, that Cassius would attend until the half term, at which I would then be withdrawing him from the school also. I sealed the envelope, ready to hand to the receptionist on Monday morning. Last week had been the final straw. I needed to get the boys out of there as soon as possible. I was devastated at leaving Cassius but reminded myself that I was not leaving him behind, instead I was trusting the process, as my friend Mimi would tell me. I discussed it with Jayde and would drop Cassius to her in the morning, before dropping Kwame to school. On the days where Cassius would be at after school club, I would collect him. All other days, he would go home with Jayde, and I would collect him from there. I couldn't possibly pick up both the boys due to the coinciding times at which they finished school. I would do this just until half term that was all.

The second letter I drafted was to my old University. A polite letter, thanking them for their previous letter, but advising them that

I had taken the decision to withdraw from the course, and would not be returning to continue my studies. I felt better after writing both letters. I would post the university letter later that afternoon and Miss O'Connor would receive her letter on Monday morning. I felt relieved I'd made the decisions and put them in writing, now I would be sticking to them. As I sat there watching the boys, I had no regrets about the decisions enclosed within the letters. I not only believed in the decisions but was certain of them. Only recently, Kwame had come to me using the same verbatim of feeling 'safe at home', to then arrive at the school and yet again, my parenting and my whole life called into question. I knew I had made the right decision. There was no way I could allow all of this to keep happening, these people were not going to destroy my sons.

CHAPTER 47

The day had finally arrived when we would board the aeroplane to soar into the skies, leaving all remains of yesterday behind us, even if just for a few weeks. The boys had slept in my bed the night before, far too excited to actually go to sleep. Besides I was excited and didn't see the point of sleeping either, I would sleep when I got to Jamaica, I told myself.

We met my mum and my brother at the airport. Luckily, we'd arrived at about the same time, thus ensuring we were seated together on the plane was easy. The boys had new Disney suitcases and were more concerned with wheeling around the cartoon cases, then an actual holiday. They were children I reminded myself. They had no idea, the amount of blood sweat, and tears that made the entire holiday possible. Getting on a plane was not similar to getting on a bus, you just get a ticket and 'bob's your uncle'. You're off. But I knew what had gone into it, and as we were seated on the plane, I began to feel strange. My head was feeling light. My body felt like it was giving way. Had the pilot required that all passengers stand at that moment, I would have been unable, because as I sat in the airplane seat. I could feel my body sinking deeper between the cushioned seats, as it enveloped me like a secret package. My body was almost floating, much like a balloon, being held between a finger and thumb. I watched attentively as tension, stress, anxiety, anger, resentment, fear, all packed their bags and vacated my being. There was no longer room left here for them to occupy. They had been the bane in our lives, in my life, long enough. It was high time they left. I sat on the plane knowing that, no matter what else happened, I would do everything in my power to prevent them from re-entering, repossessing. Everything. They had had not entered to serve or protect me, but rather to aid in ridiculing and judging me. At no point had they been good houseguests. I did not appreciate nor want to keep their company. They could all, up and leave right now. I was done with them. Onwards and upwards literally.

CHAPTER 48

The holiday was well deserved. When we returned, the sun was still shining in England, allowing us to make believe our holiday was extended somehow. The boys had told me they had had an amazing time. Spending time with family, doing tourist activities, getting to know my grandparents. Not to mention nonstop eating. They had had a ball. We all did.

Having got rid of the extra baggage before take-off, had allowed me to rekindle with my old self. Let my hair down and just be free. On holiday or 'at home' as I prefer to call it, I felt free from all the judgements that had overshadowed me in England. Here I was surrounded by people with the same or similar values to me. When I looked around everything was normal to me, when I listen to the sounds around me, everything sounded normal to me. I was not raising my eyebrows even half as much as I did, when I was out and about in England. The boys hadn't wanted to come home and I couldn't help but admit to them that neither did I.

Kwame was excited about starting a new school, Cassius wasn't best pleased about having to wait before he could join his brother at the new school.

However, when I told them they would be attending a play centre with Kevron and James the following week, Cassius forgot about his bitter disappointment. I had also received a call from a new social worker. As we had been away and had not been visited, she was keen to introduce herself to us as soon as possible. Still grateful at not having to lug around the excess baggage that I'd been carrying before, I didn't dread meeting with the new social worker. In fact, now that I was feeling a lot lighter, I was more than willing to give her a chance. I had spent a lot of time reflecting while I'd been away, and one of the things I had reminded myself of, was that there was a higher purpose to what I was experiencing, all that we were going through. There was a reason I had been pushed to the edge of my very existence. A reason I had been consumed with fear, anger, resentment and lack of understanding. It was because that was the way it had been written. This was part of my evolution. If I had been told that I would go through something like this I would have expected to crumble at the sheer thought. Yet I was still standing, still fighting, still believing. I was even stronger then I had thought I was.

This reminded me of Bible stories that my Auntie Barbara once taught me when I was just a young child. She had read me the story of Job and explained to me why Job had endured what appeared to be a traumatic experience. He was not being punished he was being tested. Strengthened. Upon reflection, even then it made perfect sense to me, of course it was a test. Strength is not gained through will but through endurance. That is where we accumulate resilience. **The best lessons in life are acquired through some of our most traumatic experiences**.

The story of the wise King Solomon when the two mothers argued over whose baby it was, after one baby died during the night, and one survived. The wise king had tested the women to try and determine whose baby had died and whose had survived. The test had proven whom the baby belonged to, after the mother of the living baby requested that the baby be given to the other mother, as not to see the child divided in two. She too had passed a test. Somehow, I had always known that human beings would be tested on their strength and their faith, yet throughout this at various points I had lost sight of that. Getting rid of the unwanted guests while on the plane allowed me to see things more clearly and decipher more astutely. I decided that I would continue to fight, minus the anger. I would do my utmost not to let my emotions get the better of me, but to stand in front of my sons and continue to fight for what I believed in.

It was still the school holidays, so our new social worker, Barbara had arranged to come and see us during the daytime, which suited me, because then, we could get on with the rest of our day after she left.

She arrived promptly at 13:00. A tall Black woman, probably about my mum's age with braids. I opened the door and she introduced herself to me. I offered Barbara a seat and sat down, so she could begin talking. Barbara went through pleasantries asking how we had been, and if we had enjoyed our holiday. I answered the questions, minus any sarcasm and let Barbara continue.

'I'll be doing announced and unannounced visits to you every two weeks. I am aware that you are not home during the day, so I will try to visit you at convenient times'

'Okay, 'I replied still being courteous. For the first time since this ordeal had begun, I didn't feel the need to defend the notion of announced and unannounced visits. Before now, before our holiday, I had found fault in the assertion that we needed to have these visits and that some would be unplanned, assuming that meant they would be trying to catch me out. However, although I still believed that the purpose of announced and unannounced visits is to see what goes on when no one is expected, it was irrelevant, because still we had nothing to hide.

If they wanted to spend time with us fine, we'll see how long before they got bored. I was trying not to stare at Barbara as she spoke. Her nose was quite prominent, even her eyes. It was like I'd seen her face before. There was something about Barbara's face that looked familiar. I was sure I didn't know her, but she looked like I should. Besides, I wasn't always good with faces, so I could barely rely on my memory. Maybe she knew my Mum, maybe I'd seen Mum talking to her before. My mum knew a lot of people. Barbara continued talking.

'Sorry Barbara to interrupt you, but I think I know you from somewhere'

Barbara looked at me puzzled.

'I don't think so Yolanda'

I told Barbara who my mum was, and the look on her face before she smiled, I knew I hit the nail on the head.

'Oh, my word' she said 'I don't think I've seen you in over 15 years. I would never have recognised you.'

It turned out I had mistaken the similarities for her sister. I explained to her that I thought she looked just like her sister, and because I occasionally see her sister when I'm out shopping, when I saw Barbara, her face looked familiar to me. They both looked alike in my opinion.

'Thank you for letting me know Yolanda'

'To be honest I thought it best, because I wouldn't want to compromise your position, and you barely even know me. So far this experience is leaving a foul taste in my mouth so the last thing I want to do is give them reason to think I'm doing something untoward. Besides, I know how these things go, so I'd rather just tell you.'

'I appreciate that Yolanda. I'll have to go back to the office now, and let my manager know, you'll probably be allocated a new social worker.'

'Another one', I said sounding exasperated.

'Yes, Barbara smiled reassuringly.

I called to the boys so Barbara could see them before she left. I knew that even though we would be allocated a new social worker, as she was here with us, she would be expected to check the boys were okay also. Now we would have to wait for another social worker. I assumed they had paid attention to my request for a culturally appropriate social worker, having sent Barbara. I only hoped that unlike the last borough, they had more than **one** culturally appropriate social worker.

CHAPTER 49

There were quite a few changes taking place at work. They were restructuring to save money. My manager seemed to be quite stressed about it. He had a wife and two young children; however, his wife did not work she was a stay at home mum. From my manager's perspective this had always worked for them, although he frequently complained about money or lack of it. Luckily non-managerial staff (like me) jobs were safe. However, management were having to reapply for their roles. I had to be grateful that this didn't apply to me because with all the current changes if I had to then start looking for another job, it would most likely invite some of those old friends back to reside in my soul. No thank you. Still no room here. I needed to hold on to this job at least until my final year. I had always said that if I needed to buckle down in my final year, I would resign from my role to do so and then find a proper job at the end of my degree. A proper job simply meant a job whereby you need to have obtained a qualification to work within that role. Unlike the role I was in. Don't get me wrong there was nothing wrong with my job and it allowed me to do what I loved, supporting young people. However, if I was qualified it wouldn't be my main job, hence why I chose to do it part-time.

The boys were at a play centre with Kevron and James. They were going on a trip to the zoo tomorrow and I needed to get them some bits for their packed lunch. I finished work and decided to stop off at the supermarket before I collected the boys, to allow us to make our way straight home afterwards. I arrived at the play centre and rung the bell. As the door opened, I couldn't ignore the blaring sound of music, thud of dancing feet, laughter and screams of children playing. As I entered it sounded like they had at least 100 children in there. I listened closely, I was sure I could hear Cassius. I spotted Kevron over by a group of older boys who were playing computer game of some kind and waved to him. Kevron waved back signalling for me to look over to the far corner of the room, where Kwame and Cassius were showing some of the other children how to do a dance. My sons we stood in front of seven or so other children demonstrating how to do the Superman dance. I stood still watching from the distance I didn't want the boys to sight me straight away just in case they stopped dancing. I wanted them to continue. I was surprised on one hand that the boys were here dancing shamelessly in front of these other people, yet, I had to take into consideration that these were their characteristics. Clearly, they were comfortable at the play centre and comfortable enough within the environment to do what they enjoy doing, I was grateful for that. It wasn't long before the boys noticed I was there.

'MUMMY' both the boys came charging towards me. I bent down hugging them.

'Are you two having fun?'

'Yes mummy. Please can we stay a bit longer?

'You can stay a bit longer while I go and speak to James and then we're going to go home.'

'Okay' they said running back to where they had come from, in case I was about to change my mind. I had already seen James look over at me with his hand in the air signalling for five minutes. It was funny because when I collected the boys from play centre and James wanted to have a word with me, anxiety was not my first reaction. I didn't feel the need to turn and run as fast as I could heading for the hills. I just took it in my stride. Ideally this is what I always wanted to feel no matter where my children were. Even if for any reason my children made a mistake and had to be sanctioned for it, I didn't want anxiety to be at the forefront of the communication. I didn't want to dread receiving feedback from schools, play-centres, nurseries whatever the provision, because everybody makes mistakes, we are only human. Sometimes we need to consider how we relay information to others because while some parents may take things in their stride other parents already have anxiety and don't need it exacerbated.

'Afternoon James, how is everything?'

'Good Yolanda, thanks for asking why don't come on through?'

James directed me into the office.

'I wanted just to have a quick chat with you your lander and let you know that your social worker has contacted me today.'

I looked at James puzzled we had only just met with Barbara who we knew was not going to remain our social worker due to the conflict of her knowing my family.

'What social worker, Barbara? Barbara is not going to remain our social worker because her family know my mum.'

'No Yolanda, it wasn't a Barbara who contacted me it was someone else. Hold on I wrote her name down somewhere.'

I waited as James ruffled through some papers on the desk.

'Jacqueline. That's her name Jacqueline Brown. She contacted me today to introduce herself to me and told me she was your newly allocated social worker.'

'Oh ok.' I replied, still trying hard to catch up. You had only been a couple of days and already they had reallocated us. I wondered if James had made a mistake.

'She asked me about the mentoring I explained to her what we do. She asked about the boys, how they were getting on, I gave her an update. Oh, she also asked if I felt there was anything else the boys would benefit from. I did explain to her Yolanda that respite during the holidays would be useful. I do think that as a single mum there are times you are finding it difficult to balance what you have to do, with what you need to do. I think having a provision the boys can attend during the holidays when you are still working will be beneficial to you and can mean a little less to worry about whilst you're at work.'

'Oh, thank you James, I really appreciate that. That's thoughtful.'

'That's fine Yolanda as we told you from the beginning, we're here for you and the boys'

'What did she say?'

'She said she didn't see any problem with it, but she would need confirmation from her manager, and she would get back to me'

'She sounded nice Yolanda.'

I gave James a look of scepticism.

'Hmmmm'

'One last thing, she also invited us to attend your next Child Protection Conference, as we have been working with yourself and the boys.'

'Oh good.' I said giving James a thumbs up.

Our new social worker had been busy. Contacting the mentoring service, inviting them to the CP hearing...ok maybe James was right, maybe this one was ok. I would reserve my judgement and wait and see.

CHAPTER 50

It was only 10:30 in the morning and already I was tired of walking around the shops. We had woken up at the crack of dawn so that I could get the boys ready and get to the shops early enough to beat the rush to buy school uniforms. Ordinarily I would have done the school uniform shopping by now, but we had been away for most of the summer and when we returned, I needed to recoup financially before I could start worrying about uniforms. As Cassius was not moving his school straight away, he would continue to wear his old uniform. Although, whilst I was buying Kwame new uniform for the new school, I made a point of buying Cassius' uniform too. I was grateful to the boys Nan and Granddad, as they had helped me with purchasing the boy's uniforms. Cassius seemed to have come to terms with the fact that he would be at the school without his brother only for a few weeks. Kwame on the other hand was excited, having found out his new school would be taking them swimming every week. Quite frankly I wasn't sure why he was so excited when he wasn't the biggest fan of swimming. However, I guessed with weekly swimming lessons he had no choice but to adjust. I was set to start university the week the boys went back to school. I still not had not received my timetable as yet and couldn't wait to get started so that I could work my new routine out. So far, I knew I couldn't drop both the boys to school and pick them up so I had sorted that out as much as I could. But without the timetable, certain elements were still left hanging in the balance.

We raced around the shops picking up everything from uniforms to vests, socks, and boxers. When I had run out of energy and the boys and I had turned into grizzly bears brought on by the onset of hunger, we grabbed our bags and headed off somewhere in search of lunch. We sat down to eat as shoppers scurried around in the background. I could hear babies crying, throwing tantrums frustrated parents. Not to mention moody teenagers' traipsing slowly behind swift walking adults. I thought about it whilst reminding myself why I prefer to do things like that first thing in the morning. This just wasn't the time of day in which I could maintain my sanity and walk around the shops. I was grateful we were sat down eating. If I wore a heart monitor, it would probably have alerted me that I was about to turn into Hulk only moments before we had arrived at the food court. I didn't envy the shoppers whizzing around behind us. Today was now done and the boys had everything they needed for school the following week, so we were done. Finito! Roll on Monday morning.

CHAPTER 51

My alarm was sounding off in my ears. I swiftly hit the snooze button and continued laying still. I welcomed the silence, the stillness of the morning. Today marked a new beginning. One for the boys and one for me also. Kwame was starting at his new school, and Cassius would be returning to the old school, alone. As I lay in bed, I started rethinking whether I had made the right decision or not. I knew I had gone through the thought process previously, having spoken at length with myself about the whys and how's. There was no good reason for me to continue beating myself up about this. I had no choice but to withdraw Kwame from that school and the only reason Cassius would remain, was because his space was not yet available. I almost willed with every part of my spirituality that Mrs Asante would call right now. At this very moment to say 'Yolanda, please bring Cassius to school we are able to take him, as of this morning', but I knew that was highly unlikely. I just had to get over it. It was only for a time. **Everything was only for a time.** I had to remind myself to trust the process. That was all I had to do now. **Trust the process**.

I sat up and turned the TV on. It was so early, GMTV had yet to start. Now what would I do with my extra time. I had set the alarm earlier than usual to allow me the added time to get dressed slowly, panic less, shout less for the boys to get a move on, be less stressed, sip my tea slowly, instead of burning my insides in a bid to drink at least half a cup of tea, before dashing out the house, perspiring like a porous fruit. Yet here I was not feeling the spring in my step that I had planned on feeling. Not celebrating the fact that Miss Reynolds and the Trenchbull could no longer seep into my sons' head like a wound unable to heal and prone to infection. Why was I not celebrating that they would no longer infect my son with a false perception of being 'unsafe at home'? Honestly, I knew I was supposed to be feeling better, but I simply wasn't. Here I was wide awake early enough to do so much and more before even waking up the boys, yet I wasn't feeling celebratory. The alarm went off again. 'OH, FOR PETES SAKE!' I hit the button so hard I feared the phone would probably stop working. I mean it had long since had its Bette days anyhow. I turned the volume right down to listen out to see if the boisterous unruly alarm had woken the boys too. There was no sign of movement coming from their room. The birds were singing outside my window. Something I had quickly become accustomed to at this new house. Being as observant as I am. I noticed the birds sang at the same time each morning. Clearly this was their ritual, their chosen way to start the day. It just so happened that their ritual at times was beginning to feel like 'our' ritual. I too marked my morning by the chirpy notes sung by whatever type of birds they were. I was certain that they were not pigeons and that's all I cared about. I despised pigeons, the flying rat bags. Although it was funny, because I had actually never seen the birds, I had only heard them. Yet they sounded ever so beautiful and that is what I told myself, that the birds that woke me up in the morning were beautiful birds. You know like mermaids or unicorns, mythical kind of beauty. I had, in only a short space of time, learned that the birds singing in chorus meant it was near time for me to be awake. I wondered why I didn't have a morning ritual of my own. I was a singer, well sort of. I mean I could sing. Why wasn't I singing my own early morning ritual? Perhaps that was what I needed in my life. To belt out some notes first thing in the morning. Maybe that would start my day off in the right direction. Not sure my new neighbours would agree though. But maybe something else would be more practical. What about the gym? No not the gym. Maybe meditation. Yes meditation. I needed to channel the superfluous emotions. That would probably help. A knock at the bedroom door interrupted my disorderly thoughts.

'Cass?' I called in the direction of the knock. I didn't need to ask. I knew the time and I knew there was no way Kwame was awake unnecessarily at this hour of the morning.

'Morning Mummy.'

Cassius looked sleepy as he entered the room and climbed into bed with me before making himself comfortable.

'Why are you awake so early dumplin?'

'I don't know Mummy.'

'Well it's not time to get up yet, so try and go back to sleep baby.'

'Are you taking me to school today Mummy?'

'I'm gonna take you to Jayde's house and Jayde will take you to school.'

'Oh okay.'

Cassius sounded disappointed. I wondered if that was the reason, he was awake this early. I put my arm around him and pulled him close.

'Remember you'll be going to school with your brother very soon baby, okay.'

Cassius didn't say anything, when I looked down at him his eyes were closed. I kissed him, smiling to myself and continued listening to the birds sing.

My plans for a stress-free morning had gone out the window! I had fallen back asleep, woke up late, and then desperately tried to get the boys ready without becoming agitated. Fat chance! I was screaming, things like, 'Are you still brushing your teeth?' And 'hurry up on the toilet'. It was a mad house. If they hadn't realised yet, the neighbours would know that we were the new family on the street. Finally, we were on our way. First stop Jayde, next stop school, then on to university. This was our first day doing the new journey to school. As soon as we were on our way, I realised that we definitely needed another fifteen minutes in order for the mornings to go in our favour every day. The traffic wasn't horrendous, but it certainly needed to be better which meant we needed to leave home earlier. I looked over at the time on my dashboard I could make it to Jayde, and then to Kwame's school on time. But that was providing all the other lights on the road instinctively turned green when they saw me approaching. If not, I may get to Jayde's late, and then end up having to drop Cassius myself. I turned the music up louder; I could feel my anxiety levels rising again.

'I can't wait to start my new school mummy,' Kwame said sounding rather excited. I looked over at him in the rear-view mirror.

'That's good baby.'

When we arrived at Jayde's house, I left Kwame in the car while I dropped Cassius off. Looking at over at Cassius he looked disheartened for a moment. I knew the change was new to him, and I hated the idea of him not having his brother at the school.

'I can't stop, Jayde, running late.'

'No problem,' she replied ironing one of her boy's shirts. 'You coming with us Cass?'

'Yaaay,' her boys replied excitedly.

I kissed Cassius goodbye and ran outside to do the second half of my new and improved school run. It didn't take long to get from Jayde's house to Kwame's new school. Kwame sang along to the songs on the radio as I drove silently, feeling apprehensive about the day ahead.

Unlike the old school the new school had a car park so parents could park off the road in the car park when they drop the children off to school. Perfect. It did mean that the boys would no longer need their scooters because there was no purpose in scooting from the car park to the school entrance. I rang the bell and we entered. Mrs Asante was there to greet us, in a bright Yellow and Blue African print dress, with a matching head wrap. My word I thought to myself now there goes a head teacher. Already the school was challenging my perceptions but satisfying my intentions all in one. On one hand, I had the belief that head teachers were actual people with character, you know characteristics that oozed character-based authority. It was that uniqueness. Mrs Asante was unique before she opened her mouth. This was what Head teachers to me should look like, they should **be** diverse they should look diverse. Families looking for perspective schools for their children should be able to walk in and feel welcomed not threatened. You see, I firmly believe that a good head teacher has positive intentions for her students. The aim is not really to intimidate the aim is to be personable. Frankly the old age perception of head master or mistress is out-dated. Can I even use that terminology anymore? Is that politically correct, I don't even know. But if you were born around the same time as me then you know that all head teachers looked the same and that isn't diversity.

'Welcome to our school Kwame.'

There was another thing about Mrs Asante she had an almost loud, assertive, prominent voice, without raising it or shouting. It was impeccable. I needed to find a way to ask her to teach me how to do that, because I was either talking, or raising my voice, or shouting. I mean I wasn't the worst; I have family members who when they speak to me, I move further away so they're not deafening me. Nevertheless, I needed to find a way to communicate like this.

'Morning Miss Asante' Kwame replied rather confidently for his first day at a new school. I felt proud. Already he seemed as though he was going to behave like the son, I knew him to be. Not the person walking aimlessly around the class at the old school. No no no, we left the spirit of that person at the old school.

Mrs Asante explained some key bits of information to myself and Kwame, before advising me that she would escort Kwame to the playground to meet the rest of his class and his teacher Mr Joseph. I kissed Kwame and walked back to the car, I unlocked the door sat down and exhaled. I didn't feel as apprehensive as I did less than twenty minutes earlier. I didn't have the same level of anxiety about Cassius being at school by himself. All of a sudden, I was able to realise that these steps were too part of the journey. I knew I had an end goal and I was very clear on what my end goal was so despite the feelings the night before and this morning, I felt as though I was on route. I had left things behind I had changed my mind made new decisions but each of which had been well considered thoroughly deliberated, that embraced with clarity and faith. I started the engine but still didn't drive away, I just needed a minute to reflect on all that was new in our lives, all that was changing. You got this Yolanda, I reminded myself. You've got this!

CHAPTER 52

I arrived at the university early enough to take a seat in the cosy open plan coffee shop and enjoy a cappuccino. As I added more sugar to the already relatively sweet beverage, I caught myself whispering that I could not make this too much of a habit. The cappuccino was going down very well, so much so I was already saying things to myself like, 'I could get used to this', when the truth was, I could not get used to this. My bank balance would not allow me to get used to this. I needed to understand today on the very first day of the new adventure that cosy little sit downs in the coffee shop cost money and cannot become too much of a habit. Yeah right, I responded to myself, knowing full well, at some point, my own advice would be blatantly ignored. The university was busy with students fluttering all over the place. Some had returned for their remaining years, you could tell, because they were talking about the previous year and the necessity for buckling down this time round. Considering this would be the first week of term some of the students already had their nose buried in books taking notes while sipping relatively tiny cups of espresso coffee. I felt like I was cheating, as I allowed the aroma of the espresso to venture into my nostrils from the neighbouring table whilst, I still enjoyed my own cappuccino. Aww well. From where I sat, I could see the University bookshop. It appeared to have an array of books and stationery. I knew I'd be exploring the bookshop at some point. I checked the time on my phone. I had no idea which direction I even needed to walk in to get to the correct lecture theatre. The University was humongous. Even from where I was seated there were various options for direction: a left a right, upstairs, outside. One may well feel overwhelmed. You know that feeling of being the only new person, when really there are hundreds, yet you feel like the sore thumb sticking out, throbbing. It was ten minutes before the induction was due to start, I reminded myself that with my poor sense of direction at the best of times, I would need all of those ten minutes and perhaps an extra five or six, so I grabbed my half-finished cappuccino and headed off in the direction of straight ahead. Who knew where that would take me, at least I could walk in a straight line and then ask for directions making believe I thought I was going the right way.

Surprisingly I arrived at the lecture room within five minutes. More surprisingly was the fact that they were at least twenty-five students in the class when I got there. I wondered if they had walked past me drinking cappuccino like I didn't have a care in the world, perhaps their concern was to rush to class and show enthusiasm. Did that mean I was not enthusiastic? That I had no desire to learn? I caught myself just in time to remind myself why I was there. What I hoped to gain from this degree. My outcome may well be different to everyone else's, but that was okay. My outcome might be demonstrated in another way, knowing me a more peculiar way that only I understood. That was also okay. After all I did have my own Individual Success Criteria, my own ISC. That meant it was impossible to compare my behaviour with the behaviour of others, my outcome with the outcomes of others, and my achievements with the achievements of others. I needed to bear that in mind for the next three years and beyond. I looked around at the eager faces. Young, mature, the group looked diverse so far. That was good. I guess different experiences during different points of our lives lead us to follow various paths. Career changes. Changes in our interests, even changes in our purpose or demonstration of such. The diversity of the group, not just in age but in culture, reaffirmed this. I was looking forward to embarking upon this challenge. Nevertheless, more than anything right now, I needed to see the timetable so I could plan my life. Not being aware of my hours meant I couldn't confirm certain shifts at work nor could I firmly arrange childcare.

'Hi I'm Alison'. The voice came from the person beside me, stretching out her hand for me to shake. I hadn't even noticed that someone was sitting beside me.

'Hi, I am Yolanda,' I replied shaking her hand and extending a friendly smile.

Alison was a tall white woman with long blonde hair that she had perfectly swept into a ponytail. I noticed she had a glasses case on her lap, but she was not wearing glasses. Alison was well equipped with a pencil case, post-its and a choice of three notepads laid out in front of her with what I assume, were her initials in silver on the front. Alison wore enthusiasm like a cologne. You couldn't miss it once you were close enough to her, as I was, at that very moment. Alison and I exchanged pleasantries and spoke about our reasons for joining the course. Alison had been a stay at home mum until recently and now that her children have started high school, she wanted to do something for herself. She told me that she had always wanted to study law, hoping that after completing this course she could go on to practice as a lawyer. I told Alison I commended her for making a decision to embark upon a challenging yet rewarding journey. Alison told me her husband had talked her into it, as she had reservations that the children were not ready for her to be without them. I could see where Alison was coming from and told her so. However I genuinely admired her decision to return to education amidst her uncertainties.

'Good morning All.'

Alison and I looked up, neither of us have noticed the lecturer enter the room. We turned to face the front and looked up attentively. The lecturer was very tall, slim, black man, Alvin. Alvin stood 10 feet high, at the front of the lecture Hall without a microphone and addressed the audience of students.

'I am your course leader…'

Alvin went on to explain how the course would run and the various divisions within the class according to minor modules selected. It was only at that point I realised why Alison and I were sat in the same lecture room, we would probably be in most classes together, however there would be modules whereby our classes would be divided. I would then go according to my minor subject and vice versa. As Alvin spoke one of the first things, I gathered about his character was that he was a straight-talking kind of guy. I did not want to get on his wrong side. I would not have liked him to politely tell me off. I say politely because something about the way he articulated himself, gave me the impression that if he did have to have harsh words with you, they would be so polite, you'd feel worse. I told myself Alvin probably didn't curse half as much as I did in frustration. Funny enough, Alvin went on to speak to the group for a further half an hour even cracking jokes, which were more hilarious because of his sense of humour, as opposed to the actual jokes being funny. On top of it he did have a habit of kind of chuckling at his own jokes, so if you weren't laughing before then you'd certainly be laughing afterwards. He seemed like a normal person, which was good. I wondered if he was a parent, or married, it was hard to tell. Of course, I had no romantic interest in him, I was just curious about the tall funny man who was going to be teaching me for the next three years. Alvin announced that we would be taking a break and handed everyone a copy of their timetable explaining which sessions were compulsory. He explained the absence procedure, attendance requirements and deadlines for assignments. Alvin was still talking while my eyes scanned through the details on the timetable. It looked better than I imagined, lectures didn't start before 10 am, we didn't have to go in every single day, in fact I could still pick the boys up, or at least Cassius every day except one. Oh. My eyes scanned across something else. One of the lectures began at 4pm, how on earth would I manage that. I would need to be in class at 4pm. There was no way I would be able to pick up the boys, or my mum for that fact. My heart sank. It was like I'd been given something in one hand whilst the other hand was snatching it right back out of my grasp. I looked up to the front of the lecture hall where Alvin had been stood. He had just left the room; the break has begun. I gathered up my belongings and headed back in the direction of the coffee shop I forbade myself from frequenting in. It was time for another coffee. I brought my coffee back to the lecture hall unaware of how long we were allocated for the break, as I had been caught up in my own thoughts when Alvin announced the times. The last thing I wanted was to return to the lecture hall late. I wasn't sure if we were allowed to bring coffee into the room, but I thought it was worth the try because I really needed it. I sat at the back of the lecture hall in hope that no one would try to talk to me, at least for ten minutes. I saw Alison renter the room and hoped she was not offended with the fact I'd now changed seats. It's just I needed quiet time, a minute to myself.

I sat on the edge of the row, took my note-pad and pen out and started writing a timetable for my school runs. I noted the days that Jayde could collect Cassius, the days he would attend after school club with Sandra, and the days that I would collect Kwame. Mrs Asante had informed me of the swimming lessons which would also take place on a Thursday, but that was fine as I worked out school would still finish at the same time on a Thursday, so it didn't affect my routine. Perhaps I could collect Kwame and drop him to my brother. Nope that wouldn't work I didn't have enough time to make it from the school to my mum's and back to university. What if I picked up Kwame and dropped him to Jayde and then picked them both up afterwards? No that still wouldn't work. No matter how I looked at it, there was no one who could pick me up from school on the Thursday except me. Alvin had already explained to everyone about absence and attendance. If I didn't attend that lecture every week my attendance would eventually decline below the 80%, I needed to pass the course. I wouldn't even make it past the first year. I slammed the notebook shut, frustrated that I still didn't have a strategy or solution. I contemplated trying to have a quiet word with Alvin at the end of the day but didn't see the point. What would I tell him that 'I was single parent with two children, enrolled on a degree but can't attend class, due to lack of childcare? No. He didn't need to know that. I wasn't trying to get pity. Yes, my current circumstances made life 100 times harder, but I didn't need sympathy. What if I attend every other week, therefore I would not be missing every class, just 50% of them. I realised how ridiculous I was sounding. 'That doesn't make sense Yolanda,' I told myself categorically. I was getting desperate; my thought process wasn't even sound anymore.

'Welcome back everyone, I hope you had a chance to stretch your legs a little and talk to your fellow peers.'

Alvin was back. I decided not to mention anything to him but to go away and see if I could somehow, miraculously find a solution.

CHAPTER 53

I left university and headed home to sit down for a few minutes, before leaving to collect Kwame and then Cassius. When I arrived at the school, I saw other parents pulling up in the car park. As I got out the car and walked towards the school entrance I smiled and said good afternoon. I watched as each of the classroom teachers escorted their children into the playground. I looked around for Mr Joseph so I could try and spot Kwame. The playground was not overrun with children, yet I couldn't see Kwame or his class. Just then Mr Joseph emerged from the building, followed by his class marching closely behind like army cadets. I caught Mr Joseph's attention and smiled at him, to let him know I was ready to take Kwame.

'One moment mum and I'll come and have a word with you', he asked politely.

Oh-oh. What now? What had gone wrong? Why did he need to speak to me?

I watched as Mr Joseph dismissed all the other children and then called for me to follow with him and Kwame.

'We had a good day today Mum, didn't we Kwame?' Mr Joseph asked looking over at Kwame now we were in the classroom.

'Yes Sir,' Kwame replied.

'This morning Kwame told me that he didn't want to do his work because it was hard. I explained it to him again, allowing him to demonstrate what was required of him, and then left him to it. Ten minutes later Kwame still had not completed his task and proceeded to tell me that he didn't know how to. So, Mum I told Kwame that I would wait until the children went out to play and then him and I would sit down and work on it together. Do you know what Kwame did then? He went on and completed his work Mum.'

I laughed. I tried not to laugh but I had to. How could I not laugh at this little boy? There you go. That was what I was talking about. This was why I wouldn't lay down and play dead when these people were trying to label my son. This was the reason why to them, I may come across as an obnoxious, ignorant and angry parent. Yet for me the reality was that my son was behaving like an opportunist. He saw an opportunity to perhaps skip doing his class work and ran with it, so to speak. Well at least ran directly into Mr Joseph who was far wiser than Kwame.

Mr Joseph continued explaining to me what had happened despite me still sniggering like a child as he spoke.

'I took the time to explain to Kwame Mum, that if he does not do his work in class, he will have to do it at playtime or at lunchtime. However, during class if there is anything he truly doesn't understand, he is to ask for my help. The work Kwame did today was impressive, and I've explained to him do not get into the habit of making people think you are incapable. Haven't I Kwame?' Mr Joseph glared at Kwame with his eyebrows raised and crossed discernibly.

'Yes Mr Joseph.'

'Thank you, sir,' I said shaking Mr Joseph's hand tightly. That was my way of saying thank you. Thank you for seeing, Mr Joseph. Thank you for believing, and most of all thank you for encouraging. I hoped Mr Joseph could feel my gratitude within the handshake.

On the way to collect Cassius Kwame and I spoke about his day.

'It was fun mummy, and I got four friends'

'Four friends already baby?' I said trying to appear shocked for maximum effect.

'Yes Mummy,' Kwame continued. 'And today we played football mummy and then do you know…'

Kwame talked me into insanity until we reached Jayde's house. I merely said, really, that's great and Kwame continued and continued. I was so grateful for his day; I hadn't heard him express this kind of joy in what seemed like so long ago. Yet just one day. One day at his new school, and my son was returning to his former excitable self. When we arrived at Jayde's house Kwame was bouncing with excitement to tell his brother all about his day. Jayde opened the door to greet us while Kwame quickly said hello, the 'o' missing as he dashed past Jayde to the living room where the three boys were playing with toys on the floor. Jayde and I stood at the doorway as Cassius jumped up and threw his arms around his brother.

'Kwame!' he exclaimed smiling from ear to ear as though Kwame had returned from a voyage at sea.

'Hi Cass,' Kwame replied wearing a smile that looked like the cat that got the cream but was trying to act like it wasn't a big deal.

'How was your new school? Did you have lunchtime? What's your teacher's name?'

Jayde and I entered the kitchen where we could still hear the boys asking a million questions a minute and Kwame, still licking the cream from his lips was loving it. We had dinner with Jayde and left at a reasonable time to allow her to get the boys ready for bed. Kwame fell asleep in the car, clearly Mr Joseph had worn him out. Another factor I could celebrate during an evening of reflection. Cassius looked as though he was following closely behind, frequently bucking if the car stopped. I pulled over and reached into the back of the car adjusting their heads to more comfortable positions and then continued on the journey home. The journey home was long, not long enough to initiate feelings of regret for the inconvenience I had willingly imposed upon us. Yet long enough to provide me with a moment. I was reminded that this would now be our daily commute every single day. However, looking into my rear-view mirror, at my sons resting their heads gently on each other while whispering a chorus of gentle snores, I was made aware that for moments like this, it was a small price to pay.

When we got home, the boys got ready for bed, said their good nights and I settled down in the sofa to relax. I remembered that there had been some letters that had come in the post, I forgot to open, and jumped up to grab them. It wasn't much. Certainly not anything of grave importance, one was addressed from the local authority. I wondered if it was from this Jacqueline person, our again, newest social worker. I opened the letter and skimmed through the contents. It was a letter introducing our new social worker, Jacqueline

Brown. The letter didn't contain much, clearly Jacqueline just wanted to advise us who she was. Besides we would be having another CP Conference any day soon, so it would be best for her to introduce herself to us, before then. At the end of the letter, Jacqueline had made a point of reminding me that the next CP conference would take place next Thursday. I couldn't recall if this had always been the date or if it had totally slipped me altogether. To be fair it was highly likely that the date had indeed escaped me as the transitions between the three of us had left me slightly more scatter brained than usual. Example, on Tuesday I turned up at the after-school club to collect Cassius, only to be told by Sandra that he wasn't supposed to be at after school club that day. Luckily, I am not a complete moron, because if it had not been for the way I feel about Sandra, I can almost picture myself morphing into some kind of Hulk-like creature demanding my son is brought to me before I destroy the world! That is, in the split second before I realise that my son is safe and sound with Jayde, as arranged previously. And my presence at the after-school facility was rapidly now giving the impression that maybe after all, I do need 'help', psychological help, because let's face it, who the hell forgets where their children are? Did I mention I happened to do all this on a day when the Trenchbull was also in the building? So just to add some clarity to my moment of shame and seemingly careless parenting. I also observed, not realising the ulterior motive behind it at the time, that the Trenchbull had very slowly followed me to the after-school club room. Obviously wondering why, I was at the school at 17:30 when neither of my sons were currently there. Of course, she saw me leave without Cassius and of course she walked right over to Sandra as I left to enquire about my mental malfunction, but that was fine. I would wait for the next CP Conference to hear about how irresponsible a mother I was, or better still, that perhaps I was misusing class A substances and that had caused me to be confused about my sons' whereabouts or something similar. As ridiculous as it sounds, I put nothing past anyone, particularly the professionals, after being subjected to the claims and allegations I had heard so far. The truth was, even though all the above propositions are ludicrous, the truth is that depending on who was speaking, ludicrous seemed to be acceptable conjecture. Elsa the idiot had already proven that. So had the uniforms in trying to discredit me whilst insinuating that my sons were in any way unsafe. That entire experience in the boardroom, the insinuations, the assumptions, conclusions, not to mention the context... would stay with me forever and serve to remind me of the length's others would go to for their own gains. That experience to this day is in part the reason why I will not accept that equality is something readily awarded to us all, irrespective of race, culture, social class and many other factors. My experience forced me to comprehend that the marathon of equality is a continuous destination. There are no ribbons, there is no world record, only the starter pistol sounding the onset in your individual race for equality. Nevertheless, I was no longer overly distracted by what would be said about me. The so-called professionals had demonstrated their idea of a 'social service' and I had come to terms with the fact the system was not working in my favour. They had displayed their intentions to me, tried to make off with my sons, tried to break me, tried to infiltrate my son's minds, attempted to discredit me for having expectations and setting high standards for my sons. At this point, I could not, and would not, be surprised by their cowardly actions. In fact, I welcomed them. I welcomed the challenge. This was not the same young Mum they had surrounded in the playground initially. No. This was the improved me. The me they had forced to evolve some more, to obtain even greater exponential strength. More fool them, for not realising that for some of us, the battles do not break us, they make us stronger. Especially when you are born with Greatness and raised by Queens. Basically, I was now like Scarface screaming 'you wanna piece of me?' Come and get it!

CHAPTER 54

It's funny that one day you can wake up and witness significant change within circumstances that once were believed capable of your demise. That was how my journey unfolded. I had gone from sobbing incessantly, feeling as though life was not worth living, and repeatedly telling myself I was not enough. I had gone from the desperation that only shock and trauma appeared to initiate to clear sound, decision making. It was at this point of my journey external influences began to wither like flowers in winter and disappear.

I cannot share with you a continued battle, because believe it or not, things slowed down a great deal. My thought process and subsequent conclusion is that just like the playground bully, once we cease to be afraid, once we learn how to stand up for ourselves defend ourselves against what seems to be a mightier strength, the warfare begins to subside. Suddenly target practice is diverted away from you as you begin to transform into an evolved you. This is what I had experienced taking place within my own life.

Kwame settled into his new school and although he sporadically challenged Mr Joseph in the classroom depending on his mood, he went on to demonstrate an alternative attitude to learning and his work. Kwame chose to buckle down that bit more now the extendable leash had been severed. Our journey although far from complete, had come as far as it would, for now. I resulted to bringing Kwame to class almost every week for at least half a term, with no mention from Alvin each time. I can however admit that once I had ceased to bring Kwame along for the delightful lecture, I found myself one day in the office with Alvin discussing a piece of work I had recently submitted. Alvin politely gave me feedback and criticism, both good bad and indifferent. However, he went on to say, that he admired my dignity, he told me that he couldn't imagine the circumstances that would cause a student to bring her son to class with her. However, he respected my conduct. He went on to say that he didn't entirely agree with me bringing Kwame along to class. I agreed that this was not ideal, yet he commended me and told me that he could see me doing great things in the future because I was very fair, and I care about people. I knew what had initiated that conversation. Alvin was referring to a particular occasion whereby Kwame had returned late from swimming. Thus, causing me to be late to class. I had raced in with Kwame behind me about to head towards my hiding place at the back when Alvin gave me the signal. I was past the allotted contingency time allowed for lateness. I stopped in my tracks, took Kwame by the hand and headed towards the car. Once inside I broke down, sobbing about the failure I was. Until I arrived home. Once home I opened my textbook and continued writing my assignment. Disappointed though I was, embarrassed though I was, I knew Alvin had been fair, and I respected him for that. So to listen to that very man commend me for conduct, I realised that too was a test and I had passed.

That conversation has lived with me all these years. At the time I remember holding back the tears, because I recall thinking if only, he knew what I was dealing with. In more ways than one; I viewed my encountering Alvin as another one of those blessings, not by chance but by way of virtue. Both spoken and unspoken Alvin's support served as motivation and encouragement on some of my most dismal days.

Cassius began school with his brother shortly afterwards. He settled well within his new class and continued to thrive. Subsequently, it was never really mentioned that he was selectively mute or otherwise. He seemed to communicate his needs quite well and quite articulately but hey: I believe in miracles. As for Kwame, well Kwame will be Kwame. Mr Joseph was the perfect teacher for Kwame, no more constant reports of him not having completed his work or wandering around the classroom instead of sitting on the mat. No that came to a halt. Then of course with the boys not having been at the old school with the Trenchbull and Miss Honey, their presence was no longer required at the Child Protection conferences. Instead they were replaced by staff from the new school, staff who were not intrinsically against us and had made a stark difference in only a short space of time.

After the first conference the uniforms decided not to attend and instead submitted reports saying something like 'no further information'. I wondered why they hadn't come to share more blasphemy but smiled at the empty seats where they had once been sat.

The new school surprisingly didn't condemn my parenting and affection towards my sons. They instead paid focus to Kwame and Cassius according to the characters they were, along with their academic effort and attainment. Suddenly I stopped attending a public flogging instead I began attending a forum on behalf of my sons, our future. With the mentoring service being commissioned, it also meant they too were invited to attend the Child Protection conferences and put their professional opinions across. They would no longer throw any eggs in my face from across the boardroom. I was far from silent, feeling empowered by each milestone irrespective of size, that we had overcome to get to this point. Kevron and James were the blessing in disguise, our modern-day Superheroes. My sons remained on the child protection register for over a year and within that time I witnessed attendance at those conferences whittle down to literally just me. No schools no educational psychologist no anybody. Just me. And I suppose at that point the Chair can only deem that my children are removed from the register because clearly there is no concern here! Oh, what a journey it has been...

We had a social worker at one point, who one day told me that I should write a book about my experience. To this day I remember the exact location of the conversation. She said, 'Yolanda, you have a story in you it would probably help other women. You should definitely consider writing a book.' It brings a tear to my eye as I remember her because she also gave me a title for the book and for the life of me, I couldn't remember it when it was time to title this book. My only wish is that somehow, she stumbles across this very book and remembers that very conversation.

My journey at times has felt like a never-ending battle. On more than one occasion, I have wanted to give up on life itself because it seemed easier than dealing with what I faced before me. I am eternally grateful for every occasion that I wanted to give up but somehow found it impossible and I thank the Almighty for that. I am grateful that I have survived enough that I can share and hopefully offer something to someone else. I give thanks, despite the journey I have survived this far with my sons in tow. To the Almighty I am eternally grateful. Without them there would be no journey. Without them I would not have learned to fight the way I did. Without them I would not have kept trying, but because of them, I refuse to give up. It does gets tough sometimes, believe me it gets tough, but I will not give up. I don't think for a moment that I possess superhuman strength. I don't believe that's what it takes to survive but I think something I have learned is that it takes faith. You really have to see the sunset before it comes through the clouds, you need to anticipate it, know that it's coming and work towards enjoying it.

ABOUT THE AUTHOR

Yolanda was born in the UK to Jamaican parents. Very much influenced by her culture, Jamaica is the place Yolanda tends to refer to as home.

Today Yolanda is married with three sons, and resides in London. Passionate about a multitude of things Yolanda devotes her time to these purposeful causes, Domestic Violence, Young people and Empowering Women.

26758624R00210

Printed in Great Britain
by Amazon